RELIGION AND LAW
How through Halakhah Judaism Sets Forth its Theology and Philosophy

SOUTH FLORIDA STUDIES IN THE HISTORY OF JUDAISM

Edited by
Jacob Neusner
William Scott Green, James Strange
Darrell J. Fasching, Sara Mandell

Number 135
RELIGION AND LAW
*How through Halakhah Judaism Sets Forth its
Theology and Philosophy*
by
Jacob Neusner

RELIGION AND LAW

How through Halakhah Judaism Sets Forth its Theology and Philosophy

by

Jacob Neusner

Scholars Press
Atlanta, Georgia

RELIGION AND LAW

How through Halakhah Judaism Sets Forth its Theology and Philosophy

by
Jacob Neusner

©1996
University of South Florida

Publication of this book was made possible by a grant from the Tisch Family Foundation, New York City. The University of South Florida acknowledges with thanks this important support for its scholarly projects.

Library of Congress Cataloging in Publication Data

Neusner, Jacob, 1932-
    Religion and law : how halakhah Judaism sets forth its theology
and philosophy / by Jacob Neuwner.
        p.   cm. — (South Florida studies in the history of Judaism ;
no. 135)
    Includes bibliographical references.
    ISBN 0-7885-0251-4 (cloth ; alk. paper)
    1. Judaism—Doctrines—History—Sources. 2. Mishnah—Criticism,
interpretation, etc. 3. Jewish law—Philosophy. I. Title.
II. Series: South Florida studies in the history of Judaism ; 135.
BM601.N496   1996
296.1'27406—dc20   96-12381
                                            CIP

Printed in the United States of America
on acid-free paper

Table of Contents

Preface

"Just as Christianity has the word religion, so other religions have concepts which, rather like religion in the Euro-Christian context, are used to express the core of what they perceive themselves as being, but this is manifested in various different aspects. Whereas Western Christianity primarily defines itself by means of a theology and a set of beliefs, other religions focus on cult rituals. In this respect, the term religion has increasingly nurtured a Christo-European reductionism, which makes it inadequate as a description of non-Christian religions...Judaism and Islam...are much like Christianity theocentric, but here religion implies far more pronounced practical components.

...Self-definition is alien to the so-called natural religions, partly because they do not make clear distinctions between the profane and the religious. Religions vary, too, in the degree to which they can compare themselves with other religions. Whereas Christianity today uses the term religion to refer to other religions as well as itself, some religions do not possess any such comparative concepts."

FROM THE CONFERENCE CALL: "RELIGION: A EURO-CHRISTIAN INVENTION?"
HAUS DER KULTUREN DER WELT, BERLIN, JULY 2-4, 1996

Both the Christian and the Reform Judaic theological critics of the Judaism of the dual Torah commonly portray as opaque and inert the role of law, halakhah, in Judaism. But an accurate understanding of the way in which, in the classical and formative age of that religion, law took a critical role in the formation of the Judaic systemic statement shows a different picture altogether. Law takes a critical and active role in the formation and formulation of that statement. It is the medium that bears the message, and, properly understood, it also constitutes the message: the deed matters as much as the word. It is through law that the larger part of the Judaic statement comes to full expression. And halakhah is never a matter of mere form, an empty formality, comprised by the letter that kills. Nor in its generative statement is the religion, Judaism, a matter of formalities of orthopraxy, as the founding theologians of Conservative Judaism maintained.

Law — norms of the right attitude and action, indicative rules of conduct and character, regulations of the social order and its primary institutions — forms one of the two principal media by which Rabbinic Judaism set forth its initial statement; the other, the exegesis of Scripture within a hermeneutics that articulated a massive theology, also spoke, in part, through its reading of the legal passages of the Torah. It follows that the law, halakhah, defines through concrete realization, embodiment in the details of the workaday world, the theology and philosophy of Judaism in its initial statement. The religion of the Torah that the world calls "Judaism" is fully realized in halakhah and can be defined only through a close and detailed reading of halakhah. But it is the simple fact that the halakhah contains within itself and forms the medium for the concrete realization of profound theological convictions. Hence the very premises of the conference call prove flawed at their foundations. Self-definition is perfectly natural to all religions, but the medium through which definition comes to expression is philosophical and theological only in a select number of instances. And in the case of Judaism, the medium of philosophy and theology is halakhah.

The essays of this book serve to give ample instantiation of that basic theory. Here I mean to indicate a productive course of systematic learning for some time to come: the analysis of the theology and philosophy that the halakhah in various areas means to embody in concrete behavior. That work of translation of deed into word, gesture into conception, forms one of the principal media of theological discourse in the religion of the Torah that the world calls Judaism. As I shall demonstrate in matters of absolutely no interest in themselves, in working out the hocus pocus of the rite of preparing purification water, our sages of blessed memory addressed profound questions about the locus of sanctity in the world. The disputes they conducted on matters of stupefyingly dull detail turn out to address the heart of Heaven.

We begin with a simple account of the point at which "the Torah" became "Judaism," which addresses the call to the Berlin conference: is "religion" a form of "Christo-European reductionism"? That account prepares the way for the sustained argument of these essays, which addresses the conference statement, "Whereas Western Christianity primarily defines itself by means of a theology and a set of beliefs, other religions focus on cult rituals." What I show in the shank of the book is that the distinction between theology and a set of beliefs, on the one side, and "cult rituals," on the other, contradicts the fundamental characteristic of Judaism, which is its utilization of halakhah to state in concrete terms the propositions that the aggadah expresses in propositional or exegetical or narrative terms. It follows that the distinction fundamental to the conference statement, between theology or a set of beliefs and "cult rituals" violates the deepest characteristics of Judaism.

We commence with a concrete example in illustration of that proposition, "ritual without myth," which shows that details of the law contain a theory of sanctification outside the framework of the Temple itself. In this way I show precisely what I mean in claiming that the halakhah forms the medium of theological thought. We then turn, in Chapter Two, to a general statement of the religious system of the halakhah as that system is put forth in the foundation-document of Judaism, which is the Mishnah. The paramount trait of the Mishnah is its philosophical character; the law puts forth a philosophy, politics, and economics, that find a comfortable place within the methods and program of Graeco-Roman philosophy, particularly in the tradition of Aristotle. Chapters Three, Four, and Five go over the way in which the halakhah of the Mishnah sets forth demonstrably-philosophical propositions. We turn, in Chapter Six, to the way in which the Mishnah puts forth a theology of history. We conclude, in Chapter Seven, with some comparative studies of the halakhah of the Judaism of the Mishnah and that of the Essene Judaism of the Dead Sea Scrolls.

While in a variety of work over the past quarter-century, partially recapitulated in these pages, I have set forth in vast detail the evidence in behalf of the propositions just now laid out, the occasion for a more systematic recapitulation of the matter came quite fortuitously. Specifically, I owe the idea of this book to the organizers of a conference, who invited me to give an address on this topic. That is why I decided to respond by a review of some of my own findings on how, through halakhah, Rabbinic Judaism makes important states on philosophical and theological topics. This retrospective involves also an account, at the outset, of the point at which "Judaism" became a religion in the Western model. Here my picture is necessarily partial, since my scholarly focus draws me to ancient, not modern times.

As Visiting Professor of Religion at Bard College, I find remarkably hospitable both my colleagues in the Department of Religion and my many friends elsewhere on the faculty. I express my thanks to the President and the Dean of the Faculty of Bard College, Dr. Leon Botstein and Dr. Stuart Levine, respectively, for their cordial interest in my serving as Visiting Professor at Bard College, so far as the rules of the University of South Florida have permitted me to do so.

That University, modest in its assessment of itself, humble in its view of the rest of the academic world, may well boast about many things, least of them the courtesy of administrators toward professors; letters are answered, questions are given replies. Indeed, no work of mine can omit reference to the exceptionally favorable circumstances in which I conduct my research. I wrote this book mainly at the University of South Florida, which has afforded me an ideal situation in which to conduct a scholarly life. I express my thanks for not only the advantage of a Distinguished Research Professorship, which must be the best job in the world for a scholar, but also of a substantial research expense fund, ample research time, and some stimulating and cordial colleagues. In the prior chapters of my career, I never knew a university that prized professors' scholarship and publication and treated with respect those professors who actively and methodically pursue research. The University of South Florida, and all ten universities that comprise the Florida State University System as a whole, exemplify the high standards of professionalism that prevail in publicly-sponsored higher education in the USA and provide the model that privately-sponsored universities would do well to emulate. Here there are rules, achievement counts, and presidents, provosts, and deans honor and respect the University's principal mission: scholarship, scholarship alone — both in the classroom and in publication. Here at last I find integrity, governing in the lives of people true to their vocation and their mission.

JACOB NEUSNER
DISTINGUISHED RESEARCH PROFESSOR OF RELIGIOUS STUDIES
UNIVERSITY OF SOUTH FLORIDA, TAMPA
AND
VISITING PROFESSOR OF RELIGION
BARD COLLEGE
ANNANDALE-ON-HUDSON, NEW YORK

Introduction

THE INTEGRATIONIST-ORTHODOX INVENTION
OF JUDAISM, THE RELIGION

"Just as Christianity has the word religion, so other religions have concepts which, rather like religion in the Euro-Christian context, are used to express the core of what they perceive themselves as being, but this is manifested in various different aspects."

FROM THE CONFERENCE CALL: "RELIGION: A EURO-CHRISTIAN INVENTION?"
HAUS DER KULTUREN DER WELT, BERLIN, 1996

The halakhah forms half of the Judaic statement of the religious system of the Judaism of the dual Torah, a.k.a., Judaism, the religion; the other half is set forth by the Aggadah, law and theology in ordinary language. The native category for "religion" in "Judaism" is the word "Torah," and the Torah is comprised by halakhah, norms of behavior, and aggadah, norms of belief. From the time that the academic study of religion took up the task of defining not religions but religion, people have taken for granted, the Torah/Judaism belongs in the classification of religion. At issue, however, is the point at which, within the circles of the faithful, that same classification served to define and classify that "Judaism" or "the Torah" — when did the Torah become "Judaism, the religion"?

One component of the answer is contributed by the formation, in nineteenth-century Germany, of a self-conscious and articulate integrationist-Orthodox Judaism, which, practicing the Torah, also insisted that areas of human endeavor might be differentiated, so that some fell within the realm of religion, and others did not. Segregationist-Orthodox Judaisms before, at that time, and afterward, conceded no such point of differentiation, maintaining that all dimensions and aspects of everyday life belonged within the governance of the Torah. From that perspective, there would be, and now is, no distinguishing the religious from the secular; all things come under the dominion of the Torah, and the Torah recognizes no reality beyond itself.

INTEGRATIONIST-ORTHODOXY AND THE DIFFERENTIATION
OF RELIGION FROM SECULARITY

To define the terms just now used: integrationist Orthodox Judaism is
that Judaic system that mediates between the received Judaism of the dual Torah
and the requirements of living a life integrated in modern circumstances.
Segregationist Orthodox Judaisms, and they are many, do not distinguish the
religious from the secular and also do not accord recognition to the claims of any
other rule but that of God through the Torah. Integrationist Orthodoxy maintains
the world-view of the received dual Torah, constantly citing its sayings and adhering
with only trivial variations to the bulk of its norms for the everyday life. At the
same time integrationist Orthodoxy holds that Jews adhering to the dual Torah
may wear clothing that non-Jews wear and do not have to wear distinctively Jewish
(even: Judaic) clothing; live within a common economy and not practice distinctively
Jewish professions (however, in a given setting, these professions may be defined),
and, in diverse ways, take up a life not readily distinguished in important
characteristics from the life lived by people in general. Above all, integrationist
Orthodoxy affirms the value of secular learning, and segregationist Orthodoxy does
not affirm any learning but study of the Torah.

So for integrationist Orthodoxy a portion of Israel's life may prove secular,
in that the Torah does not dictate and so sanctify all details under all circumstances.
Since the Judaism of the dual Torah presupposed not only the supernatural entity,
Israel, but also a way of life that in important ways distinguished that supernatural
entity from the social world at large, the power of that particular Orthodoxy to find
an accommodation for Jews who valued the received way of life and world view
and also planned to make their lives in an essentially integrated social world proves
formidable. The difference between Orthodoxy and the system of the dual Torah
therefore comes to expression in social policy: integration, however circumscribed,
versus the total separation of the holy people. This is the point at which the category
"religion" comes to pertain, that is, when the category "secular" or "neutral" is
invoked. The former without the latter makes no sense at all.

Many see Orthodox Judaism as the same as "the tradition," what is natural
and normal, holding that Orthodoxy now stands for how things always were, for
all time. But the term Orthodoxy" takes on meaning only in the contrast to Reform,
so in a simple sense, Orthodoxy owes its life to Reform Judaism. The term first
surfaced in 1795,[1] and over all covers all Jews who believe that God revealed the
dual Torah at Sinai, and that Jews must carry out the requirements of Jewish law
contained in the Torah as interpreted by the sages through time. Obviously, so
long as that position struck as self-evident the generality of Jewry at large, Orthodoxy

---

[1] Nathaniel Katzburg and Walter S. Wurzburger, "Orthodoxy," *Encyclopaedia Judaica*
(Jerusalem, 1971: Keter) 12:1486-1493.

as a distinct and organized Judaism did not exist. It did not have to. What is interesting is the point at which two events took place: first, the recognition of the received system, "the tradition" as Orthodoxy, second, the specification of the received system as religion. The two of course go together. So long as the Judaism of the dual Torah enjoys recognition as a set of self-evident truths, those truths add up not to something so special as "religion," but to a general statement of how things are: all of life explained and harmonized in one whole account.

The former of the two events—the view that the received system was "traditional" — came first. (The matter of the self-aware recognition of "Judaism" as "religion" comes later.) That identification of truth as tradition came about when the received system met the challenge of competing Judaisms. Then, in behalf of the received way of life and world view addressed to supernatural Israel, people said that the Judaism of the dual Torah was established of old, the right, the only way of seeing and doing things, how things have been and should be naturally and normally: "Tradition." But that is a category that contains within itself an alternative, namely, change, as in "tradition and change."

INTEGRATIONIST ORTHODOXY AND EMANCIPATION OF THE JEWS

Integrationist Orthodoxy responded to the social facts in which German Jews found themselves. They found self-evident the requirement to accommodate themselves to the changing political climate that defined their existence, a climate in which (so they perceived) a place was opening up to Jews, who now aspired to "Emancipation" and "citizenship." It is when the system as a matter of social fact lost its power of self-evidence that it entered, among other apologetic categories, the classification, "the Tradition." Orthodox theologians denied that change was ever possible, so Walter Wurzburger: "Orthodoxy looks upon attempts to adjust Judaism to the 'spirit of the time' as utterly incompatible with the entire thrust of normative Judaism which holds that the revealed will of God rather than the values of any given age are the ultimate standard."[2] To begin with the issue important to the Reformers, the value of what was called "Emancipation," meaning, the provision to Jews of civil rights, defined the debate.

When the Reform Judaic theologians took a wholly one-sided position affirming Emancipation, numerous Orthodox ones adopted the contrary view. The position outlined by those theologians followed the agenda laid forth by the Reformers. If the Reform made minor changes in liturgy and its conduct, the Orthodox rejected even those that, under other circumstances, might have found acceptance. Saying prayers in the vernacular, for example, provoked strong opposition. But everyone knew that some of the prayers, said in Aramaic, in fact were in the vernacular of the earlier age. The Orthodox thought that these changes,

---

[2] *op. cit.*, col. 1487.

not reforms at all, represented only the first step of a process leading Jews out of the Judaic world altogether, so, as Wurzburger says, "The slightest tampering with tradition was condemned."

If we ask where did the received system of the dual Torah prevail, and where, by contrast, did Orthodoxy with its recognition of the difference between the religious and the secular come to full expression, we may follow the spreading out of railway lines, the growth of new industry, the shifts in political status accorded to, among other citizens, Jews, changes in the educational system, in all, the entire process of political change, economic and social, demographic and cultural shifts of a radical and fundamental nature. Where the changes came first, there Reform Judaism met them in its way—and Orthodoxy in its way. Where change came later in the century, as in the case of Russian Poland, the eastern provinces of the Austro-Hungarian Empire, and Russia itself, there, in villages contentedly following the old ways, the received system endured.

Again, in an age of mass migration from Eastern Europe to America and other western democracies, those who experienced the upheaval of leaving home and country met the challenge of change either by accepting new ways of seeing things or articulately and in full self-awareness reaffirming the familiar ones, once more, Reform or Orthodoxy. We may, therefore, characterize the received system as a way of life and world view wedded to an ancient peoples' homelands, the villages and small towns of central and eastern Europe, and Orthodoxy as the heir of that received system as it came to expression in the towns and cities of central and Western Europe and America. That rule of thumb, with the usual exceptions, allows us to distinguish between the piety of a milieu and the theological conviction of a self-conscious community. Or we may accept the familiar distinction between tradition and articulate Orthodoxy, a distinction with its own freight of apologetics to be sure.

The beginnings of Orthodoxy took place in the areas where Reform Judaism had already made its way, hence in the major cities of Germany and in Hungary. In Germany, where Reform attracted the majority of not a few Jewish communities, the Orthodox faced a challenge indeed. Critical to their conviction was the notion that "Israel," all of the Jews, bore responsibility to carry out the law of the Torah. But the community's institutions in the hands of the Reform did not obey the law of the Torah as the Orthodox understood it. So, in they end, Orthodoxy took that step that marked it as a self-conscious Judaism. Orthodoxy separated from the established community altogether. The Orthodox set up their own organization and seceded from the community at large. The next step prohibited Orthodox from participating in non-Orthodox organizations altogether. Isaac Breuer, a leading theologian of Orthodoxy, would ultimately take the position that "refusal to espouse the cause of separation was interpreted as being equivalent to the rejection of the absolute sovereignty of God."[3]

---

[3] op. cit., col. 1488.

The matter of accommodating to the world at large, of course, did not allow for so easy an answer as mere separation. The specific issue—integration or segregation—concerned preparation for life in the large politics and economic life of the country, and that meant secular education, involving not only language and science, but history and literature, matters of values. Orthodoxy proved diverse, with two wings to be distinguished, one rejecting secular learning as well as all dealing with non-Orthodox Jews, the other cooperating with non-Orthodox and secular Jews and accepting the value of secular education. That position in no way affected loyalty to the law of Judaism, e.g., belief in God's revelation of the one whole torah at Sinai. The point at which the received system and Orthodox split requires specification. In concrete terms we know the one from the other by the evaluation of secular education. Proponents of the received system never accommodated themselves to secular education, while the Orthodox in Germany and Hungary persistently affirmed it. That represents a remarkable shift, since central to the received system of the dual Torah is study of Torah—Torah, not philosophy.

Explaining where we find the one and the other, Katzburg works with the distinction we have already made, between an unbroken system and one that has undergone a serious caesura with the familiar condition of the past. He states:

> In Eastern Europe until World War I, Orthodoxy preserved without a break its traditional ways of life and the time-honored educational framework. In general, the mainstream of Jewish life was identified with Orthodoxy, while Haskalah [Jewish Enlightenment, which applied to the Judaic setting the skeptical attitudes of the French Enlightenment] and secularization were regarded as deviations. Hence there was no ground wherein a Western type of Orthodoxy could take root....European Orthodoxy in the 19th and the beginning of the 20th centuries was significantly influenced by the move from small settlements to urban centers...as well as by emigration. Within the small German communities there was a kind of popular Orthodoxy, deeply attached to tradition and to local customs, and when it moved to the large cities this element brought with it a vitality and rootedness to Jewish tradition..[4]

Katzburg's observations provide important guidance. He authoritatively defines the difference between Orthodoxy and "tradition." So he tells us how to distinguish the received system accepted as self-evident, and an essentially selective, therefore by definition new system, called Orthodoxy. In particular he guides us in telling the one from the other and where to expect to find, in particular, the articulated, therefore, self-conscious affirmation of "tradition" that characterizes Orthodoxy but does not occur in the world of the dual Torah as it glided in its eternal orbit of the seasons and of unchanging time.

---

[4] Katzburg, col. 1490.

JUDAISM ENTERS THE CATEGORY, RELIGION

The category "religion," with its counterpart, "secular," recognizes as distinct from "all of life" matters having to do with the church, the life of faith, the secular as against the sacred. Those distinctions were lost on the received system of the dual Torah, which legislated for matters we should today regard as entirely secular or neutral, for example, the institutions of state (e.g., king, priest, army). In the received system as it took shape in Eastern and Central Europe, Jews wore garments regarded as distinctively Jewish, and some important traits of these garments indeed derived from the Torah. They pursued sciences that only Jews studied, for instance, the Talmud and its commentaries. In these and other ways, the Torah encompassed all of the life of Israel, the holy people. The recognition that Jews were like others, that the Torah fell into a category into which other and comparable matters fell—that recognition was long in coming.

From the wars of the Reformation and the parlous settlements thereof, for Christians it had become a commonplace in Germany and other Western countries to see "religion" as distinct from other components of the social and political system. While the Church in Russia identified with the Tsarist state, or with the national aspirations of the Polish people, for example, in Germany two churches, Catholic and Protestant, competed. The terrible wars of the Reformation in the sixteenth and seventeenth centuries, which ruined Germany, had led to the uneasy compromise that the prince might choose the religion of his principality, and, from that self-aware choice, people understood that "the way of life and world view" in fact constituted a religion, and that one religion might be compared with some other. By the nineteenth century, moreover, the separation of church and state ratified the important distinction between religion, where difference would be tolerated, and the secular, where citizens were pretty much the same.

That fact of political consciousness in the West reached the Judaic world only in the late eighteenth century for some intellectuals, and in the nineteenth century for large numbers of others. It registered, then, as a fundamental shift in the understanding and interpretation of "the Torah," now seen, among Orthodox as much as among Reform, as "Judaism," an *-ism* along with other *-isms*. A mark of the creative power of the Jews who formed the Orthodox Judaic system derives from their capacity to shift the fundamental category in which they framed their system. The basic shift in category is what made Orthodoxy a Judaism on its own, not simply a restatement, essentially in established classifications, of the received system of the dual Torah.

If we ask how Orthodox Judaism, so profoundly rooted in the canonical writings and received convictions of the Judaism of the dual Torah, at the same time made provision for the issues of political and cultural change at hand, we recognize the importance of the shift in category contributed by Orthodoxy. For Orthodoxy, within the sector of the received system, made provision for the difference between sacred and secular, so within Judaic systems identified as a religion, Judaism, what the received system had called the Torah, encompassing and symmetrical with the whole of the life of Judaic society. Specifically, Orthodox Judaism took the view that one could observe the rules of the Judaic system of the ages and at the same time keep the laws of the state. More important, Orthodox Judaism took full account of the duties of citizenship, so far as being a good citizen imposed the expectation of conformity in certain aspects of everyday life. So a category, "religion," could contain the Torah, and another category, "the secular," could allow Jews a place in the accepted civic life of the country. The importance of the category-shift therefore lies in its power to accommodate the political change so important, also, to Reform Judaism. The Jews' differences from others would fit into categories in which difference was (in Jews' minds at any rate) acceptable, and would not violate those lines to which all citizens had to adhere.

To review the fundamental shift represented by the distinction between secular and religious, we recall our original observation that Jews no longer wished to wear distinctively Jewish clothing, for example, or to speak a Jewish language, or to pursue only Jewish learning under Jewish auspices. Yet the received system, giving expression to the rules of sanctification of the holy people, did entail wearing Jewish clothing, speaking a Jewish language, learning only, or mainly, Jewish sciences. So clothing, language, and education now fell into the category of the secular, while other equally important aspects of everyday life remained in the category of the sacred. Orthodox Judaism, as it came into existence in Germany and other Western countries, therefore found it possible by recognizing the category of the secular to accept the language, clothing, and learning of those countries. And these matters serve only to exemplify a larger acceptance of gentile ways, not all but enough to lessen the differences between the Holy People and the nations. Political change of a profound order, which made Jews call into question some aspects of the received system—if not most or all of them, as would be the case for Reform Judaism—presented to Jews who gave expression to Orthodox Judaism the issues at hand: how separate, how integrated? And the answers required picking and choosing, different things to be sure, just as much as, in principle, the Reform Jews picked and choose. Both Judaisms understood that some things were sacred, others not, and that understanding marked these Judaisms off from the system of the dual Torah.

Once the category-shift had taken place, the difference was to be measured in degree, not kind. For Orthodox Jews maintained those distinctive beliefs of a political character in the future coming of the Messiah and the reconstitution of the Jewish nation in its own land that Reform Jews rejected. But, placing these convictions in the distant future, the Orthodox Jews nonetheless prepared for a protracted interim of life within the nation at hand, like the Reform different in religion, not in nationality as represented by citizenship. What follows for our inquiry is that Orthodoxy, as much as Reform, signals remarkable changes in the

Jews' political situation and—more important—aspiration. They did want to be different, but not so different as the received system would have made them.

Still, Orthodoxy in its nineteenth century formulation laid claim to carry forward, in continuous and unbroken relationship, "the tradition." That claim assuredly demands a serious hearing, for the things that Orthodoxy taught, the way of life it required, the Israel to whom it spoke, the doctrines it deemed revealed by God to Moses at Sinai—all of these conformed more or less exactly to the system of the received Judaism of the dual Torah as people then new it. So any consideration of the issue of a linear and incremental history of Judaism has to take at face value the character, and not merely the claim, of Orthodoxy. But we do not have without reflection to concede that claim. Each Judaism, after all, demands study not in categories defined by its own claims of continuity, but in those defined by its own distinctive and characteristic choices. For a system takes shape and then makes choices—in that order. But the issue facing us in Orthodoxy is whether or not Orthodoxy can be said to make choices at all. For is it not what it says it is, "just Judaism"? Indeed so, but the dual Torah of the received tradition hardly generated the base-category, "Judaism." And "Judaism," Orthodox or otherwise, is not "Torah."

That is the point at which making self-conscious choices enters discourse. For the Orthodoxy of the nineteenth century — that is, the Judaism that named itself "Orthodox" — exhibited certain traits of mind that marked its framers as distinctive, that is, as separate from the received Judaism of the dual Torah as the founders of Reform Judaism. To state the matter simply: by adopting for themselves the category, religion, and by recognizing a distinction between religion and the secular, the holy and other categories of existence, the founders of Orthodoxy performed an act of choice and selectivity. And that fact defines them as self-conscious, rendering the received system for them not self-evident, therefore definitive of the very facts of being as it was for those for whom it was self-evident.

The Torah found itself transformed into an object, a thing out there, a matter of choice, deliberation, affirmation. In that sense Orthodoxy recognized a break in the line of the received "tradition": and proposed to repair the break: a self-conscious, a modern decision. The issues addressed by Orthodoxy, the questions its framers found ineluctable—these take second place. The primary consideration in our assessment of the claim of Orthodoxy to carry forward, in a straight line, the incremental history of a single Judaism, carries us to the fundamental categories within which Orthodoxy pursued its thought, but the Judaism of the dual Torah did not. How so? The Judaism of the dual Torah had no word for Judaism, and Orthodoxy did (and does).

JUDAISM, A SPECIES OF THE GENUS, RELIGION

So let us dwell on this matter of the category, Judaism, a species of the genus, religion. The fact is that those Jews for whom the received Judaism retained the standing of self-evident truth in no way recognized the distinctions implicit in the category, religion. Those distinctions separated one dimension of existence from others, specifically, the matter of faith and religious action from all other matters, such as politics, economic life, incidental aspects of every day life such as clothing, vocation and avocation, and the like. As I have stressed, the Judaism of the dual Torah, for its part, encompasses every dimension of human existence, both personal and public, both private and political. The Jews constitute a supernatural people; their politics form the public dimension of their holiness, and their personal lives match the most visible and blatant rules of public policy. The whole forms a single fabric, an indivisible and totally coherent entity, at once social and cultural, economic and political—and, above all, religious. The recognition, therefore, that we may distinguish the religious from the political, or concede as distinct any dimension of a person's life or of the life of the community of Judaism, forms powerful evidence that a fresh system has come into existence.

For nineteenth century Reform and Orthodox theologians alike, the category "Judaism" defined what people said when they wished all together and all at once to describe what the Jews believe, or the Jewish religion, or similar matters covering religious ideas viewed as a system and as a whole. It therefore constituted a philosophical category, an -*ism*, instructing thinkers to seek the system and order and structure of ideas: the doctrine of this, the doctrine of that, in Juda-*ism*. The nineteenth century Judaic religious thinkers invoked the category, Judaism, when they proposed to speak of the whole of Judaic religious existence. Available to the Judaism of the dual Torah are other categories, other words, to tell how to select and organize and order data: all together, all at once to speak of the whole.

To the Jews who abided within the received Judaism of the dual Torah, the discovery of Orthodoxy therefore represented an innovation, a shift from the perceivedly self-evident truths of the Torah. For their word for Judaism was Torah, and when they spoke of the whole all at once, they used the word Torah—and they also spoke of different things from the things encompassed by Judaism. For the received Judaism of the dual Torah did not use the word the nineteenth century theologians used when speaking of the things of which they spoke when they said, Juda-*ism*. The received system not only used a different word, but in fact referred to different things. The two categories—Judaism and Torah—which are supposed to refer to the same data in the same social world, in fact encompass different data from those taken in categorically, by Judaism. So we contrast the two distinct categories, Judaism and Torah.

Judaism falls into the classification of a philosophical or ideological or theological one, a logos: a word, while *Torah* fell into the classification of a symbol, that is, a symbol that in itself encompassed the whole of the system that the category at hand was meant to describe. The species -ism falls into the classification of the genus, logos, while the species, Torah, while using words, transcends words. It falls into a different classification, a species of the genus symbol. How so? The -*ism*-category does not invoke an encompassing symbol but a system of thought.

Judaism is an it, an object, a classification, an action. Torah, for its part, is an everything in one thing, a symbol. I cannot imagine a more separate and unlike set of categories than Judaism and Torah, even though both encompassed the same way of life and world view and addressed the same social group. So Torah as a category serves as a symbol, everywhere present in detail and holding all the details together. Judaism as a category serves as a statement of the main points: the intellectual substrate of it all.

The conception of Judaism as an organized body of doctrine, as in the sentence, *Judaism teaches*, or *Judaism says*, derives from an age in which people further had determined that Judaism belonged to the category of religion, and, of still more definitive importance, a religion was something that *teaches* or *says*. That is to say, Judaism is a religion, and a religion to begin with is (whatever else it is) a composition of beliefs. That age is the one at hand, the nineteenth century, and the category of religion as a distinct entity emerges from Protestant theological thought. For In Protestant theological terms, one is saved by faith. But the very components of that sentence, one—individual, not the people or holy nation, saved—personally, not in history, and saved, not sanctified, faith—not commandments—in fact prove incomprehensible in the categories constructed by Torah. Constructions of Judaic dogmas, the specification of a right doctrine—an ortho-doxy—and the insistence that one can speak of religion apart from such adventitious matters as clothing and education (for the Orthodox of Germany who dressed like other Germans and studied in Universities, not only in yeshivas) or food (for the Reform) testify to the same fact: the end of self-evidence, the substitution of the distinction between religion and secularity, the creation of *Judaism* as the definitive category.

In fact in the idiomatic language of Torah-speech one cannot make such a statement in that way about, or in the name of, Judaism—not an operative category at all. In accord with the modes of thought and speech of the received Judaism of the dual Torah, one has to speak as subject of Israel, not one, to address not only individual life but all of historical time, so saved by itself does not suffice, further to invoke the verb, since the category of sanctification, not only salvation must find its place, and, finally, one native to the speech of the Torah will use the words of commandments, not of faith alone. So the sentence serves for Protestant Christianity but not for the Torah. Of course "Judaism," Orthodox or Reform, for its part will also teach things and lay down doctrines, even dogmas.

The counterpart, in the realm of self-evidence comprised by the received Judaism of the dual Torah, of the statement, *Judaism teaches*, can only be, *the Torah requires*, and the predicate of such a sentence would be not, *...that God is one*, but, *...that you say a blessing before eating bread*. The category, Judaism, encompasses, classifies and organizes, doctrines: the faith, which, by the way, an individual adopts and professes. The category, Torah, teaches what "we," God's holy people, are and what "we" must do. The counterpart to the statement of Judaism, "God is one," then is, "...who has sanctified us by his commandments and commanded us to...." The one teaches, that is, speaks of intellectual matters and beliefs, the latter demands — social actions and deeds of us, matters of public consequence—including, by the way, affirming such doctrines as God's unity, the resurrection of the dead, the coming of the Messiah, the revelation of the Torah at Sinai, and on and on: "we" can rival the Protestants in heroic deeds of faith.. So it is true, the faith demands deeds, and deeds presuppose faith. But, categorically, the emphasis is what it is: Torah on on God's revelation, the canon, to Israel and its social way of life, Judaism on a system of belief. That is a significant difference between the two categories, which, as I said, serve a single purpose, namely, to state the thing as a whole.

THEOLOGY AND PHILOSOPHY VS. TORAH-STUDY

Equally true, one would (speaking systemically) also *study Torah*. But what one studied was not an intellectual system of theology or philosophy, rather a document of revealed Scripture and law. That is not to suggest that the theologians of Judaism, Orthodox or Reform, of the nineteenth century, did not believe that God is one, or that the philosophers who taught that "Judaism teaches ethical monotheism" did not concur that, on that account, one has to say a blessing before eating bread. But the categories are different, and, in consequence, so too the composites of knowledge. A book on Judaism explains the doctrines, the theology or philosophy, of Judaism. A book of the holy Torah expounds God's will as revealed in "the one whole Torah of Moses, our rabbi," as sages teach and embody God's will. I cannot imagine two more different books, and the reason is that they represent totally different categories of intelligible discourse and of knowledge. Proof, of course, is that the latter books are literally unreadable. They form part of a genuinely oral exercise, to be cited sentence by sentence and expounded in the setting of other sentences, from other books, the whole made cogent by the speaker. That process of homogenization is how Torah works as a generative category. It obscures other lines of structure and order.

True, the two distinct categories come to bear upon the same body of data, the same holy books. But the consequent compositions—selections of facts, ordering of facts, analyses of facts, statements of conclusion and interpretation and above all, modes of public discourse, meaning who says what to whom—bear no relationship to one another, none whatsoever. Indeed, the compositions more likely than not do not even adduce the same facts, or even refer to them.

How is it that the category I see as imposed, extrinsic, and deductive, namely, "Judaism," attained the status of self-evidence? Categories serve because they are self-evident to a large group of people. In the case at hand, therefore, Judaism serves because it enjoys self-evidence as part of a larger set of categories that are equally self-evident. In all of these categories, religion constitutes a statement of belief distinct from other aspects and dimensions of human existence, so religions form a body of well-composed -isms. So whence the category, "Judaism"? The source of the categorical power of "Judaism" derives from the

Protestant philosophical heritage that has defined scholarship, including category formation, from the time of Kant onward. *"Juda"* + *"ism"* do not constitute self-evident, let alone definitive, categories—except where they do. Judaism constitutes a category asymmetrical to the evidence adduced in its study. The category does not work because the principle of formation is philosophical and does not emerge from an unmediated encounter with the Torah. Orthodoxy can have come into existence only in Germany, and, indeed, only in that part of Germany in which the philosophical heritage of Kant and Hegel defined the categories of thought, also, for religion.

TORAH AND SECULAR EDUCATION AFFIRMED: SAMSON RAPHAEL HIRSCH

The importance of Hirsch (1808-1888), first great intellect of Orthodoxy, derives from his philosophy of joining Torah with secular education, producing a synthesis of Torah and modern culture. He represents the strikingly new Judaism at hand, exhibiting both its strong tie to the received system but also its innovative and essentially new character. Sometimes called "neo-Orthodoxy,"[5] Hirsch's position laid stress on the possibility of living in the secular world and sustaining a fully Orthodox life rallied the Jews of the counter-reformation. But Hirsch and his followers took over one principal position of Reform, the possibility of integrating Jews in modern society. What made Hirsch significant was that he took that view not only on utilitarian grounds, as Samet says, "but also through the acceptance of its scale of values, aiming at creating a symbiosis between traditional Orthodoxy and modern German-European culture; both in theory and in practice this meant abandonment of Torah study for its own sake and adopting instead an increased concentration on practical halakhah."[6] On that basis we rightly identify Orthodoxy as a distinct Judaism from the system of the dual Torah. Hirsch himself studied at the University of Bonn, specializing in classical languages, history, and philosophy.[7] So, as we noted, he did not think one had to spend all his time studying Torah, and in going to a university he implicitly affirmed that he could not define, within Torah-study, all modes of learning. Gentile professors knew things worth knowing. But continuators of the Judaism of the dual Torah thought exactly the opposite: whatever is worth knowing is in the Torah.

In his rabbinical posts, Hirsch published a number of works to appeal to the younger generation. His ideal for them was the formation of a personality that would be both enlightened and observant, that is to say, educated in Western knowledge and observant of the Judaic way of life. This ideal took shape through

---

[5] Moshe Shraga Samet, "Neo-Orthodoxy," *Encylopaedia Judaica* 12:956-958.
[6] op. cit., col. 957.
[7] Simha Katz, "Samson (ben) Raphael Hirsch," *Encyclopaedia Judaica* (Jerusalem, 1971) 8:508-515.

an educational program that encompassed Hebrew language and holy literature, and also German, mathematics, sciences, and the like. In this way he proposed to respond to the Reformers view that Judaism in its received form constituted a barrier between Jews and German society. The Reformers saw the received way of life as an obstacle to the sort of integration they thought wholesome and good. Hirsch concurred in the ideal and differed on detail. Distinctive Jewish clothing, in Hirsch's view, enjoyed a low priority. Quite to the contrary, he himself wore a ministerial gown at public worship, which did not win the approbation of the traditionalists, and when he preached, he encompassed not only the law of the Torah but other biblical matters, equally an innovation. Hirsch argued that Judaism and secular education could form a union. This would require the recognition of externals, which could be set aside, and the emphasis on the principles, which would not change. So Hirsch espoused what, in the ideas of those fully within the mentality of self-evidence, constituted selective piety, and, while the details differed, therefore fell within the classification of reform.

In his selections Hirsch included changes in the conduct of the liturgy, involving a choir, congregational singing, sermons in the vernacular—a generation earlier sure marks of Reform. He required prayers to be said only in Hebrew and Jewish subjects to be taught in that language. He opposed all changes in the Prayer Book. At the same time he sustained organizational relationships with the Reformers and tried to avoid schism. By mid-career, however, toward the middle of the century, Hirsch could not tolerate the Reformers' abrogation of the dietary laws and those affecting marital relationships, and he made his break, accusing the Reformers of disrupting Israel's unity. In the following decades he encouraged Orthodox Jews to leave the congregations dominated by Reform, even though, in the locale, such was the only synagogue. Separationist synagogues formed in the larger community.

We come now to Hirsch's framing of issues of doctrine. He constructed an affirmative system, not a negative one. His principal argument stressed that the teachings of the Torah constitute facts beyond all doubt, as much as the facts of nature do not allow for doubt. This view of the essential facticity—the absolute givenness—of the Torah led to the further conviction that human beings may not deny the Torah's teachings even when they do not grasp the Torah's meaning. Wisdom is contained within the Torah, God's will is to be found there. Just as the physical laws of nature are not conditioned by human search, so the rules of God's wisdom are unaffected by human search. The Torah constitutes an objective reality, and, in Katz's words, its laws form "an objective disposition of an established order that is not dependent on the will of the individual or society, and hence not even on historical processes."[8] Humanity nonetheless may through time gain religious truth.

What makes Israel different is that they gain access to the truth not through experience but through direct revelation. Gentile truth is truth, but derives from

---

[8] *op. cit.*, col. 512-513.

observation and experience. What Israel knows through the Torah comes through a different medium. That people then stands outside of history and does not have to learn religious truth through the passage of history and changes over time. Israel then forms a supernatural entity, a view certainly in accord with the Judaism of the dual Torah. But when it came to explaining the way of life at hand, Hirsch went his own way. Hirsch pursued a theory of the practice of the religious life through concrete deeds—the commandments—in a highly speculative and philosophical way. What he maintained was that each of the deeds of the way of life represented something beyond itself, served as a symbol, not as an end in itself. So when a Jew carries out a holy deed, the deed serves to make concrete a revealed truth. This mode of thought transforms the way of life into an exercise in applied theology and practical, practiced belief.

Specifically, in Katz's words, "the performance of a commandment is not determined by simple devotion but by attachment to the religious thought represented in symbolic form by the commandment. Symbolic meanings must be attributed...particular to commandments which are described by the Torah itself as signs...and commandments which are established as pointing to historical events...and commandments whose entire content testifies to their symbolic character."9 The diverse commandments all together stand for three principles: justice, love, and "the education of ourselves and others."

Hirsch's theory of who is Israel stood at the opposite pole from that of Geiger and the Reformers. To them, as we have seen, Israel fell into the classification of a religious community, that alone. To Hirsch Israel constituted a people, not a religious congregation, and Hirsch spoke of "national Jewish consciousness: "The Jewish people, though it carries the Torah with it in all the lands of its dispersion, will never find its table and lamp except in the Holy Land." Israel performs a mission among the nations, to teach "that God is the source of blessing." Israel then falls between, forming its own category, because it has a state system, in the land, but also a life outside.10 In outlining this position, Hirsch of course reaffirmed the theory of the supernatural Israel laid forth in the dual Torah. The power of the national ideal for Hirsch lay in its polemical force against the assimilationists and Reformers, whom he treated as indistinguishable:

> The contempt with which the assimilationists treat David's [fallen] tabernacle and the prayer for the sacrificial service clearly reveals the extent of their rebellion against Torah and their complete disavowal of the entire realm of Judaism. They gather the ignorant about them to whom the Book of Books, the Divine national document of their Jewish past and future, is closed with seven seals. With a conceit engendered by stupidity and a perfidy born

---

9 *op. cit.*, col. 513.

10 *op. cit.*, col. 514.

from hatred they point to God's Temple and the Divine Service in Zion as the unholy center of the 'bloody cult of sacrifices.' Consequently, they make certain to eliminate any reference to the restoration of the Temple service from our prayers...The 'cultured, refined' sons and daughters of our time must turn away with utter disgust from their 'pre-historic, crude' ancestors who worship their god with bloody sacrifices...

Hirsch reviews the long line of exalted leaders who affirmed sacrifice and who were not crude, e.g., Moses, Isaiah, Jeremiah, and on. Then he concludes:

> The Jewish sacrifice expresses the highest ideal of man's and the nation's moral challenge Blood and kidney, head and limbs symbolize our service of God with every drop of b.blood, every emotion, every particle of our being. By performing the act of sacrifice at the place chosen by God as the site of His Law, we proclaim our determination to fulfill our lofty moral and ethical tasks to enable God to bless the site of the national vow with the presence of this glory and with the fullness of this love and grace.[11]

Hirsch's spiritualization of the sacrifices, in an ample tradition of precedent to be sure, derives from the challenge of Reform. Demanding an acceptance at face value of the Torah as the revelation of God's wisdom, Hirsch nonetheless made the effort to appeal to more than the givenness of the Torah and its commandments.

On the contrary, he entered into argument in the same terms—spiritualization, lofty moral and ethical tasks — as did the Reformers. That marks his thought as new and responsive to a fresh set of issues. As to the Reformers, he met them on their ground, as he had to, and his principal points of insistence to begin with derived from the issues defined by others. That is why we may find for him a suitable place in the larger setting of discourse among the Judaisms of the nineteenth century, all of them products of the end of self-evidence and the beginning of a self-conscious explanation for what had formerly, and elsewhere in the age at hand, the authority of the absolutely given. We see that fact most clearly when we take up a single stunning instance of the possibility of locating the several Judaisms on a single continuum: the doctrine of the Torah, what it is, where it comes from.

THE CONCEPTION OF THE RELIGION, JUDAISM, AND THE BIRTH OF A JUDAISM

That Hirsch's Orthodoxy flows directly out of the received system no one doubts. But it also takes a position separate from that system in both doctrine and method. Hirsch spent much energy defending the practice of the religious duties called commandments, such as circumcision, the wearing of fringes on garments,

---

[11] Samson Raphael Hirsch, *The Collected Writings* (N.Y. and Jerusalem, 1984: Philipp Feldheim, Inc.) 1:388-389.

the use, in morning worship, of *tefillin* (commonly translated phylacteries), and the sacrificial cult and Temple. These he treats not as utter data—givens of the holy life. Rather, he transforms them into symbols of a meaning beyond. And that exercise, in his context, testifies to the utter self-consciousness of the Judaism at hand, hence to the formation of a new Judaism out of received materials, no less than Reform Judaism constituted a new Judaism out of those same received materials. For the sole necessity for making up such symbolic explanations derived from decision: defend these, at all costs. Equivalent explanations and a counterpart process of articulated defense of the holy way of life hardly struck as equivalently urgent the contemporaries of Hirsch living in the villages of the East.

When, therefore, Hirsch invoked the parallel, to which we have already alluded, between the study of nature and the study of the Torah, he expressed the freshness, the inventiveness, of his own system, thereby testifying to the self-consciousness at hand. A sizable abstract provides a good view of Hirsch's excellent mode of thought and argument:

> One word here concerning the proper method of Torah investigation. Two revelations are open before us, that is, nature and the Torah. In nature all phenomena stand before us as indisputable facts, and we can only endeavor a posteriori to ascertain the law of each and the connection of all. Abstract demonstration of the truth, or rather, the probability of theoretical explanations of the acts of nature, is an unnatural proceeding. The right method is to verify our assumptions by the known facts, and the highest attainable degree of certainty is to be able to say: 'The facts agree with our assumption'—that is, all the phenomena observed can be explained according to our theory. A single contradictory phenomenon will make our theory untenable. We must, therefore, acquire all the knowledge possible concerning the object of our investigation and know it, if possible, in its totality. If, however, all efforts should fail in disclosing the inner law and connection of phenomena revealed to us as facts in nature, the facts remain, nevertheless, undeniable and cannot be reasoned away.
>
> The same principles must be applied to the investigation of the Torah. In the Torah, even as in nature, God is the ultimate cause. In the Torah, even as in nature, no fact may be denied, even though the reason and the connection may not be understood. What is true in nature is true also in the Torah: the traces of divine wisdom must ever be sought. Its ordinances must be accepted in their entirety as undeniable phenomena and must be studied in accordance with their connection to each other, and the subject to which they relate. Our conjectures must be tested by their precepts, and our highest certainty here also can only be that everything stands in harmony with our theory.

> In nature the phenomena are recognized as facts, though their cause and relationship to each other may not be understood and are independent of our investigation. So too the ordinances of the Torah must be law for us, even if we do not comprehend the reason and the purpose of a single one. Our fulfillment of the commandments must not depend on our investigations.[12]

Here we have the counterpart, in argument, to Hirsch's theory of Torah and worldly learning. Just as Hirsch maintained the union of the two, so in the deepest structure of his thought he worked out that same union. Natural science dictated rules of inquiry, specifically, the requirement that we explain phenomena through a theory that we can test. The phenomenon is the given. Then, for the Torah, the requirements of the Torah constitute the givens, which demand explanation, but which must be accepted as facts even when explanation fails. Clearly, Hirsch addressed an audience that had come to doubt the facticity of the facts of the Torah in a way in which none doubted the facticity of the facts of nature.

Once we compare the Torah to nature, the Torah no longer defines the world-view and the way of life at hand. Rather, the Torah takes its place as part of a larger world-view and way of life, one in which the Israelite-human being (in Hirsch's happy concept) has to accommodate both the received of the Torah and the given of nature. The insistence that the process of accommodation—"studied in accordance with their connection..and the subject to which they relate"—testifies to a world view essentially distinct from the one of the received system of the dual Torah. In this new world view the Torah demands explanation, its rules find themselves reduced to the lesser dimensions of an apologia of symbolism, so that they form not givens in an enduring and eternal way of life, but objects of analysis, defense, above all, reasoned decision. True, Hirsch insisted, "Our fulfillment of the commandments must not depend on our investigations." But the investigations must go forward, and that, in and of itself, tells us we deal with a new Judaism.

Integrationist Orthodoxy never claimed to mark the natural next step in the history of Judaism. That Orthodoxy saw itself as nothing other than Judaism. In its near-total symmetry with the received system, integrationist Orthodoxy surely made a powerful case for that claim. But the fact that the case had to be made, the context and conditions of contention—these form the indicators that another Judaism was coming into being. The asymmetrical points, moreover, demand attention, though, on their own, they should not decisively refute the position of that Orthodoxy. What does is the existence of an Orthodoxy at all. The single most interesting instance of a Judaism of self-consciousness, Orthodoxy defends propositions that, in the received system, scarcely reached a level of articulate discourse, for instance, the absolute necessity to conform to the holy way of life of the Torah. The necessity for making such an argument testifies to the fact that

---

[12] Samson Raphael Hirsch, III. *Jewish Symbolism,* pp. xiii-xiv.

people, within Orthodoxy, thought they confronted the need to choose and did choose. True, the choices, from the viewpoint of Orthodoxy, fell in the right direction.

But integrationist Orthodoxy formed an act of restoration and renewal, therefore an act of innovation. The modes of argument of Hirsch, representative as they are of the mentality of the Orthodoxy he defined, call into question the linear descent of Orthodoxy from what people called "tradition." An incremental progress, perhaps, but a lineal and unbroken journey, no. But even the incremental theory of the history of Judaism, which, in the case of Orthodoxy, identifies Hirsch's Orthodoxy with the system of the dual Torah, fails to take note of facts, and, as Hirsch himself argues, that failure suffices. The facts that people, Hirsch included, made clearcut choices, identifying some things as essential, others not (clothing, for one important instance). If the piety of Reform proved selective, the selections that Hirsch made place him into the classification, also, of one who sorted out change and made changes.

1

Ritual without Myth:
How Halakhah Addresses Theology

While some religions, Christianity and Islam for example, are rich in theological writings, and others in myth, still others make their statements about the nature of being and of the realm of the sacred primarily through law.[1] In the case of early rabbinic Judaism, upon which we shall concentrate, we have a considerable corpus of laws which prescribe the way things are done but make no effort to interpret what is done. These constitute ritual entirely lacking in mythic, let along theological, explanation. Accordingly, the processes and modes of thought of earlier rabbinic Judaism, the Mishnah, in fact was not practiced; indeed, the earlier rabbis scarcely claim that it was. For example, we have two immense sections of Mishnah, one third of the whole, devoted to the conduct of the cult of the Temple on the one side, and rules of purity, on the other, and the rabbis of whom we speak, who lived from A.D. 70 to A.D. 200, flourished after the destruction of the Temple and in no way could have legislated for the conduct of the actual cult. Further, the laws about ritual cleanness or purity, so far as they had to be kept so that a person could enter the Temple, bore no more concrete relevance to everyday life than did the cultic laws, and only a small part of the Jewish population of Palestine was expected to keep those laws outside of the cult. Accordingly, we have before us the paradox presented by most serious effort to create a corpus of laws to describe a ritual life which did not exist. I shall try to show that the processes of making those laws themselves constituted the rabbis' mode of thinking about the same issues investigated, in other circumstances, through rigorous theological thought, on the one side, or profound mythic speculation, on the other.

My primary point is that *so far as the laws describe a ritual, the ritual itself is myth,* in two senses. First, the ritual is myth in the sense that it was not real, was not carried out. Second, while lacking in mythic articulation, the ritual expresses important ideas and points of view on the structure of reality. What people are supposed to do, without a stage of articulation of the meaning of what they do, itself expresses what they think. The explanation of the ritual, the drawing out of

---

[1] The Seventh Annual Religious Studis Lecture, University of Minnesota, 1975.

1

that explanation of some sort of major cognitive statement, is skipped. The world is mapped out through gesture, the boundaries of reality are laid forth through norms on how the boundaries of reality are laid forth.

Accordingly, we deal with laws made by people who never saw or performed the ritual described by those laws. It is through thinking about the laws that they shape and express their ideas, their judgments upon transcendent issues of sacred and profane, clean and unclean, It follows that thinking about the details of the law turns out to constitute reflection on the nature of being and the meaning of the sacred. The form, the ritual lacking in myth, is wholly integrated to the content, the mythic substructure. The structure of the ritual is its meaning.

We turn now to a particular ritual, the burning of the red cow for the preparation of ashes, to be mixed with water, and sprinkled upon a person who has became unclean through contact with a corpse. The ritual is described in two sources, Numbers 19:1-10, and the tractate of Mishnah called Parah, the cow.

Let us first consider the way the priestly author of Numbers 19:1-10 described the rite, the things he considers important to say about it:

> Tell the people of Israel to bring you a red cow without defect, in which there is no blemish, and upon which a yoke has never come. And you shall give her to Eleazar the priest, and she shall be taken outside the camp and slaughtered before him. And Eleazar the priest shall take some of her blood with his finger and sprinkle some of her blood toward the front of the tent of meeting seven times. And the heifer shall be burned in his sight; her skin, her flesh, and her blood, with her dung, shall be burned; and the priest shall take cedarwood and hyssop and scarlet stuff and cast them into the midst of the burning of the heifer. Then the priest shall wash his clothes and bathe his body in water, and afterwards he shall come into the camp and the priest shall be unclean until evening. He who burns the heifer shall wash his clothes in water and bathe his body in water and shall be unclean until evening. And a man who is clean shall gather up the ashes of the heifer and deposit them outside the camp in a clean place; and they shall be kept for the congregation of the people of Israel for the water for impurity, and the removal of sin. And he who gathers the ashes of the heifer shall wash his clothes and be unclean until evening (Num. 19:1-10a).

How is the ash used? Num. 19:17 states:

> For the unclean they shall take some ashes of the burnt sin-offering and running water shall be added in a vessel; then a clean person shall take hyssop and dip it in the water and sprinkle it upon the tent...(in which someone has died, etc.).

Let us now ask, what to the biblical writer are the important traits of the burning of the cow and the mixing of its ashes into water?

The priestly author stresses, first of all, that the rite takes place outside of the camp, which is to say, in an unclean place. He repeatedly tells us that anyone involved in the rite is made unclean by his participation in the rite, thus, 19:7, the priest shall wash his clothes; Num. 19:8, "the one who burns the heifer shall wash his clothes"; Num. 19:10, "and he who gathers the ashes of the heifer shall wash his clothes and be unclean until evening." The priestly legislator therefore takes for granted that the rules of purity which govern rites in the Temple simply do not apply to the rite of burning the cow. Not only are the participants not in a state of cleanness, but they are in a state of uncleanness, being required to wash their clothes, remaining unclean until the evening, only then allowed back into the camp which is the Temple. Accordingly, the world outside the Temple cannot be clean; only to the Temple do the cleanness taboos pertain; and it follows that a rite performed outside of the Temple is by definition not subject to the Temple's rules and is not going to be clean.

What is interesting, when we turn to the Mishnah tractate on the burning of the red cow, Parah, is its distinctive agendum of issues and themes. If I may now summarize rapidly the predominant concerns of Mishnah-Tosefta Parah, they are two: first, the degree of cleanness required of those who participate in the rite and how these people become unclean; second, how the water used for the rite is to be drawn and protected, with special attention directed to not working between the drawing the water and the mixing of the ashes referred to in Num. 19:17. The theoretical concerns of Mishnah-Tosefta Parah thus focus upon two important matters of no interest whatever to the priestly author of Numbers 19:1-10, because the priestly author assumes the rite produced uncleanness, is conducted outside of the realm of cleanness, and therefore does not involve the keeping of the levitical rules of cleanness required for participation in the Temple cult. By contrast, Mishnah-Tosefta Parah is chiefly interested in that very matter. An important body of opinion in our tractate demands a degree of cleanness higher than that required for the Temple cult itself. Further, the matter of drawing water, protecting it, and mixing it with the ash, is virtually ignored by the priestly author, while it occupies much of our tractate and, even more than in quantity, the quality and theoretical sophistication of the laws on that topic form the apex of our tractate. Accordingly, the biblical writer on the rite of burning the red cow wishes to tell us that the rite takes place outside the camp, understood in Temple times as outside the Temple. The rite is conducted in an unclean place. And it follows that people who are going to participate in the rite, slaughtering the cow, collecting its ashes, and the like, are not clean. The mishnaic authorities stress exactly the opposite conception, that people who will participate in the rite must be clean, not unclean, as if they were in the Temple. And they add a further important point, that the water which is to be used for mixing with the ashes of the cow must be mixed with the ashes without an intervening act of labor, not connected with the rite.

At the outset I pointed to two facts. First, the authorities of the Mishnah describe a ritual which, in fact, they have never seen, and about which they claim to have few historical traditions. The ritual under description is, as I said, a myth in two senses. The first has just now been stated: it is something which is not part of observed reality. But the second remains to be spelled out. The laws of the ritual themselves contain important expressions about the nature of the sacred and the clean, I shall now attempt to illustrate how the articulation of the laws, through the standard legal disputes of the late first- and second-century authorities, contains within itself statements about the most fundamental issues of reality, statements which, in describing the form of the ritual, also express the content of the ritual, its myth.

The first dispute concerns which hand one uses for sprinkling the blood toward the door of the Holy of Holies; the second asks about how we raise the cow up to the top of the pyre of wood on which it is going to be burned; and the third deals with whether intending to do the wrong thing spoils what one actually does. The texts are simple and pose no problems of interpretation. The first is at Mishnah Parah 3:9:

> They bound it with a rope of bast and place it on the pile of wood, with its head southward and its face westward.
> The priest, standing at the east side, with his face turned toward the west slaughtered it with his right (northern) hand and received the blood with his left (southern) hand.
> R. Judah says, 'With his right hand did he receive the blood and he put it into his left hand, and he sprinkled with (the index finger of) his right hand.'

Before analyzing the pericope, I should add the corresponding Tosefta supplement (Tosefta Parah 3:9):

> They bound it with a rope of bast and put it onto the wood pile.
> And some say, "It went up with a mechanical contraption."
> R. Eliezer b. Jacob says, "They made a causeway on which it ascended.
> Its head was to the south and its face to the west."

In the present set, therefore, are the first two of the issues mentioned earlier: which hand we use for sprinkling the blood, and how we raise the cow to the top of the pyre of wood.

Let us notice, first of all, the placing of the cow and the priest. The rite takes place on the Mount of Olives, that is, to the east and north of the Temple Mount in Jerusalem. Accordingly, we set up a north-south-east-west grid. The cow is placed with its head to the south, pointing in the direction of the Temple Mount, slightly to the south of the Mount of Olives, and its face is west – that is, toward the Temple. The priest then is set east of the cow, so that he too will face the Temple.

He faces west – toward the Temple. When he raises his hand to slaughter the cow, he reaches over from north and east to south and west, again, toward the Temple. We have, therefore, a clear effort to relate the location and slaughter of the red cow, which takes place outside the Temple, toward the Temple itself. In fact each gesture is meant to be movement toward the Temple. Just as Scripture links the cow, outside the camp, to the camp, by having the blood sprinkled in the direction of the camp (a detail which Mishnah takes for granted), so that the sprinkling of the blood, which is the crucial and decisive action which effects the purpose of the rite – accomplishes atonement, or *kapparah,* in mishnaic language – so all other details of the rite here are focused upon the Temple.

This brings us to Judah's opinion, which disagrees about slaughter with the left hand. As observed, we have to set up a kind of mirror to the Temple, with the whole setting organized to face and correspond to the Holy Place. The priest in the Temple slaughtered with his right hand, and received the blood in his left. Likewise, the anonymous rule holds, the priest now does the same. In other words, our rite in all respects replicates what is done in the Temple setting: What is done there is done here. Judah, by contrast, wants the blood received with the right hand and slaughtered with the left. Why? Because we are not in the Temple itself. We are facing it. Thus if we want to replicate the cultic gestures, we have to do each thing in exactly the opposite direction. Just as, in a mirror, one's left is at the right, and the right is at the left, so here, we set up a mirror. Accordingly, he says, if in the Temple the priest receives the blood in his left hand, on the Mount of Olives and facing the Temple, he receives the blood in his right hand. All parties to the dispute, therefore, agree on this fundamental proposition, that the effort is to replicate the Temple's cult in every possible regard.

This brings us to the dispute about how we get the beast up to the top of the wood pile. The anonymous rule, shared by Mishnah and Tosefta, is that we bind the sacrificial cow and somehow drag it up to the top. But in the Temple the sacrifices were not bound; they would be spoiled if they were bound. Accordingly, Eliezer b. Jacob, a contemporary of Judah, imposes the same rule. He says that there was a causeway constructed from the ground to the top of the woodpile on which the cow will be slaughtered and burned, and the cow walks up on its own. Self-evidently, both parties cannot be right, and the issue is not what really was done in "historical" times – let us say, seventy-five years earlier. As in the dispute between Judah and the anonymous narrator, the issue is precisely how we shall do the rite, on the Mount of Olives, so as to conform to the requirements of the rite on the Temple Mount itself. To state matters in general terms, it is taken for granted by all parties to the present pericope that the rite of the cow is done in the profane world, outside the cult, *as if* it were done in the sacred world constituted by the Temple itself.

How is the contrary viewpoint expressed? The simplest statement is in Mishnah Parah 2:3B-D:

B.   The harlot's hire and the price of a dog – it is unfit.

That is to say, if the red cow is purchased with funds deriving from money spent to purchase the services of a prostitute or to buy a dog, the cow is unfit for the rite. The pericope continues:

C.   R. Eliezer declares fit,
D.   since it is said, 'You will not bring the harlot's hire and the price of a dog to the house of the Lord your God (Deut. 23:18). But this (cow) does not come to the house (of the Lord, namely, the Temple).

The issue could not be drawn more clearly than does the glossator (D). Eliezer holds that since the burning of the cow takes place outside of the Temple, the Temple's rules as to the acquisition of the cow simply do not apply.

A more subtle question appears at Mishnah Parah 4:1 and 4:3. The manuscript evidence here is in conflict. Some manuscripts give us the operative ruling in the name of Eliezer, others read Eleazar, a different authority; and in point of fact, there are several Eliezers and Eleazars. Tosefta supplies a parallel which gives us Eleazar b. R. Simeon, and I am inclined to think that the Mishnah's Eliezers and Eleazars are Eleazar b. R. Simeon. But it hardly matters, since the viewpoint is identical to that assigned to Eliezer (certainly b. Hyrcanus, ca. 70-90) in the foregoing passage. The first item, Mishnah Parah 4:1, is as follows:

The cow of purification which one slaughtered not for its own name (meaning, not as a cow of purification, but for some other offering), or the blood of which one received and sprinkled not for its own name, etc., is unfit.
     R. Eliezer (Eleazar) declares fit.

What is at issue? In the sanctuary, we have correctly to designate the *purpose* of a sacrifice. Eleazar holds that this is not a rite subject to the rule of the Temple cult. The rule continues,

     And if this was done by a priest whose hands and feet were not washed,
it is unfit.
     R. Eliezer declared fit.

Priests of the Temple of course had to be properly washed. Since the rite is not in the Temple, Eliezer says that the priest need not even be washed. In this connection, Tosefta supplies:

If one whose hands and feet were not washed burned it, it is unsuitable.

And R. Eleazar b. R. Simeon declares fit, as it is said 'When they come to the Tent of Meeting, they will wash in water and not die' (Ex. 30:20) – So the washing of the hands applies only inside (the Temple, and not on the Mount of Olives).

The issue seems to me fully articulated, and the glosses in both the matter of the harlot's hire and the matter of washing spell out the implications. The law which describes the ritual – the *structure* of the ritual itself – also expresses the meaning of the ritual. The form imposed upon the ritual fully and completely states the content of the ritual. If now we ask, What is this content? we may readily answer. The ritual outside of the cult is done in a state of cleanness, as is the ritual done inside the cult. The laws of the cult, furthermore, apply not only to the conduct of the slaughtering of the cow (the cases I have given here), but also to the preservation of purity by those who will participate in the slaughtering (cases not reviewed here).

Mishnah presupposes what Scripture takes for granted is not possible, namely, that the rules of purity apply outside of the Temple, just as the rules of Temple slaughter apply outside of the Temple. And the reason is, of course, that the Mishnah derives, in part from the Pharisees, whose fundamental conviction is that the cleanness taboos of the Temple and its priesthood apply to the life of all Israel, outside of the Temple and not of priestly caste. When Israelites eat their meals in their homes, they must obey the cleanness taboos as if they were priests at the table of God in the Temple. This larger conception is expressed in the acute laws before us.

Let us now proceed to a matter which is by no means self-evident, and which was not understood in the way in which I shall explain it even by the second-century authorities. It concerns the issue of drawing the water. The rule is that if I draw water for mixing with the ashes of the red cow, and, before actually accomplishing the mixture, I do an act of labor not related to the rite of the mixing of the ashes, I spoil the water. This is stated very succinctly, "An act of extraneous labor spoils the water." This conception is likely to have originated before the destruction of the Second Temple in 70, because a very minor gloss on the basic rule is attributed to the authorities of the period immediately after 70, of Yavneh:

He who brings the borrowed rope in his hand (after drawing the water with bucket suspended on a rope, the man plans to return the rope to the owner) – if (he returns it to the owner) on his way (to the rite of adding ashes to the water), it is suitable (that is, the bucket of water has not been spoiled by the act of extraneous labor), and if it is not on his way, it is unfit.

Appended is the following observation:

> (On this matter) someone went to Yavneh three festival seasons (to ask the law), and at the third festival season, they declared it fit for him, as a special dispensation.

Taken for granted, therefore, is the principle, evidently deriving from Pharisaism before 70, that an act of extraneous labor done between the drawing of the water and the mixing of ashes and water spoils the drawn water.

The rule lies far beyond the imagination of the priestly writer of Numbers, because he tells us virtually nothing about the water into which the ashes are to be mixed. But that is of no consequence. What is interesting, second, is the language which is used, *unfit,* not *unclean.* So the matter of the cleanness of the water – its protection against sources of contamination – is not at issue. Some other consideration has to be involved. Third, the drawing of the water is treated as intrinsic to the rite. That is: I burn the cow. I go after water for mixing with the ashes of the cow. That journey – outside of the place in which the cow is burned – is assumed to be part of the larger rite.

Now this matter of extraneous labor is exceedingly puzzling. We have to ask, to begin with, for some sort of relevant analogy. Do we know about other rites in which we distinguish between acts of labor which are intrinsic and those which are not? And on what occasion is such a distinction made? The answer to these questions is obvious. We do distinguish between acts of labor required for the conduct of the sacrificial cult, and those which are not required for the conduct of the sacrificial cult, in particular we make that distinction *on the Sabbath.* On the Sabbath day labor is prohibited. But the cult is continued. How? Labor intrinsic to the sacrifices required on the Sabbath is to be done, and that which is not connected with the sacrifice is not to be done.

When we introduce the issue of extraneous labor (and the issue extends to the burning of the cow itself, but I think this is secondary), what do we say about the character of the sanctity of the rite? Clearly, we take this position: The rite is conducted by analogy to the sacrifices which take place in the Temple, so that the place of the rite and all its participants must be clean, exactly as the place of the Temple and all the participants in the Temple sacrifices must be clean. So too with the matter of labor. When we impose the Temple's taboos, we state that the rite is to be conducted in clean space. When we introduce the issue of labor, we forthwith raise the question of holy time, the Sabbath. For it is solely to the Sabbath that the matter of labor or no labor, labor which is intrinsic or labor which is extrinsic, applies. When we impose the taboos applicable to the Temple on the Sabbath, we state that the rite is to be conducted in holy *time.*

The cleanness laws in the present instance create in the world outside of the cult a *place of cleanness* analogous to the cult. The Sabbath laws in the present instance create in the world outside of the cult a *time of holiness* analogous to the locus of the cult. The ritual constructs a structure of clean cultic space and holy Sabbath time in the world to which, by the priestly definition, neither cleanness nor holiness (in the limited sense of the present discussion) applies.

The laws, it is clear, do not contain explanations. The issues themselves are trivial, ritualistic, yet even the glossators at the outset introduced into the consideration of legal descriptions of ritual extra-legal conceptions of fundamental importance. Accordingly, the processes of thought which produce the rabbis' legal dicta about ritual matters also embody the rabbis' judgments about profound issues. The final stage in my argument is to consider other sorts of sayings, in which the rabbis speak more openly and directly about matters we should regard as theological, not ritual, in character. These sayings are general, not specific, treat questions of salvation, not of the conduct of a ritual, and constitute a quite distinct mode of expression about these same questions, These theological sayings contrast, therefore, to the ones about ritual law, showing a separate way in which the authorities of the same period form and express their ideas. The issue at hand, in particular, is the relationship between cleanness and holiness. We have already considered the matter in our interpretation of the ritual laws, showing that cleanness is distinct from holiness, and the two are related to and expressed by the laws about burning the red cow. Pinhas b. Yair gives us a statement (translated following ms. Kaufman) which links the issue of cleanness and holiness to salvation:

> R. Pinhas b. Yair says, "Attentiveness leads to (hygienic) cleanliness, cleanliness to (ritual) cleanness, cleanness to holiness, holiness to humility, humility to fear of sin, fear of sin to piety, and piety to the holy spirit, the holy spirit to the resurrection of the dead, and the resurrection of the dead to Elijah of blessed memory."

Pinhas therefore sees cleanness as a step in the ladder leading to holiness, thence to salvation: the resurrection of the dead and the coming of the Messiah. Maimonides, much later, introduces into the messianic history the burning of the cow of purification. Referring to the saying that nine cows in all were burned from the time of Moses to the destruction of the Second Temple, he states (*Red Heifer* 3:4):

> Now nine red heifers were prepared from the time this commandment was received until the Temple was destroyed the second time...and a tenth will King Messiah prepare – may he soon be revealed.

Maimonides thus wishes to link the matter of the burning the red cow which produces water for ritual purification to the issue of the coming of the Messiah. Both sayings, those of Pinhas b. Yair and Maimonides, show that is is entirely possible to speak directly and immediately, not through the language of ritual law, about fundamental questions. And when we do find such statements, we no longer are faced with ritual laws at all. Yet it seems to be clear that Pinhas b. Yair and Maimonides saw in the issues of purity, even in the very specific questions addressed by the rabbinic lawyers who provide the ritual law, matters of transcendent, even salvific, weight and meaning.

Let us now return to the issues raised at the outset and summarize the entire argument. It is now clear that the mishnaic rabbis express their primary cognitive statements, their judgments upon large matters, through ritual law, not through myth or theology. Indeed, we observe a curious disjuncture between ritual laws and theological sayings concerned with the *heilsgeschichtliche* meanings of the laws. The ritual laws themselves describe a ritual.

Since the ritual was not carried out by the authorities of the law, the purpose and meaning of legislation in respect to the ritual of burning the cow are self-evidently not to describe something which has been done, but to create – if only in theory – something which, if done, will establish limits and boundaries to sacred reality. The issue of the ritual is *cleanness* outside of the Temple, and, if I am right about the taboo connected with drawing the water, *holiness* outside of the Temple as well. The lines of structure, converging upon, and emanating from, the Temple, have now to be discerned in the world of the secular, the unclean, and the profane. Where better to discern, to lay out these lines of structure, than in connection with the ritual of sacrifice not done in the Temple but outside of it, in that very world of the secular, unclean, and profane. As I have stressed, the priestly author of Numbers cannot imagine that cleanness is a prerequisite of the ritual. He says the exact opposite. The ritual produces contamination for those who participate. The second-century rabbis who debated the details of the rite held that the rite is performed just as it would have been done in the Temple. Or, in the mind of Eliezer and Eleazar b. R. Simeon, the rite is performed in a way different from the way it would have been done in the Temple. The laws which describe the ritual therefore contain important judgments upon its meaning. With remarkably little exegesis of those laws – virtually none not coming to us from the glossators themselves – we are able to see that their statements about law deal with metaphysical reality, revealing their effort to discern and to define the limits of both space and time.

The structure of the ritual contains its meaning. Form and content are wholly integrated. Indeed, we are unable to dissociate form from content. It follows that what is done in the ritual, the sprinkling with one hand or other other, the binding of the cow or the use of a causeway to bring it to the pyre, the purchase of cows with the wrong sort of money, the employment of unwashed priests, the exclusion of the issue of the wrong intention – all of these matters of rite and form *alone* contain whatever the rabbis will tell us about the meaning of the rite and its forms. The reason, as I have stressed, is that the rabbis think about transcendent issues primarily through rite and form. When, as I showed at the end, they choose another means of discourse and a different mode of thought entirely, matters of rite and form fall away. Theological and mythic considerations to which ritual is irrelevant take their place. Judah, Eliezer, Eleazar b. R. Simeon, Eliezer b. Jacob, and the others cited, however, refer to no myth, make use of neither mythic nor theological language, because they think about reality and speak about it through the norms of the law. Since, as I have stressed, the law concerns a ritual which these authorities have never seen and certainly would never perform, *the law itself constitutes its own myth,* the fabulous myth of a ritual no one has ever done, and the transcendent myth of the realm of the clean and the sacred constructed through ritual and taboo in the world of the unclean and the secular. That is why I claim that the ritual *is* the myth. What people are told to do is what they are supposed to think, the gestures and taboos of the rite themselves express the meaning of the rite, without the mediation of myth.

2

Max Weber Revisited:
Religion and Society in Ancient Judaism

with Special Reference to the Late First
and Second Centuries

A scholar's journey moves in ever-widening circles, down familiar paths towards frontiers of knowledge and across. For the study of religion in general, and Judaism as an example of the general, Max Weber laid out one road from the known even to the outer bounds of understanding. We do well again and again to walk on the road he laid out. There are two points of interest today in Weber's thought, one which serves to define my problem, and the other which shows the way in which I propose to solve it. First, Weber's interest in the relation between social stratification and religious ideas presents an enduring perspective for the analysis of the place of religion in society and of the relationship between religion and society. Second, Weber's mode of formulating ideal types for the purposes of analysis provides a model for how we may think about the castes, professions, and classes of society and the religious ideas they hold. The former is the fundamental issue. If we ask about whether we may discern congruence between the religious ideas to be assigned to a given group, described in gross terms as an ideal type, in ancient Israelite society, and the class status of that group, we use a mode of thought shaped by Weber in the analysis of a question raised by Weber.

It is in that sense alone that we revisit Weber. I do not propose to enrich the vast literature of interpretation of his writings, let alone discuss the enduring or transient value of his work on ancient Judaism, which is important only in the study of Weber. I shall simply take the road laid out by Weber, in order to cross frontiers of problems of interpretation not known to the world of learning in the time of Weber's *Ancient Judaism,* I mean, describing and explaining the character of Judaism as it took shape in the late first and second centuries. My purpose, stated simply, is to explore that paramount theme in Weber's great work, as expressed by Reinhard Bendix:

In order to understand the stability and dynamics of a society we should attempt to understand these efforts in relation to the ideas and values that are prevalent in the society; or, conversely, for every given idea or value that we observe we should seek out the status group whose material and ideal way of life it tends to enhance. Thus, Weber approached the study of religious ideas in terms of their relevance for collective actions, and specially in terms of the social processes whereby the inspirations of a few become the convictions of the many (Reinhard Bendix, *Max Weber. An Intellectual Portrait* (New York, 1962: Doubleday), p. 259).

The question then is how to relate the religious ideas held by an important group of Jews in the late first and second centuries to the social world imagined by that group.

The group under discussion is that handful of sages who, from before 70, through the period between the second war against Rome, in 132-135, and down to the end of the second century, worked out the principal themes of Israelite life and law and produced the Mishnah, their systematic account of the way in which Israel, the Jewish people in the Holy Land, should construct its life.[1] Taking up, in succession, the holiness of the Land, the proper conduct of cult and home on holy days, the holiness of family life with special reference to the transfer of women from the father's house to the husband's bed, the stable conduct of civil life, the conduct of the cult on ordinary days, and the bounds of holiness in a world of cultic uncleanness, the Mishnah designed the formative categories of reality and designated their contents.

Our work is to generalize about fundamental religious perspectives and collective actions. Now it is not difficult to take up one teaching or another within that law code and speculate about who may have said it, for what material or ideal purpose, and as an expression of which social status or context. But that sort of unsystematic and unmethodical speculation is hardly worthy of the question presented to us by Max Weber, because in the end the answers are beside the point. We wish to ask how and why "the inspirations of a few" – the sages of the document

---

[1] Weber's formulation of the problem – the relationship of religious ideas to the group which held them – justifies our concentrating on a given book of the character of the Mishnah. First, we assume only that the Mishnah speaks for its authorities, with no presuppositions, at this point, about their prospective audience. Second, since the Mishnah to begin with is a collective document, carefully effacing the signs of individual authorship or authority, we are justified in deeming it to speak for a group. Third, as we shall now see, the Mishnah most certainly is a corpus of religious conceptions, framed, in some measure, through the medium of civil law to be sure. So it would be wrong to suppose that at hand is an exercise in treating a book as a religious community (!). Within the framework of Weber's paradigm, the Mishnah constitutes an ideal program for description and analysis of one suggestive aspect of the relationship between religion and society.

under discussion and the people who stand behind the document – become "the convictions of the many." For that purpose, episodic speculation on discrete sayings is not really pertinent, even if it *were* to be subject to the controls and tests of verification and falsification.

Rather I wish to turn to a more fundamental matter, which is the mode of thought of the group as a whole. That mode of thought is revealed, in particular, in the way in which questions are formulated. For what is telling is the asking; what is revealing is how people define what they wish to know. If we may discover the key to the system by which questions are generated and by which the logic for forming and answering those questions is made to appear to be self-evident, and if we may then relate that mode of logic and inquiry to its social setting, then I believe we may claim to speak to that program of thought laid forth by Weber in his effort "to analyze the relation between social stratification and religious ideas" (Bendix, p. 258). In this regard, individual ideas, let alone the ideas of individual thinkers, are not important. The great classical historian, Harold Cherniss, says, "The historian is concerned to comprehend the individuality of a work of art only in order that he may eliminate it and so extract for use as historical evidence those elements which are not the creation of the author" (Harold Cherniss, "The Biographical Fashion in Literary Criticism," *University of California Publications in Classical Philology,* ed. by J. T. Allen, W. H. Alexander, and G. M. Calhoun, vol. XII, No. 15, pp. 279-292; quotation, pp. 279-280). We must do the same. That is, we are not helped to know the ideas of individuals or even the concrete and specific doctrines of the document. We wish, rather, to eliminate not only individuality, but also all specificity. So we turn to what is most general. That is, as I said, we want to discover the systemic motive behind asking a question, the power which generates and defines both problems and the logic by which they will be solved.

Let me now state the proposition of this lecture at the outset. The issues which occupy the Mishnah's philosophical mode of forming ideas and defining questions to be taken up will be seen to emerge from the social circumstance of the people of Israel in the Land of Israel. Specifically, the Mishnah's systematic preoccupation with sorting out uncertainties, with pointing up and resolving points of conflict, and with bringing into alignment contradictory principles, corresponds in thought to the confusion and doubt which then disordered Israelite social existence in the aftermath of defeat and catastrophe. In every line the Mishnah both expresses the issue of confusion in the wake of the end of the old mode of ordering life above and below, and also imposes order by sorting out confused matters. The Mishnaic message is that Israel's will is decisive. What the Israelite proposes is what disposes of questions, resolves conflict, settles doubt. Everything depends upon Israelite will, whether this thing of which we speak be expressed in terms of wish, intention, attitude, hope, conception, idea, aspiration, or other words which speak of parts of the whole entity of heart and mind. So the medium is a sequence of problems of conflict and confusion, and the message is that things are what you will them to be.

In a moment of deep despair and doubt such as the late first and second centuries, this appeal to the heart and mind of Israel penetrated to the depths of the dilemma.

I. The Mishnah in its Social Setting

The Mishnah presents a "Judaism," that is, a coherent world view and comprehensive way of living. It is a world view which speaks of transcendent things, a way of life expressive of the supernatural meaning of what is done, a heightened and deepened perception of the sanctification of Israel in deed and in deliberation. Sanctification means two things: first, distinguishing Israel in all its dimensions from the world in all its ways; second, establishing the stability, order, regularity, predictability, and reliability of Israel at moments and in contexts of danger, meaning instability, disorder, irregularity, uncertainty, and betrayal. Each topic of the Mishnah's system of Judaism as a whole takes up a critical and indispensable moment or context of social being. Through what is said in regard to each of the Mishnah's principal topics, what the system as a whole wishes to declare is fully expressed. Yet if the parts both severally and jointly give the message of the whole, the whole cannot exist without all of the parts, so well-joined and carefully crafted are they all together.

The critical issue in economic life, which means, in farming, is in two parts. First, Israel, as tenant on God's Holy Land, maintains the property in the ways God requires, keeping the rules which make the Land and its crops as holy. Second, at the hour at which the sanctification of the Land comes to form a critical mass, namely, in the ripened crops, comes the moment ponderous with danger and heightened holiness. Israel's will so affects the crops as to mark a part of them as holy, the rest of them as available for common use. The human will is determinative in the process of sanctification. Second, what happens in the Land at certain times, at Appointed Times, marks off spaces of the Land as holy in yet another way. The center of the Land and the focus of its sanctification is the Temple. There the produce of the Land is received and given back to God, the One who created and sanctified the Land. At these unusual moments of sanctification, the inhabitants of the Land in their social being in villages enter a state of spatial sanctification. This is expressed in two ways. First, the Temple itself observes and expresses the special, recurring holy time. Second, the villages of the Land are brought into alignment with the Temple, forming a complement and completion to the Temple's sacred being. The advent of the appointed times precipitates a spatial reordering of the Land, so that the boundaries of the sacred are matched and mirrored in village and in Temple. At the heightened holiness marked by these moments of appointed times, therefore, the occasion for an effective sanctification is worked out. Like the harvest, the advent of an appointed time, a pilgrim festival also a sacred season, is made to express that regular, orderly, and predictable sort of sanctification for Israel which the system as a whole seeks.

If for a moment we bypass the next two divisions, we come to the counterpart of the divisions of Agriculture and Appointed Times, that is, Holy Things and Purities. These divisions deal with the everyday and the ordinary, as against the special moments of harvest, on the one side, and special time or season, on the other. The Temple, the locus of continuous, as against special, sanctification, is conducted in a wholly routine and trustworthy, punctilious manner. the one thing which may unsettle matters is the intention and will of the human actor. The division of Holy Things generates its companion, the one on cultic cleanness, Purities. The relationship between the two is like that between Agriculture and Appointed Times, the former locative, the latter utopian, the former dealing with the fields, the latter with the interplay between fields and altar. Here too, once we speak of the one place of the Temple, we address, too, the cleanness which pertains to every place. A system of cleanness, taking into account what imparts uncleanness and how this is done, what is subject to uncleanness, and how that state is overcome – that system is fully expressed, once more, in response to the participation of the human will. Without the wish and act of a human being, the system does not function. It is inert. Sources of uncleanness, which come naturally and not by volition, and modes of purification, which work naturally and not by human intervention, remain inert until human will has imparted susceptibility to uncleanness, that is, introduced into the system, that food and drink, bed, pot, chair, and pan, which to begin with form the focus of the system. The movement from sanctification to uncleanness takes place when human will and work precipitate it.

The middle divisions, the third and fourth, on Women, on family law, and Damages, on civil law, finally, take their place in the structure of the whole by showing the congruence, within the larger framework of sanctification through regularity and the perfection of social order, of human concerns of family and farm, politics and workaday transactions among ordinary people. For without attending to these matters, the Mishnah's system does not encompass what, at its foundations, it is meant to comprehend and order. What is at issue is fully cogent with the rest. In the case of Women, attention focuses upon the point of disorder marked by the transfer of that disordering anomaly, woman, from the regular status provided by one man, to the equally trustworthy status provided by another. That is the point at which the Mishnah's interests are aroused: once more, predictably, the moment of disorder. In the case of Damages, there are two important concerns. First, there is the paramount interest in preventing, so far as possible, the disorderly rise of one person and fall of another, and in sustaining the *status quo* of the economy of the household Israel, the holy society in perfect stasis. Second, there is the necessary concomitant in the provision of a system of political institutions to carry out the laws which preserve the balance and steady state of persons.

The divisions which take up topics of concrete and material concern, the formation and dissolution of families and the transfer of property in that connection, the transactions, both through torts and through commerce, which lead to exchanges of property and the potential dislocation of the state of families in society, are both locative and utopian. They deal with the concrete locations in which people make their lives, household and street and field, the sexual and commercial exchanges of a given village. But they pertain to the life of all Israel, both in the Land and otherwise. These two divisions, together with the household ones of Appointed Times, constitute the sole opening outward toward the life of utopian Israel, that diaspora in the far reaches of the ancient world. This community from the Mishnah's perspective is not merely in exile, but unaccounted for; it is simply outside the system, for the Mishnah declines to recognize and take it into account. Israelites who dwell in the land of (unclean) death instead of in the Land simply fall outside of the realm and range of (holy) life.

Now if we ask ourselves about the sponsorship and source of special interest in the topics just now reviewed, we come up with obvious answers.

So far as the Mishnah is a document about the holiness of Israel in its Land, it expresses that conception of sanctification and theory of its mode which will have been shaped among those to whom the Temple and its technology of joining Heaven and holy Land through the sacred place defined the core of being, I mean, the caste of the priests.

So far as the Mishnah takes up the way in which transactions are conducted among ordinary folk and takes the position that it is through documents that transactions are embodied and expressed (surely the position of the relevant tractates on both Women and Damages), the Mishnah expresses what is self-evident to scribes. Just as, to the priest, there is a correspondence between the table of the Lord in the Temple and the locus of the divinity in the heavens, so, to the scribe, there is a correspondence between the documentary expression of the human will on earth, in writs of all sorts, in the orderly provision of courts for the predictable and just disposition of exchanges of persons and property, and Heaven's judgment of these same matters. When a woman becomes sanctified to a particular man on earth, through the appropriate document governing the transfer of her person and property, in heaven as well, the woman is deemed truly sanctified to that man. A violation of the writ therefore is not merely a crime. It is a sin. That is why the Temple rite involving the wife accused of adultery is integral to the system of the division of Women.

So there are these two social groups. But they are not symmetrical with one another. For one is the priestly caste, and the other is the scribal profession. We know, moreover, that in time to come, the profession would become a focus of sanctification too. The scribe would be transformed into the rabbi, locus of the holy through what he knew, just as the priest had been, and would remain, locus of the holy through what he could claim for genealogy. The tractates of special interest to scribes-become-rabbis and to their governance of Israelite society, those of Women and Damages, together with certain others particularly relevant to utopian Israel beyond the system of the Land – those tractates would grow and grow. Others would remain essentially as they were with the closure of the Mishnah. So we must notice that the Mishnah, for its part, speaks about the program of topics important to the priests. It does so in the persona of the scribes, speaking through their voice and in their manner.

Now what we do not find is astonishing in the light of these observations. It is sustained and serious attention to the matter of the caste of the priests and of the profession of the scribes. True, scattered through the tractates are exercises, occasionally important exercises, on the genealogy of the priestly caste, their marital obligations and duties, as well as on the things priests do and do not do in the cult, in collecting and eating their sanctified food, and other topics of keen interest to priests. Indeed, it would be no exaggeration to say that the Mishnah's system, seen whole is not a great deal more than a handbook of how the priestly caste wished to design its life in Israel and the world. And this is what makes amazing the fact that in the fundamental structure of the document, its organization into divisions and tractates, there is no place for a division of the Priesthood. There is no room even for a complete tractate on the rules of the priesthood, except, as we have seen, for the pervasive way of life of the priestly caste, which is everywhere. This absence of sustained attention to the priesthood is striking, when we compare the way in which the Priestly Code at Leviticus chapters one through fifteen spells out its triplet of concerns: the priesthood, the cult, the matter of cultic cleanness. Since we have divisions for the cult and for cleanness at Holy Things and Purities, we are struck by the absence of a parallel to the third division.

We must, moreover, be equally surprised that, for a document so rich in the importance lent to petty matters of how a writ is folded and where the witnesses sign, so obsessed with the making of long lists and the organization of all knowledge into neat piles of symmetrically arranged words, the scribes who know how to make lists and match words nowhere come to the fore. They speak through the document. But they stand behind the curtains. They write the script, arrange the sets, design the costumes, situate the players in their place on the stage, raise the curtain – and play no role at all. We have no division or tractate on such matters as how a person becomes a scribe, how a scribe conducts his work, who forms the center of the scribal profession and how authority is gained therein, the rights and place of the scribe in the system of governance through courts, the organization and conduct of schools or circles of masters and disciples through which the scribal arts are taught and perpetuated. This absence of even minimal information on the way in which the scribal profession takes shape and does its work is stunning, when we realize that, within a brief generation, the Mishnah as a whole would fall into the hands of scribes, called rabbis,[2] both in the Land of Israel and in Babylonia.

---

[2] But the title, "rabbi," cannot be thought particular to those who served as judges and administrators in small-claims courts and as scribes and authorities in the Jewish community, called "rabbis" in the talmudic literature and afterward. The title is clearly prior to its particularization in the institutions of the talmudic community.

These rabbis would make of the Mishnah exactly what they wished. Construed from the perspective of the makers of the Mishnah, the priests and the scribes who provide contents and form, substance and style, therefore, the Mishnah turns out to omit all reference to actors, when laying out the world which is their play.

The metaphor of the theater for the economy of Israel, the household of holy Land and people, space and time, cult and home, leads to yet another perspective. When we look out upon the vast drama portrayed by the Mishnah, lacking as it does an account of the one who wrote the book, and the one about whom the book was written, we notice yet one more missing component. In the fundamental and generative structure of the Mishnah, we find no account of that other necessary constituent: the audience. To whom the document speaks is never specified. What group ("class") generates the Mishnah's problems is not at issue. True, it is taken for granted that the world of the Mishnah expresses the sanctified being of Israel in general. So the Mishnah speaks about the generality of Israel, the people. But to whom, within Israel, the Mishnah addresses itself, and what groups are expected to want to know what the Mishnah has to say are matters which never come to full expression.

Yet there can be no doubt of the answer to the question. The building block of Mishnaic discourse, the circumstance addressed whenever the issues of concrete society and material transactions are taken up, is the householder and his context. The Mishnah knows all sorts of economic activities. But for the Mishnah the center and focus of interest lie in the village. The village is made up of households, each a unit of production in farming. The households are constructed by, and around, the householder, father of an extended family, including his sons and their wives and children, his servants, his slaves, the craftsmen to whom he entrusts tasks he does not choose to do. The concerns of householders are in transactions in land. Their measurement of value is expressed in acreage of top, middle, and bottom grade. Through real estate critical transactions are worked out. The marriage settlement depends upon real property. Civil penalties are exacted through payment of real property. The principal transactions to be taken up are those of the householder who owns beasts which do damage or suffer it; who harvests his crops and must set aside and so by his own word and deed sanctify them for use by the castes scheduled from on high; who uses or sells his crops and feeds his family; and who, if he is fortunate, will acquire still more land. It is to householders that the Mishnah is addressed: the pivot of society and its bulwark, the units of production of which the village is composed, the corporate component of the society of Israel in the limits of the village and the land. The householder, as I said, is the building block of the house of Israel, of its *economy* in the classic sense of the word.

So, to revert to the metaphor which has served us well, the great proscenium constructed by the Mishnah now looms before us. Its arch is the canopy of heaven. Its stage is the holy Land of Israel, corresponding to heaven. Its actors are the holy people of Israel. Its events are the drama of unfolding time and common transactions, appointed times and holy events. Yet in this grand design we look in vain for the three principal participants: the audience, the actors, and the playwright. So we must ask why.

The reason is not difficult to discover, when we recall that, after all, what the Mishnah really wants is for nothing to happen. The Mishnah presents a tableau, a wax museum, a diorama. It portrays a world fully perfected and so wholly at rest. The one thing the Mishnah does not want to tell us is about change, how things come to be, or cease to be, what they are. That is why there can be no sustained attention to the caste of the priesthood and its rules, the scribal profession and its constitution, the class of householders and its interests. The Mishnah's pretense is that all of these have come to rest. They compose a world in stasis, perfect and complete, made holy because it is complete and perfect. It is an economy – again in the classic sense of the word – awaiting the divine *act* of sanctification which, as at the creation of the world, would set the seal of holy rest upon an again-complete creation, just as in the beginning. There is no place for the actors when what is besought is no action whatsoever, but only perfection, which is unchanging. There is room only for a description of how things are: the present tense, the sequence of completed statements and static problems. All the action lies within, in how these statements are made. Once they come to full expression, with nothing left to say, there also is nothing left to do, no need for actors, whether scribes, priests, or householders.

We have now to ask how the several perspectives joined in the Mishnah do coalesce. What the single message is which brings them all together, and how that message forms a powerful, if transient, catalyst for the social groups which hold it – these define the task in portraying the Judaism for which the Mishnah is the whole evidence. Integral to that task, to be sure, is an account of why, for the moment, the catalyst could serve, as it clearly did, to join together diverse agents, to mingle, mix, indeed unite, for a fleeting moment, social elements quite unlike one another, indeed not even capable of serving as analogies for one another.

One of the paramount, recurring exercises of the Mishnaic thinkers is to give an account of how things which are different from one another become part of one another, that is, the problem of mixtures. This problem of mixtures will be in many dimensions, involving cases of doubt; cases of shared traits and distinctive ones; cases of confusion of essentially distinct elements and components; and numerous other concrete instances of successful and of unsuccessful, complete and partial catalysis. If I had to choose one prevailing motif of Mishnaic thought, it is this: the joining together of categories which are distinct, the distinguishing among those which are confused. The Mishnaic mode of thought is to bring together principles and to show both how they conflict and how the conflict is resolved; to deal with gray areas and to lay down principles for disposing of cases of doubt; to take up the analysis of entities into their component parts and the catalysis of distinct substances into a single entity; to analyze the whole, to synthesize the parts. The motive force behind the Mishnah's intellectual program of cases and examples, the thing the authorship of the Mishnah wants to do with all of the facts it has in its hand, is described within this inquiry into mixtures. Now the reasons for this deeply typical, intellectual concern with confusion and order, I think, are probably to be found here and there and everywhere.

For, after all, the basic mode of thought of the priests who made up the priestly creation legend (Gen. 1:1-2:4a) is that creation is effected through the orderly formation of each thing after its kind and correct location of each in its place. The persistent quest of the Mishnaic subsystems is for stasis, order, the appropriate situation of all things.

A recurrent theme in the philosophical tradition of Graeco-Roman antiquity, current in the time of the Mishnah's formative intellectual processes, is the nature of mixtures,[3] the interpenetration of distinct substances and their qualities, the juxtaposition of incomparables. The types of mixture were themselves organized in a taxonomy: a mechanical composition, in which the components remain essentially unchanged, a total fusion, in which all particles are changed and lose their individual properties, and, in-between, a mixture proper, in which there is a blending. So, concern for keeping things straight and in their place is part of the priestly heritage, and it also is familiar to the philosophical context in which scribes can have had their being. Nor will the householders have proved disinterested in the notion of well-marked borders and stable and dependable frontiers between different things. What was to be fenced in and fenced out hardly requires specification.

And yet, however tradition and circumstances may have dictated this point of interest in mixtures and their properties, in sorting out what is confused and finding a proper place for everything, I think there is still another reason for the recurrence of a single type of exercise and a uniform mode of thought. It is the social foundation for the intellectual exercise which is the Mishnah and its Judaism. In my view the very condition of Israel, standing, at the end of the second century, on the limns of its own history, at the frontiers among diverse peoples, on both sides of every boundary, whether political or cultural or intellectual – it is the condition of Israel itself which attracted attention to this matter of sorting things out. *The concern for the catalyst which joins what is originally distinct, the powerful attraction of problems of confusion and chaos, on the one side, and order and form, on the other – these form the generative problematic of the Mishnah as a system because they express in intellectual form the very nature and essential being of Israel in its social condition at that particular moment in Israel's history.* It is therefore the profound congruence of the intellectual program and the social and historical realities taken up and worked out by that intellectual program, which accounts for the power of the Mishnah to define the subsequent history of Judaism.

---

[3] I refer to S. Sambursky, *The Physics of the Stoics.*

That is why the inspirations of the few in time would become the convictions of the many. It is what Weber's questions generate for answers.

II. THE MISHNAH'S METHODS OF THOUGHT

Now that the tributaries to the Mishnah have been specified, we have to turn to those traits of style and substance in which the Mishnah vastly exceeds the flood of its tributaries, becomes far more than the sum of its parts. The Mishnah in no way presents itself as a document of class, caste, or profession. It is something different. The difference comes to complete statement in the two dimensions which mark the measure of any work of intellect: style and substance, mode of thought, medium of expression, and message. These have now to be specified with full attention to recurrent patterns to be discerned among the myriad of detailed rules, problems, and exercises, of which the Mishnah is composed.[4]

Let us take up, first of all, the matter of style. The Mishnah's paramount literary trait is its emphasis on disputes about the law. Nearly all disputes, which dominate the rhetoric of the Mishnah, derive from bringing diverse legal principles into formal juxtaposition and substantive conflict. So we may say that the Mishnah as a whole is an exercise in the application to a given case, through practical reason, of several distinct and conflicting principles of law. In this context, it follows, the Mishnah is a protracted inquiry into the intersection of principles. It maps out the gray areas of the law delimited by such limns of confusion. An example of this type of "mixture" of legal principles comes in the conflict of two distinct bodies of the law. But gray areas are discerned not only through mechanical juxtaposition, making up a conundrum of distinct principles of law. On the contrary, the Mishnaic philosophers are at their best when they force into conflict laws which, to begin with, scarcely intersect. This they do, for example, by inventing cases in which the secondary implications of one law are brought into conflict with the secondary implications of some other. Finally, nothing will so instantly trigger the imagination of the Mishnah's exegetical minds as matters of ambiguity. A species of the genus of gray areas of the law is the excluded middle, that is, the creature or substance which appears to fall between two distinct and definitive categories. The Mishnah's framers time and again allude to such an entity, because it forms the excluded middle which inevitably will attract attention and demand categorization. There are types of recurrent middles among both human beings and animals as well as vegetables. Indeed, the obsession with the excluded middle leads the Mishnah to invent its own examples, which have then to be analyzed into their definitive components and situated in their appropriate category. What this does is to leave no area lacking in an appropriate location, none to yield irresoluble doubt.

---

[4] Documentation for the general statements made in this section will be found in my *Judaism: The Evidence of the Mishnah* (Chicago, 1981: The University of Chicago Press).

The purpose of identifying the excluded middle is to allow the lawyers to sort out distinct rules, on the one side, and to demonstrate how they intersect without generating intolerable uncertainty, on the other. For example, to explore the theory that an object can serve as either a utensil or a tent, that is, a place capable of spreading the uncleanness of a corpse under its roof, the framers of the Mishnah invent a "hive." This is sufficiently large so that it can be imagined to be either a utensil or a tent. When it is whole, it is the former, and if it is broken, it is the latter. The location of the object, e.g., on the ground, off the ground, in a doorway, against a wall, and so on, will further shape the rules governing the cases (M. Ohalot 9:1-14). Again, to indicate the ambiguities lying at the frontiers, the topic of the status of Syria will come under repeated discussion. Syria is deemed not wholly sanctified, as is the Land of Israel, but also not wholly outside of the frame of Holy Land, as are all other countries. That is why to Syria apply some rules applicable to Holy Land, some rules applicable to secular land. In consequence, numerous points of ambiguity will be uncovered and explored (M. Sheb. 6:1-6).

Gray areas of the law in general, and the excluded middle in particular, cover the surface of the law. They fill up nearly every chapter of the Mishnah. But underneath the surface is an inquiry of profound and far-reaching range. It is into the metaphysical or philosophical issues of how things join together, and how they do not, of synthesis and analysis, of fusion and union, connection, division, and disintegration. What we have in the recurrent study of the nature of mixtures, broadly construed, is a sustained philosophical treatise in the guise of an episodic exercise in ad hoc problem solving. It is as if the cultic agendum, laid forth by the priests, the social agendum, defined by the confusing status and condition of Israel, and the program for right categorization of persons and things, set forth for the scribes to carry out – all were taken over and subsumed by the philosophers who proposed to talk abstractly about what they deemed urgent, while using the concrete language and syntax of untrained minds. To put it differently, the framers of the Mishnah, in their reflection on the nature of mixtures in their various potentialities for formation and dissolution, shape into hidden discourse, on an encompassing philosophical-physical problem of their own choosing, topics provided by others.

In so doing, they phrased the critical question demanding attention and response, the question in dimensions at once social, political, metaphysical, cultural, and even linguistic, but above all, historical: the question of Israel, standing at the outer boundaries of a long history now decisively done with. That same question of acculturation and assimilation, alienation and exile, which had confronted the sixth century B.C. priests of the Priestly Code, from 70 to 200 was raised once more. Now it is framed in terms of mechanical composition, fusion, and something in between, mixtures. But it is phrased in incredible terms of a wildly irrelevant world of unseen things, of how we define the place of the stem in the entity of the apple, the affect of the gravy upon the meat, and the definitive power of a bit of linen in a fabric of wool. In concrete form, the issues are close to comic. In abstract form, the answers speak of nothing of workaday meaning. In reality, at issue is Israel in its Land, once the lines of structure which had emanated from the Temple had been blurred and obliterated. It is in this emphasis upon sorting out confused things that the Mishnah becomes truly Mishnaic, distinct from modes of thought and perspective to be assigned to groups represented in the document. To interpret the meaning of this emphasis, we must again recall that the Priestly Code makes the point that a well-ordered society on earth, with its center and point of reference at the Temple altar, corresponds to a well-ordered canopy of heaven. Creation comes to its climax at the perfect rest marked by completion and signifying perfection and sanctification. Indeed, the creation-myth represents as the occasion for sanctification a perfected world at rest, with all things in their rightful place. Now the Mishnah takes up this conviction, which is located at the deepest structures of the metaphysic of the framers of the Priestly Code and, therefore, of their earliest continuators and imitators in the Mishnaic code. But the Mishnah does not frame the conviction that in order is salvation through a myth of creation and a description of a cult of precise and perfect order, such as is at Gen. 1:1-2:4a. True, the Mishnah imposes order upon the world through lines of structure emanating from the cult. The verses of Scripture selected as authoritative leave no alternative.

Yet, the Mishnah at its deepest layers, taking up the raw materials of concern of priests and farmers and scribes, phrases that concern after the manner of philosophers. That is to say, the framers of the Mishnah speak of the physics of mixtures, conflicts of principles which must be sorted out, areas of doubt generated by confusion. The detritus of a world seeking order but suffering chaos now is reduced to the construction of intellect. If, therefore, we wish to characterize the Mishnah when it is cogent and distinctive, we must point to this persistent and pervasive mode of thought. For the Mishnah takes up a vast corpus of facts and treats these facts, so to speak, "mishnaically," that is, in a way distinctive to the Mishnah, predicable and typical of the Mishnah. That is what I mean when I refer to the style of the Mishnah: its manner of exegesis of a topic, its mode of thought about any subject, the sorts of perplexities which will precipitate the Mishnah's fertilizing flood of problem-making ingenuity. Confusion and conflict will trigger the Mishnah's power to control conflict by showing its limits, and, thus, the range of shared conviction too.

For by treating facts "mishnaically," the Mishnah establishes boundaries around, and pathways through, confusion. It lays out roads to guide people by ranges of permissible doubt. Consequently, the Mishnah's mode of control over the chaos of conflicting principles, the confusion of doubt, the improbabilities of a world out of alignment, is to delimit and demarcate. By exploring the range of interstitial conflict through its ubiquitous disputes, the Mishnah keeps conflict under control. It so preserves that larger range of agreement, that pervasive and shared conviction, which is never expressed, which is always instantiated, and which, above all, is forever taken for granted. The Mishnah's deepest convictions about what lies beyond confusion and conflict are never spelled out; they lie in the preliminary, unstated exercise prior to the commencement of a sustained exercise of inquiry, a tractate. They are the things we know before we take up that exercise and study that tractate.

Now all of this vast complex of methods and styles, some of them intellectual, some of them literary and formal, may be captured in the Mishnah's treatment of its own, self-generated conflicts of principles, its search for gray areas of the law. It also may be clearly discerned in the Mishnah's sustained interest in those excluded middles it makes up for the purpose of showing the limits of the law, the confluence and conflict of laws. It further may be perceived in the Mishnah's recurrent exercise in the study of types of mixtures, the ways distinct components of an entity may be joined together, may be deemed separate from one another, may be shown to be fused, or may be shown to share some traits and not others. Finally, the Mishnah's power to sort out matters of confusion will be clearly visible in its repeated statement of the principles by which cases of doubt are to be resolved. A survey of these four modes of thought thus shows us one side of the distinctive and typical character of the Mishnah, when the Mishnah transcends the program of facts, forms, and favored perspectives of its tributaries. We now turn to the side of substance. What causes and resolves confusion and chaos is the power of the Israelite's will. As is said in the context of measurements for minimum quantities to be subject to uncleanness, "All accords with the measure of the man" (M. Kel. 17:11).

The Mishnah's principal message is that Israelite man is at the center of creation, the head of all creatures upon earth, corresponding to God in Heaven, in whose image man is made. The way in which the Mishnah makes this simple and fundamental statement is to impute power to the Israelite to inaugurate and initiate those corresponding processes, sanctification and uncleanness, which play so critical a role in the Mishnah's account of reality. The will of man, expressed through the deed of man, is the active power in the world. Will and deed – these constitute those actors of creation which work upon neutral realms, subject to either sanctification or uncleanness: the Temple and table, the field and family, the altar and hearth, woman, time, space, transactions in the material world and in the world above as well. An object, a substance, a transaction, even a phrase or a sentence, is inert but may be made holy, when the interplay of the will and deed of man arouses and generates its potential to be sanctified. Each may be treated as ordinary or (where relevant) made unclean by neglect of the will and inattentive act of man. Just as the entire system of uncleanness and holiness awaits the intervention of man, which imparts the capacity to become unclean upon what was formerly inert, or which removes the capacity to impart cleanness from what was formerly in its natural and puissant condition, so in the other ranges of reality, man is at the center on earth, just as is God in Heaven. Man is counterpart and partner in creation, in that, like God he has power over the status and condition of creation, putting everything in its proper place, calling everything by its rightful name.

So, stated briefly, the question taken up by the Mishnah is, What can a man do? And the answer laid down by the Mishnah is, Man, through will and deed, is master of this world, the measure of all things. Since when the Mishnah thinks of man, it means the Israelite, who is the subject and actor of its system, the statement is clear. This man is Israel, who can do what he wills. In the aftermath of the two wars, the message of the Mishnah cannot have proved more pertinent – or poignant and tragic. The principal message of the Mishnah is that the will of man affects the material reality of the world and governs the working of those forces, visible or not, which express and effect the sanctification of creation and of Israel alike. This message comes to the surface in countless ways. At the outset a simple example of the supernatural power of man's intention suffices to show the basic power of the Israelite's will to change concrete, tangible facts. The power of the human will is nowhere more effective than in the cult, where, under certain circumstances, what a person is thinking is more important than what he does. The basic point is that if an animal is designated for a given purpose, but the priest prepares the animal with the thought in mind that the beast serves some other sacrificial purpose, then, in some instances, in particular involving a sin offering and a Passover on the fourteenth of Nisan, the sacrifice is ruined. In this matter of preparation of the animal, moreover, are involved the deeds of slaughtering the beast, collecting, conveying, and tossing the blood on the altar, that is, the principal priestly deeds of sacrifice. Again, if the priest has in mind, when doing these deeds, to offer up the parts to be offered up on the altar, or to eat the parts to be eaten by the priest, in some location other than the proper one (the altar, the courtyard, respectively), or at some time other than the requisite one (the next few hours), the rite is spoiled, the meat must be thrown out. Now that is the case, even if the priest did not do what he was thinking of doing. Here again we have a testimony to the fundamental importance imputed to what a person is thinking, even over what he actually does, in critical aspects of the holy life (M. Zebahim 1:1-4:6, Menahot 1:1-4:5).

Once man wants something, a system of the law begins to function. Intention has the power, in particular, to initiate the processes of sanctification. So the moment at which something becomes sacred and so falls under a range of severe penalties for misappropriation or requires a range of strict modes of attentiveness and protection for the preservation of cleanness is defined by the human will. Stated simply: at the center of the Mishnaic system is the notion that man has the power to inaugurate the work of sanctification, and the Mishnaic system states and restates that power. This assessment of the positive power of the human will begins with the matter of uncleanness, one antonym of sanctification or holiness. Man alone has the power to inaugurate the system of uncleanness.

From the power of man to introduce an object or substance into the processes of uncleanness, we turn to the corresponding power of man to sanctify an object or a substance. This is a much more subtle matter, but it also is more striking. It is the act of designation by a human being which "activates" that holiness inherent in crops from which no tithes have yet been set aside and removed. Once the human being has designated what is holy within the larger crop, then that designated portion of the crop gathers within itself the formerly diffused holiness and becomes holy, set aside for the use and benefit of the priest to whom it is given. So it is the interplay between the will of the farmer, who owns the crop, and the sanctity inherent in the whole batch of the crop itself, which is required for the processes of sanctification to work themselves out.

In addition to the power to initiate the process of sanctification and the system of uncleanness and cleanness, man has the power, through the working of his will, to differentiate one thing from another. The fundamental category into which an entity, which may be this or that, is to be placed is decided by the human will for that entity. Man exercises the power of categorization, so ends confusion. Once more, the consequence will be that, what man decides. Heaven confirms or ratifies. Once man determines that something falls into one category and not another, the interest of Heaven is provoked. Then misuse of that thing invokes heavenly penalties. So man's will has the capacity so to work as to engage the ratifying power of Heaven. Let us take up first of all the most striking example, the deed itself. It would be difficult to doubt that what one does determines the effect of what one does. But that position is rejected. The very valence and result of a deed depend, to begin with, on one's prior intent. The intent which leads a person to do a deed governs the culpability of the deed. There is no intrinsic weight to the deed itself. Human will not only is definitive. It also provides the criterion for differentiation in cases of uncertainty or doubt. This is an overriding fact. That is why I insisted earlier that the principal range of questions addressed by the Mishnah – areas of doubt and uncertainty about status or taxonomy – provokes an encompassing response. This response, it now is clear, in the deep conviction of the Mishnaic law, present at the deepest structures of the law, is that what man wills or thinks decides all issues of taxonomy.

To conclude: The characteristic mode of thought of the Mishnah thus is to try to sort things out, exploring the limits of conflict and the range of consensus. The one thing which the Mishnah's framers predictably want to know concerns what falls between two established categories or rules, the gray area of the law, the excluded middle among entities, whether persons, places, or things. This obsession with the liminal or marginal comes to its climax and fulfillment in the remarkably wide-ranging inquiry into the nature of mixtures, whether these are mixtures of substance in a concrete framework or of principles and rules in an abstract one. So the question is fully phrased by both the style of the Mishnaic discourse and its rhetoric. It then is fully answered. The question of how we know what something is, the way in which we assign to its proper frame and category what crosses the lines between categories, is settled by what Israelite man wants, thinks, hopes, believes, and how he so acts as to indicate his attitude. With the question properly phrased in the style and mode of Mishnaic thought and discourse, the answer is not difficult to express. What makes the difference, what sets things into their proper category and resolves those gray areas of confusion and conflict formed when simple principles intersect and produce dispute, is man's will. Israel's despair or hope is the definitive and differentiating criterion.

III. THE CONVICTIONS OF THE MANY

Passionate concern for order and stability, for sorting things out and resolving confusion, ambiguity, and doubt – these may well characterize the mind of priests, scribes, and householders. The priests, after all, emerge from a tradition of sanctification achieved through the perfection of the order of creation – that is the theology of their creation-myth. The scribes with their concern for the correspondence between what they do on earth and what is accorded approval and confirmation in Heaven, likewise carry forward that interest in form and order characteristic of a profession of their kind. But if I had to choose that single group for whom the system speaks, it would be neither of these. We noted at the outset that the scribe and the priest are noteworthy by their absence from the fundamental structure and organization of the Mishnah's documents. By contrast, the householder forms the focus of two of the six divisions, those devoted to civil law and family. Let us then reflect for a moment on the ways in which the householder will have found the Mishnah's principal modes of concern congruent with his own program. We speak now of the householder in a courtyard, for he is the subject of most predicates. He is the proprietor of an estate, however modest, however little. He also is a landholder in the fields, an employer with a legitimate claim against lazy or unreliable workers, the head of a family, and the manager of a small but self-contained farm. He is someone who gives over his property to craftsmen for their skilled labor, but is not a craftsman himself. He also is someone with a keen interest in assessing and collecting damages done to his herds and flocks, or in paying what he must for what his beasts do. The Mishnah speaks for someone who deems thievery to be the paltry, petty thievery ("Oh! the servants!") of watchmen of an orchard and herdsmen of a flock, and for a landowner constantly involved in transactions in real property.

The Mishnah's class perspective, described merely from its topics and problems, is that of the undercapitalized and overextended upper-class farmer, who has no appreciation whatsoever for the interests of those with liquid capital and no understanding of the role of trading in commodity futures. This landed proprietor of an estate of some size sees a bushel of grain as a measure of value. But he does not concede that, in the provision of supplies and sustenance through the year, from one harvest to the next, lies a kind of increase no less productive than the increase of the fields and the herd. The Mishnah is the voice of the head of the household, the pillar of society, the model of the community, the arbiter and mediator of the goods of this world, fair, just, honorable, above all, reliable.

The Mishnah therefore is the voice of the Israelite landholding, proprietary class (compare *Soviet Views of Talmudic Judaism. Five Papers by Yu. A. Solodukho in English Translation,* edited with a commentary by this writer (Leiden, 1973: E. J. Brill)). Its problems are the problems of the landowner, the householder, as I said, the Mishnah's basic and recurrent subject for nearly all predicates. Its perspectives are his. Its sense of what is just and fair expresses his sense of the givenness and cosmic rightness of the present condition of society. Earth matches Heaven. The Mishnah's hope for Heaven and its claim on earth, to earth, corresponding to the supernatural basis for the natural world, bespeak the imagination of the surviving Israelite burgherdom of the mid-second century Land of Israel – people deeply tired of war and its dislocation, profoundly distrustful of messiahs and their dangerous promises. These are men of substance and means however modest, aching for a stable and predictable world in which to tend their crops and herds, feed their families and workers, keep to the natural rhythms of the seasons and the lunar cycles, and, in all, live out their lives within strong and secure boundaries, on earth and in Heaven.

Now when we turn away from the Mishnah's imagined world to the actual context of the Israelite community after the destruction of the Temple in 70 and still later after Bar Kokhba, we are able to discern what it is that the Mishnah's sages have for raw materials, the slime they have for mortar, the bricks they have for building. The archaeological evidence of the later second and third century reveals a thriving Israelite community in Galilee and surrounding regions, a community well able to construct for itself synagogues of considerable aesthetic ambition, to sustain and support an internal government and the appurtenances of an abundant life. What that means is that, while the south was permanently lost, the north remained essentially intact. Indeed, it would be on the sturdy and secure foundations of that stable community of the northern part of the Land of Israel that Israelite life for the next three or four hundred years – a very long time – would be constructed.

So when the Mishnah's sages cast their eyes out on the surviving Israelite world, their gaze must have rested upon that thing which had endured, and would continue to endure, beyond the unimaginable catastrophe brought on by Bar Kokhba and his disruptive messianic adventure. Extant and enduring was a world of responsible, solid farmers and their slaves and dependents, the men and women upon the backs of whom the Israelite world would now have come to rest. They, their children, slaves, dependents could yet make a world to endure – if only they could keep what they had, pretty much as they had it – no more, but also no less. Theirs was not a society aimed at aggrandizement. They wanted no more than to preserve what had survived out of the disorderly past. That is why the Mishnah's is not a system respectful of increase. It asks no more than that what is to be is to be. The Mishnah seeks the perfection of a world at rest, the precondition of that seal of creation's perfection sanctified on the seventh day of creation and perpetually sanctified by the seventh day of creation.

But if the philosophers of Israelite society refer to a real world, a world in being, the values of which were susceptible of protection and preservation, the boundaries of which were readily discerned, they also defied that real world. They speak of location but have none. For Israelite settlement in the Land then was certainly not contiguous. There was no polity resting on a homogeneous social basis. All Israel had was villages, on a speckled map of villages of many peoples. There was no Israelite nation, in full charge of its lands or Land, standing upon contiguous and essentially united territories. This locative polity is built upon utopia: no one place. The ultimate act of will is forming a locative system in no particular place, speaking nowhere about somewhere, concretely specifying utopia. This is done – in context – because Israel wills it.

At the end, Weber's problem points the way for further inquiry: how do the inspirations of a few become the convictions of the many? For, we observe, while the Mishnah came into the world ás the law book of a class of scribes and small-claims court judges, it in time to come formed the faith and piety of the many of Israel, the Jews at large, the workers and craftsmen. And these, it must be emphasized, were not landholders and farmers. They were in the main landless craftsmen and workers, but they took over this book of landholders and farmers and accepted it as the other half, the oral half, of the whole Torah of God to Moses at Mount Sinai.

That is to say, in somewhat less mythological terms, the Mishnah began with some one group, in fact, with a caste, a class, and a profession. But it very rapidly came to form the heart and center of the imaginative life and concrete politics, law, and society of a remarkably diverse set of groups, that is, the Jewish people as a whole. So the really interesting question, when we move from the account of Israelite religion and society in the first and second centuries, represented by the Mishnah, to religion and society in the third and fourth centuries, represented by the Talmuds, and in the fifth and later centuries, represented by the Midrashim, is how the Mishnah was transformed in social context from one thing into something else. If, as I said at the outset, we locate "the status group whose material and ideal way of life a given idea or value tends to enhance," then we must ask why that same idea or value served, as it did, to enhance a far wider and more encompassing group within Israelite society. We must investigate how it came about that, in time to come, Judaism, the world view and way of life resting upon the Scriptures and upon the Mishnah and in due course upon the Talmuds, came to constitute the world view and way of life of nearly all Israel.

For the difficult question before us is the truly historical one: the question of change, of why things begin in one place but move onward, and of how we may account for what happens. The weak point of sociology of religion, in Weber's powerful formulation, emerges from its strong point. If we begin by asking about the relevance of religious ideas to collective actions, we must proceed to wonder about the continuing relevance of religious ideas within a changing collectivity and context. If as Bendix says, Weber emphasizes the issue of how a given idea or value enhances the way of life of a "status group," then we must wonder why that given idea or value succeeds in maintaining its own free-standing, ongoing life among and for entirely other status groups and types of social groups. The history of Judaism from the formation of the Mishnah onward through the next four centuries, amply documented as is that period, provides an important arena for inquiry into yet another constituent of Weber's grand program. But this next set of questions will have to be taken up in another lecture. For the honor of the invitation to give this one, I thank my host, and for the gracious hospitality and hearing according to me on this visit, I thank you all.

3

How the Mishnah Expresses its Philosophy:

A Theory of Intentionality or (Mere) Obsession with Whether Wheat Gets Wet?

Concrete exercises, rather than abstract argument, show what is at stake in the insistence that through halakhah the Judaic religious system of the dual Torah sets forth a systematic response to critical questions of philosophy and theology. Only in the concrete and material details of halakhah can the full intellectual measure of the halakhah be assessed. For the case, I choose an arid and unpromising instance of the working of the law of purities. Surely that arcane and recondite area of law presents a fine occasion to test the claim that in details of a hermetic character important and fundamental issues of theory inhere. Indeed, the character of the law under analysis proves so formal and meaningless as to allow for a null-hypothesis: if we do not find a profound layer of intellectual reflection in the law here, then my claim will not have passed the test in the most difficult material of all.

One fundamental principle of the system of Judaism attested in the Mishnah is that God and the human being share traits of attitude and emotion. They want the same thing. For example, it is made clear in Mishnah-tractate Maaserot, man and God respond in the same way to the same events, since they share not only ownership of the Land but also viewpoint on the value of its produce. When the farmer wants the crop, so too does God. When the householder takes the view that the crop is worthwhile, God responds to the attitude of the farmer by forming the same opinion. The Mishnah's theological anthropology that brings God and the householder into the same continuum prepares the way for understanding what makes the entire Mishnaic system work. But in what kind of language, and precisely through what sort of discourse, does the authorship of the Mishnah set forth principles that motivate the entire system of the Mishnah? Here

33

I shall show that through little that authorship says much, and in discourse on matters of no consequence at all, indeed, matters that, in the setting of the writers of the document, had no practical bearing at all, principal conceptions emerge.

At stake in this presentation is not the particular proposition, but the mode of discourse in which the proposition is set forth. I maintain we have philosophy and theology in a very odd idiom; others find here nothing more than obsessive formalism expressing a religion of pots and pans, and so they want the authorship of the Mishnah to be represented in other ways than in the way in which I have described them. What we shall see in striking ways is a way of expressing a principle and of exploring conflicting positions that is quite odd. Our authorship, specifically, talks only in picayune details. Great issues of philosophy are spelled out in exchanges on matters of no consequence. Only when we see the whole do we perceive that, through arguments about nothing very much, our authorship has laid forth a variety of positions on a fundamental issue, a concern that animates the entire system they propose to construct. Let me first spell out the positions, then we shall turn to a sustained and concrete example of the manner in which these positions are laid out in the to us unfamiliar mode of discourse at hand.

The Mishnah's authorship's discussion on intention works out several theories concerning not God and God's relationship to humanity but the nature of the human will, a decidedly philosophical topic. The human being is defined as not only sentient but also a volitional being, who can will with effect, unlike beasts and, as a matter of fact, angels (which do not, in fact, figure in the Mishnah at all). On the one side, there is no consideration or will or attitude of animals, for these are null. On the other side, will and attitude of angels, where these are represented in later documents, are totally subservient to God's wishes. Only the human being, in the person of the farmer, possesses and also exercises the power of intentionality. And it is the power that intentionality possesses that forms the central consideration. Because a human being forms an intention, consequences follow, whether or not given material expression in gesture or even in speech. An account of the Mishnah's sages' philosophical anthropology — theory of the structure of the human being — must begin with the extraordinary power imputed by the Mishnah's system to the will and intentionality of the human being.

But that view comes to expression with regard to human beings of a particular sort. The householder-farmer (invariably represented as male) is a principal figure, just as the (invariably male) priest in the Temple is another. The attitude of the one toward the crop, like that of the other toward the offering that he carries out, affects the status of the crop. It classifies an otherwise-unclassified substance. It changes the standing of an already-classified beast. It shifts the status of a pile of grain, without any physical action whatsoever, from one category to another. Not only so, but as we shall now so, the attitude or will of a farmer can override the effects of the natural world, e.g., keeping in the status of what is dry and so insusceptible to cultic uncleanness a pile of grain that in fact has been rained upon and wet down. An immaterial reality, shaped and reformed by the householder's attitude and plan, overrides the material effect of a rain-storm. And that example brings us to the way in which these profound philosophical issues are explored. It is in the remarkable essay on theories of the relationship between action and intention worked out in Mishnah-tractate Makhshirin and exemplified by Chapter Four of that tractate.

The subject-matter that serves as medium for sages' theories of human will and intention hardly appears very promising. Indeed, the topic of the tractate before us on its own hardly will have led us to anticipate what, in fact, will interest sages. The subject matter of tractate Makhshirin, to which we now turn, is the affect of liquid upon produce. The topic derives from the statement of Lev. 11:37: "And if any part of their carcass [a dead creeping thing] falls upon any seed for sowing that is to be sown, it is clean; but if water is put on the seed and any part of their carcass falls on it, it is unclean for you." Sages understand this statement to mean that seed that is dry is insusceptible to uncleanness, while seed that has been wet down is susceptible. They further take the view — and this is the point at which intention or human will enters in — that if seed, or any sort of grain, is wet down without the assent of the farmer who owns the grain, then the grain remains insusceptible, while if seed or grain is wet down with the farmer's assent, then the grain is susceptible to uncleanness. The upshot is that that grain that a farmer wets down and that is touched by a source of uncleanness, e.g., a dead creeping thing, is then deemed unclean and may not be eaten by those who eat their food in a state of cultic cleanness in accord with the laws of the book of Leviticus pertaining to the priests' food in the temple.

Once we agree that what is deliberately wet down is susceptible and what is wet down not with the farmer's assent or by his intention is insusceptible, then we work out diverse theories of the interplay between intention and action. And that is the point, over all, at which the authorship of Mishnah-tractate Makhshirin enters in and sets forth its ideas. Tractate Makhshirin is shown to be formed of five successive layers of generative principles, in sequence:

1. Dry produce is insusceptible, a notion which begins in the plain meaning of Lev. 11:34, 37.
2. Wet produce is susceptible only when *intentionally* wet down, a view expressed in gross terms by Abba Yosé as cited by Joshua.
3. Then follow the refinements of the meaning and effects of *intention,* beginning in 'Aqiba's and Tarfon's dispute, in which the secondary matter of what is tangential to one's primary motive is investigated.
4. This yields the contrary views, assuredly belonging to second-century masters, that what is essential imparts susceptibility and what is peripheral to one's primary purpose does not; and that both what is essential and what is peripheral impart susceptibility to uncleanness.

(A corollary to this matter is the refinement that what is wet down under constraint is not deemed wet down by deliberation.)

5.   The disputes on the interpretation of intention – Is it solely defined by what one actually does or modified also by what one has wanted to do as well as by what one has done? – belonging to Yosé and Judah and his son Yosé.

We see from this catalogue of successive positions, assigned to authorities who lived in successive generations, that the paramount theme of the tractate is the determination of the capacity of the eligible liquids to impart susceptibility to uncleanness. The operative criterion, whether or not the liquids are applied intentionally, obviously is going to emerge in every pericope pertinent to the theme. If I now summarize the central and generative theme of our tractate, we may state matter as follows.

First, liquids are capable of imparting susceptibility to uncleanness only if they are useful to men, e.g., drawn with approval, or otherwise subject to human deliberation and intention. The contrary view is that however something is wet down, once it is wet, if falls within the rule of Lev. 11:34, 38, and is subject to uncleanness.

Second, if we begin with the fundamental principle behind the tractate, thus: it is

(1) that which is given in the name of Abba Yosé-Joshua (M. Makhshirin 1:3M): Water imparts susceptibility to uncleanness only when it is applied to produce intentionally or deliberately. This yields a secondary and derivative rule:

(2) Aqiba's distinction at M. Makhshirin Makhshirin 4:9 and M. Makhshirin 5:4: Water intrinsic to one's purpose is detached with approval, but that which is not essential in accomplishing one's primary purpose is not under the law, If water be put. What 'Aqiba has done is to carry to its logical next stage the generative principle. If water applied with approval can impart susceptibility to uncleanness, then, it follows, only *that part* of the detached and applied water is essential to one's intention is subject to the law, If water be put. Items in the name of second-century authorities that develop 'Aqiba's improvement of Abba Yosé's principle raise an interesting question:

(3) What is the relationship between intention and action? Does intention to do something govern the decision in a case, even though one's action has produced a different effect? For example, if I intend to wet down only part of an object, or make use of only part of a body of water, but then wet down the whole or dispose of the whole, is the whole deemed susceptible? Does my consequent action revise the original effects of my intention?

The deep thought on the relationship between what one does and what one wants to see happen explores the several possible positions. Judah and his son, Yosé, take up the position that ultimate deed or result is definitive of intention.

What happens is retrospectively deemed to decide what I wanted to happen (M. Makhshirin 3:5-7). Other Ushans, Yosé in particular (M. Makhshirin 1:5), maintain the view that, while consequence plays a role in the determination of intention, it is not exclusive and definitive. What I wanted to make happen affects the assessment of what actually has happened. Now the positions on the interplay of action and intention are these:

1. Judah has the realistic notion that a person changes his mind, and therefore we adjudge a case solely by what he does and not by what he says he will do, intends, or has intended, to do. If we turn Judah's statement around, we come up with the conception predominant throughout his rulings: *A case is judged in terms solely of what the person does.* If he puts on water, that water in particular that he has deliberately applied imparts susceptibility to uncleanness. If he removes water, only that water he actually removes imparts susceptibility to uncleanness, but water that he intends to remove but that is not actually removed is not deemed subject to the person's original intention. And, it is fair to add, we know it is not subject to the original intention, because the person's action has not accomplished the original intention or has placed limits upon the original intention. What is done is wholly determinative of what is originally intended, and that is the case whether the result is that the water is deemed capable or incapable of imparting susceptibility to uncleanness.

' 2. Yosé at M. Makhshirin 1:5 expresses the contrary view. Water that has been wiped off is detached with approval. But water that has remained on the leek has not conformed to the man's intention, and that intention is shown by what the man has actually done. Accordingly, the water remaining on the leek is not subject to the law, If water be put. The upshot is to reject the view that what is done is wholly determinative of what is originally intended. We sort things out by appeal to nuances of effect.

3. Simeon's point at M. Makhshirin 1:6 is that the liquid is the breath or left on the palm of the hand is not wanted and not necessary to the accomplishment of one's purpose. Simeon's main point is that liquid not essential in accomplishing one's purpose is not taken into account and does not come under the law, If water be put. Why not? Because water is held to be applied with approval *only* when it serves a specific purpose. That water which is incidental has not been subjected to the man's wishes and therefore does not impart susceptibility to uncleanness. Only that water that is necessary to carry out the farmer's purpose imparts susceptibility to uncleanness. If a pile of grain has been wet down, then water that the farmer has deliberately applies effects susceptibility to uncleanness to that part of the grain-pile that it has touched. But water that is incidental and not subject to the farmer's initial plan has no effect upon the grain, even though, as a matter of fact, grain at some other point in the pile may be just as wet as grain the farmer has deliberately watered.

Simeon and Yosé deem water to have been detached and applied with approval only when it serves a person's essential purpose, and water that is not necessary in accomplishing that purpose is not deemed subject to the law, If water be put. That is why Simeon rules as he does. Yosé states a different aspect of the same conception. Water that actually has dripped of the leek in no way has fallen under the person's approval. This is indicated by the facts of the matter, the results of the person's actual deed. And this brings us to the concrete exposition of the chapter at hand. With the positions and principles just now outlined, the reader can follow the discussion with little difficulty. We begin with the simple distinction between water that I want for the accomplishment of my purpose, and water that I do not want, and that category of water does not have the power to impart susceptibility to uncleanness.

The recurrent formula, "If water be put," alludes to Lev. 11:34, 37, and refers to the deliberate watering down of seed or produce. But at stake is the classification of the water. The kind of water to which allusion is made is in the category of "If water be put," meaning that that water, having served the farmer's purpose, has the power to impart susceptibility to uncleanness should it fall on grain. Water that is not in the category of "If water be put," should it fall on grain by some sort of accident, does not impart susceptibility to uncleanness to grain that is otherwise kept dry. It remains to observe that the reason the farmer wets down grain is that the grain is going to be milled, and milling grain requires some dampening of the seed. Accordingly, we have the counterpart to the issue of tithing. When the farmer plans to make use of the (now-tithed) grain, and indicates the plan by wetting down the grain, then the issue of cultic cleanness, that is, preserving the grain from the sources of cultic uncleanness listed in Leviticus Chapters Eleven through Fifteen, is raised. Before the farmer wants to use the produce, the produce is null. The will and intentionality of the farmer, owner of the grain, are what draws the produce within the orbit of the immaterial world of uncleanness and cleanness.

Now to the actual texts I have chosen for illustrating not only the issues but the way in which the issues are set forth and analyzed: arguments about very picayune questions indeed, and, furthermore, questions lacking all concrete relevance in the world in the second century in which the Mishnah's philosophers actually lived.

4:1

A. He who kneels down to drink –

B. the water that comes up on his mouth and on his moustache is under the law, If water be put. [That water imparts susceptibility to uncleanness should it drip on a pile of grain, since the farmer has accomplished his purpose — getting a drink — by stirring up that water and getting it into his mouth or on his moustache.]

C. [The water that comes up] on his nose and on [the hair of] his head and on his beard is not under the law, "If water be put." [That water does not have the power to impart susceptibility to uncleanness should it fall on a pile of dry produce.]

D.   He who draws [water] with a jug –

E.   the water that comes up on its outer parts and on the rope wound round its neck and on the rope that is needed [in dipping it] – lo, this is under the law, If water be put on.

F.   And how much [rope] is needed [in handling it]?

G.   R. Simeon b. Eleazar says, "A handbreadth."

H.   [If] one put it under the water-spout, [the water on its out parts and on the rope, now not needed in drawing water] is not under the law, If water be put.

M. Makhshirin 4:1

What must get wet in order to accomplish one's purpose if deemed wet down by approval. But water not needed in one's primary goal is not subject to approval. The pericope consists of A-C and D-H, the latter in two parts, D-E + F-G, and H. The point of A-C is clear. Since, D-E, in dipping the jug into the water, it is not possible to draw water without wetting the outer parts and the rope, water on the rope and the outer pats is deemed affected by one's wishes. Simeon b. Eleazar glosses. At H one does not make use of the rope and does not care to have the water on the outer parts, since he can draw the water without recourse to either. Accordingly, water on the rope and on the outer parts does not impart susceptibility to uncleanness.

4:2

A.   He on whom rains fell,

B.   even [if he is] a Father [principal source] of uncleanness –

C.   it [the water] is not under the law, If water be put [since even in the case of B, the rainfall was not wanted].

D.   But if he shook off [the rain], it [the water that is shaken off] is under the law, If water be put.

E.   [If] he stood under the water-spout to cool off,

F.   or to rinse off,

G.   in the case of an unclean person [the water] is unclean.

H.   And in the case of a clean person, [the water] is under the law, If water be put.

M. Makhshirin 4:2

The pericope is in two parts, A-D and E-H, each in two units. The point of A + C is that the rain does not come under the person's approval. Therefore the rain is not capable of imparting susceptibility to uncleanness. If by some action, however, the person responds to the rain, for example, if he shook off his garments, then it falls under his approval. B is certainly a gloss, and not an important one. The principal source of uncleanness, e.g., the *Zab* of Leviticus, Chapter Fifteen, derives no benefit from the rain and therefore need not be explicitly excluded. At E, however, the person obviously does want to make use of the water. Therefore it is rendered both susceptible to uncleanness and capable of imparting susceptibility to other tings. G makes the former point, H, the latter. Perhaps it is G that has generated B, since the distinction between unclean and clean is important at G-H and then invites the contrast between A + B and E + G, that is, falling rain *versus* rain-water pouring through the waterspout and deliberately utilized.

4:3

A.   He who puts a dish on end against the wall so that it will rinse off, lo, this [water that flows across the plate] is under the law, If water be put.

B.   If [he put it there] so that it [rain] should not harm the wall, it [the water] is not under the law, If water be put

M. Makhshirin 4:3

The established distinction is repeated one more, with reference to an inanimate object. Now we make use of the water for rinsing off the plate. Accordingly, the water is detached with approval. But if the plate is so located as to protect the wall, then the water clearly is not wanted and therefore does not have the capacity to impart susceptibility to uncleanness.

4:4-5

I.   A.   A jug into which water leaking from the roof came down –

B.   The House of Shammai say, "It is broken."

C.   The House of Hillel say, "It is emptied out."

D.   And they agree that he puts in his hand and takes pieces of fruit from its inside, and they [the drops of water, the pieces of fruit] are insusceptible to uncleanness.

M. Makhshirin 4:4

II.   F.   A trough into which the rain dripping from the roof flowed [without approval] –

G.   [water in the trough and (GRA)] the drops [of water] that splashed out and those that overflowed are not under the law, If water be put.

H.   [If] one took it to pour it out –

I.   The House of Shammai say, "It is under the law, If water be put." [Since he poured the water away only when the tub was moved to another place, it may be said that he did not object to the water when the tub was in its original place.]

J.   The House of Hillel say, "It is not under the law, If water be put."
      [His pouring away showed that he did not want the water even in the
      tub's original place.]

III. K.   [If] one [intentionally] left it out so that the rain dripping from the
      roof would flow into it –

L.   the drops [of water] that splashed out and those that overflowed –

M.   The House of Shammai say, "They are under the law, If water be
      put" [all the more so what is in the trough].

N.   The House of Hillel say, "They [the drops that splashed or overflowed]
      are not under the law, If water be put.

O.   [If] one took it in order to pour it out, these and those agree that [both
      kinds of water] are under the law, If water be put. [For since the
      owner did not empty it where it stood, the water is deemed to be
      detached with his approval.]

P.   He who dunks the utensils,
      and he who washes his clothing in a cave [pond] –

Q.   the water that comes up on his hands is under the law, If water be put.

R.   [And the water that comes up] on his feet is not under the law, If
      water be put.

S.   R. Eleazar says, "If it is impossible for him to go down [into the
      water] unless his feet become muddy, even [the drops of water] that
      come up on his feet are under the law, If water be put [since he wants
      to clean his feet]."

M. Makhshirin 4:5

The composite is in the following parts: A-D, a complete and well balanced
Houses' dispute, in which the apodosis exhibits exact balance in the number of
syllables, F-G, which set the stage for the second Houses' dispute, at H-J; K-L, the
protasis for the third dispute, which depends upon F (+ G = L) – a trough that
happens to receive rain *versus* one deliberately left out to collect rain, and the
standard apodosis, M-N; and a final agreement, O, parallel to D. R-S form a separate
pericope entirely. The issue of A-D is this: We have left a jug containing fruit in
such a position that water leaking from the roof fills it. We want to empty the fruit
out of the jug. But we want to do so in such a way that the water in the jug does not
received the capacity to impart susceptibility to uncleanness to the fruit contained
in the jug. There are these considerations.

(1) Clearly, in its present location, the water is insusceptible. Why?
Because it did not fall into the jug with approval.

(2) If then we break the jug, we accomplish the purpose of treating the
water as unwanted and this is what the Shammaites say we should to (B).

(3) But if we merely empty out the fruit, we stir the water with approval;
the fruit in the jug forthwith is wet down by the water, with approval, and becomes
susceptible.

The Hillelites (C) say that if we pour out the fruit, that suffices. Why? Because the man wants the fruit, not the water. So the water does not have the capacity to impart susceptibility to uncleanness. In its original location it is not subject to approval. The Shammaites and Hillelites agree that, so long as the fruit in the jug is unaffected by the water, the fruit is insusceptible to uncleanness. It is not made susceptible even by the water which is removed with the fruit. Maimonides *(Uncleanness of Foodstuffs,* 12:7) at the italicized words adds a valuable clarification:

> If a jar is full of fruit and water leaking from the roof drips into it, the owner may pour off the water from the fruit, and it does not render the fruit susceptible, *even though it was with his approval that the water remained in the jar until he should pour it off the fruit.*

Accordingly, Maimonides not only follows the Hillelite position but (quite reasonably) imposes that position upon the Shammaite agreement at D.

The second Houses' dispute, F-J, goes over the ground of the first. There is no significant difference between water that has leaked into the jug and water that has fallen into the trough, A/F. But the issue, G, is different. Now we ask about water that overflows. Does this water flow with approval? Certainly not, both parties agree. None of this water is wanted. What if the man then takes up the trough with the intention of pouring the water out? We already know the Hillelite position. It is the same as at C. There is no reason to be concerned about moving the trough in order to empty it. The man pours out the water. By his deed he therefore indicates that he does not want it. The Shammaites are equally consistent. The man has raised the trough to pour out the water. In moving the water, he (retrospectively) imparts the stamp of approval on the original location of the water. The reference at G is only to set the stage for K-L, since the water in the trough of F itself is insusceptible.

At K the problem is that the man deliberately does collect the water. Accordingly, he certainly has imparted his approval to it. The problem of L is that part of the water splashes out or overflows. Clearly, the man wanted the water and therefore, what overflowed or splashed out has not conformed to his original wishes. That is, if he shook the tree to bring down the water, all parties agree that the water that falls is subject to the man's approval. But the water that does not fall is a problem. Here too the Shammaites say that what has been in the trough and overflowed has been subject to the man's intention. Therefore, like the water in the trough, the drops that splash out or overflow are under the law, If water be put. But the House of Hillel maintain that the water not in the location where the man has desired it is not subject to this wishes, and therefore does not impart susceptibility to uncleanness.

O completes the elegant construction by bringing the Hillelites over to the Shammaite position. If the man lifted up a trough of water that he *himself* has collected, then his is water that at one point in its history has surely conformed to the man's wishes and therefore has the capacity to impart insusceptibility to uncleanness. The Hillelites of N clearly will agree that the water in the trough is subject to the law, If water be put, just as the Shammaites at L-M will maintain the same. The dispute of M-N concerns only the liquid referred to at L. P-R go over the ground of M. 4:1. That is, water necessary to accomplish the man's purpose is subject to the law, If water be put. That which is not important in the accomplishment of his purpose is not subject to the law. Eleazar's gloss, S, adds that if the man's feet grow muddy in the process of getting the water, then he will want to clean his feet, and even the water on his feet therefore is subject to the law, If water be put. There is nothing surprising in this unit, but the exposition is elegant indeed.

4:6

A. A basket that is full of lupines and [that happens to be] placed into an immersion-pool –

B. one puts out his hand and takes lupines from is midst, and they are insusceptible to uncleanness.

C. [If] one took them out of the water [while still in the basket] –

D. the ones that touch the [water on the sides of the] basket are susceptible to uncleanness.

E. And all the rest of the lupines are insusceptible to uncleanness.

F. A radish that is in the cave-[water] –

G. a menstruant rinses it off, and it is insusceptible to uncleanness.

H. [If] she brought it out of the water in any measure at all, [having been made susceptible to uncleanness in the water], it is unclean.

M. Makhshirin 4:6

We go over the point at which the Houses agree at M. Makhshirin 4:4D. The lupines in the basket are wet on account of the water in the pool, but that does not render them susceptible to uncleanness. Accordingly, since the water is not detached with approval, when one takes the lupines out of the basket, they remain insusceptible. The water on the basket, however, is detached with approval, since presumably the basket has been immersed to render it clean from uncleanness. (The lupines — being food — in any event cannot be cleaned in the pool.) Accordingly, at C, the ones in the basket that touch the sides of the basket are in contact with water capable of imparting susceptibility to uncleanness, having been used with approval. The others, however, although wet, remain clean. Why? Because they have not touched water that has been detached with approval. The sentence-structure is slightly strange, since A sets the stage for a thought, but the thought begins afresh at B. This is then extreme apocopation at A-B, less clear-cut apocopation at C-D.

The same form is followed at F-H. The radish in the water is insusceptible to uncleanness. The menstruant rinses it off. While the radish is in the water, it remains insusceptible. But the woman has rinsed her hands and the radish. Accordingly, the water on the radish is detached with approval. It renders the radish susceptible to uncleanness, and as soon as the radish is taken out of the water, the woman's touch imparts uncleanness.

4:7

A.   Pieces of fruit that fell into a water-channel –

B.   he whose hands were unclean reached out and took them –

C.   his hands are clean, and the pieces of fruit are insusceptible to uncleanness.

D.   But if he gave thought that his hands should be rinsed off [in the water], his hands are clean, and the [water on the] pieces of fruit is under the law, If water be put.

M. Makhshirin 4:7

The pericope is in the severe apocopation characteristic of the present set, A, B, and C being out of clear syntactical relationship to one another. We should have to add, at A *as to pieces...,* then at B, *if he whose hands...,* and C would follow as a complete sentence. But A is not continued at B-C. Rather, we have apocopation. We have a further illustration of the principle of the foregoing. The owner wants to retrieve the fruit. Even though his hands are unclean, he reaches out and takes the fruit. What is the result? The hands are made clean by the water-flow. But the fruit remains insusceptible to uncleanness. Why? Because it was not the man's intent to rinse off his hands in the water channel and so to clean them. If, D adds, that was his intent, then his hands of course are clean, but the fruit now has been rendered susceptible to uncleanness.

4:8

A.   A [clay] dish that is full of water and placed in an immersion-pool,

B.   and into [the airspace of] which a Father of uncleanness put his hand,

C.   is unclean [but the water remains clean].

D.   [If he was unclean only by reason of] contact with unclean things, it is clean.

E.   And as to all other liquids – they are unclean.

F.   For water does not effect cleanness for other liquids.

M. Makhshirin 4:8

The present pericope is not phrased in the expected apocopation, for C refers to the dish and so completes the thought of A. We have an exercise in several distinct rules. First, a clay pot is made unclean only by a Father of uncleanness. Second, it is not cleaned by immersion in the pool but only by breaking. But the sides of the pot are porous, as at M. Makhshirin 3:2. Therefore, third, the water in the pot is deemed in contact with the immersion-pool. The dish is touched by a Father of uncleanness and is therefore made unclean. But, D, someone in the first remove of uncleanness is not able to contaminate the pot. The liquid in the pot is not referred to at A-D, but E demands that we understand the liquid in A-C and D to be clean. Why? Because the water referred to at A certainly is cleaned and kept clean in the pool, along the lines of M. Makhshirin 4:6-7. E then simply registers the fact that liquids apart from those enumerated at M. Makhshirin 6:4 are not cleaned in an immersion-pool. E-F should also tell us that if other liquids are in the pot, the pot also is unclean, because liquids in the first remove of uncleanness do impart uncleanness to clay or earthenware utensils. Accordingly, E-F form either a slightly awry gloss, taking for granted that A-C have said *the water is clean, even though it* [the pot] *is unclean,* or they belong to a pericope other than the present one, which is highly unlikely.

4:9

A. He who draws water with a swape-pipe [or bucket] [and pieces of fruit later fell into the moisture or water remaining in the pipe or bucket],

B. up to three days [the water] imparts susceptibility to uncleanness. [Afterward it is deemed to be unwanted (Maimonides).]

C. R. 'Aqiba says, "If it has dried off, it is forthwith incapable of imparting susceptibility to uncleanness, and if it has not dried off, up to thirty days it [continues to] impart susceptibility to uncleanness."

M. Makhshirin 4:9

The dispute poses A-B against C. We deal now with a wooden pipe or bucket. Do we deem the bucket to be dried off as soon as it is empty? No, B says, the water in the bucket, detached with approval (by definition) remains able to impart susceptibility for three days. 'Aqiba qualifies the matter. If the water drawn with approval was dried out of the bucket, whatever moisture then is found in the bucket is not wanted; the man has shown, by drying out the bucket or pipe, that he does not want moisture there. If it is not dried out, then whatever liquid is there is deemed to be detached from the pool with approval and therefore able to impart uncleanness for a very long time. Only after thirty days do we assume that the wood is completely dry of the original water detached with approval.

4:10

A. Pieces of wood on which liquids fell and on which rains fell –

B. if [the rains] were more [than the liquids], [the pieces of wood] are insusceptible to uncleanness.

C.   [If] he took them outside so that the rains might fall on them, even
      though they [the rains] were more [than the liquids], they [the pieces
      of wood] are [susceptible to uncleanness and] unclean.

D.   [If] they absorbed unclean liquids, even though he took them outside
      so that the rains would fall on them, they are clean [for the clean rain
      has not had contact with the unclean absorbed liquid].

E.   But he should kindle them only with clean hands alone [to avoid
      contaminating the rain-water of D].

F.   R. Simeon says, "If they were wet [freshly cut] and he kindled them,
      and the liquids [sap] that exude from them were more than the liquids
      that they had absorbed, they are clean"

                                                                M. Makhshirin 4:10

The pericope is in the following parts: A-B balanced by C; and D, qualified
by E. F is an important gloss of D-E. The point of A-B is familiar from M.
Makhshirin 2:3. If we have a mixture of unclean and clean liquids, we determine
matters in accord with the relative quantity of each. If the clean liquids are the
greater part, the whole is deemed clean. Accordingly, since the rain, which is
insusceptible and does not impart susceptibility to uncleanness unless it falls with
approval, forms the greater part, B, the liquids on the pieces of wood are deemed
clean. But if, C, the man deliberately arranged for the rain to fall on the pieces of
wood, then the rain falls on the wood with approval, is susceptible to uncleanness,
and is made unclean by the unclean liquids already on the wood.

D raises a separate question. What if pieces of wood have absorbed unclean
liquids? The answer is that what is absorbed does not have contact with what is on
the surface – that is the meaning of absorption. Therefore if rain falls on wood that
has absorbed unclean liquids, the rain does not impart susceptibility to uncleanness
if it has not fallen with approval. D does not treat that matter; it wishes to say
something additional. Even if the rain falls with approval, the wood remains clean.
Why? Because nothing has made the rain unclean. That secondary point then
invites E — or E imposes the detail, *even if,* on D: Even though he took them
outside, so the rain falls with approval, E adds, since the rain *has* fallen with
approval, it is susceptible to uncleanness. Accordingly, the man should kindle the
wood only with clean hands, lest he make the rain-water unclean.

Simeon deals then with a still further point. If the wood is freshly cut
when kindled, then the unclean absorbed liquids are deemed neutralized by the
sap. If the exuded liquid caused by the heat is more than the still-absorbed liquid,
then the clean, exuded liquid forms the greater part, and the whole is clean, just as
at A-B. Simeon, Maimonides says, differs from D (+ E). We hold, as at A-D, that
if unclean liquids are absorbed by the wood, they are deemed clean and do not
impart uncleanness to the oven, *only* in the case in which the wood is wet. Then,
when it is heated, it produces sap in greater quantity than the unclean liquids that it

absorbed. But if not, the wood imparts uncleanness to the oven when it is heated because of the unclean liquid that has been absorbed.

Now if we reflect on the detailed rules we have observed, one thing will have struck the reader very forcefully. What Scripture treats as unconditional the authorship of the Mishnah has made contingent upon the human will. Specifically, when Scripture refers at Lev. 11:34, 37, to grain's being made wet, it makes no provision for the attitude of the owner of the grain, his intention in having wet the grain, or his will as to its disposition. What is wet is susceptible, what is dry is insusceptible. The effect of the water is *ex opere operato*. Yet, as we see, that very matter of the attitude of the householder toward the grain's being made wet forms the centerpiece of interest. The issue of intentionality thus forms the precipitating consideration behind every dispute we have reviewed, and, it is clear, the Priestly authors of Leviticus could not have conceived such a consideration. The introduction of that same concern can be shown to characterize the Mishnah's treatment of a variety of biblical rules and to form a systemic principle of profound and far-reaching character. We may draw a simple and striking contract, for instance, between the following bald statements:

1. Whatever touches the altar shall become holy" (Ex. 29:37)

It would be dffficult to find a less ambiguous statement. But here is the rule of the Mishnah's sages:

2. "The altar sanctifies that which is appropriate to it" (M. Zebahim 9:1)...."And what are those things which, even if they have gone up, should go down [since they are not offered at all and therefore are not appropriate to the altar]? "The flesh for the priests of Most Holy Things and the flesh of Lesser Holy Things [which is designated for priestly consumption]" (M. Zeb. 9:5).

To understand the conflict between statement No. 1 and statement No. 2 we have to understand how an animal enters the category of Most Holy Things or Lesser Holy Things. It is by the action of the farmer, who owns the beast and designates it for a purpose, within the cult, that imparts to the beast that status of Most Holy Things or Lesser Holy Things. In both cases, the rule is that such a beast yields parts that are burned up on the alter, and other parts that are given to the priests to eat or to the farmer, as the case may be.

Now the point is that it is the farmer who has designated a beast owned by him for sacrifice in the status of Most Holy Things or Lesser Holy Things. His disposition of the offering then places that offering into the classification that yields meat for the officiating priest out of the carcass of the sacrificial beast. Here is, in principle, something that is *surely* appropriate to the altar. But because of the designation, that is, the realization of the act of intentionality, of the householder, the owner of the beast, the beast has fallen into a classification that must yield meat to be eaten, and that meat of the carcass that is to be eaten is taken off the altar, though it is fit for being burnt up as an offering to God, and given to the owner or to the priest, as the rule may require.

It would be difficult to find a more profound difference, brought about by a keen appreciation for the power of the human will, between the Scripture's unnuanced and uncontingent rule and the Mishnah's clear revision of it. It would carry us far afield to catalogue all of the innumerable rules of the Mishnah in which intentionality forms the central concern. The rather arcane rules of Mishnah-tractate Makhshirin show us how sages thought deeply and framed comprehensive principles concerning will and intentionality and then applied these principles to exceedingly picayune cases, as we should, by now, expect. A simple conclusion seems well justified by the chapter we have examined in its broader conceptual context.

From the cases at hand, we may generalize as follows: will and deed constitute those actors of creation which work upon neutral realms, subject to either sanctification or uncleanness: the Temple and table, the field and family, the altar and hearth, woman, time, space, transactions in the material world and in the world above as well. An object, a substance, a transaction, even a phrase or a sentence is inert but may be made holy, when the interplay of the will and deed of the human being arouses or generates its potential to be sanctified. Each may be treated as ordinary or (where relevant) made unclean by the neglect of the will and inattentive act of the human being. Just as the entire system of uncleanness and holiness awaits the intervention of the human being, which imparts the capacity to become unclean upon what was formerly inert, or which removes the capacity to impart cleanness from what was formerly in its natural and puissant condition, so in the other ranges of reality, the human being is at the center on earth, just as is God in heaven. And all of this comes to us in arguments about the status of some drops of water.

The upshot is very simple. A central problem in the interpretation of the Mishnah, the foundation-document of Judaism, is to explain this very strange mode of discourse. Specifically, we want to know why its philosophical authorship has chosen such a strikingly concrete and unphilosophical manner for the expression of what clearly are abstract and profoundly reflective philosophical positions on the nature of human intention in relationship to metaphysical reality. To answer that question, it seems to me, sustained attention to modes of philosophical discourse in the age of the Mishnah, which is to say, the second century, will be required. Here then is a task awaiting attention: to explain why philosophers have chosen the petty and banal mode of discourse of rule-making bureaucrats.

4

PHILOSOPHY IN THE MISHNAIC MODE:
Mixtures, Doubts, and Establishing a Grid

FOR SORTING OUT RELATIONSHIPS
AMONG DISTINCT BUT INTERSECTING PRINCIPLES

The authorship of the Mishnah addressed long-standing philosophical issues, taking up these issues within its own idiom. When we grasp that fact, we shall appreciate the Mishnah as not a tedious statement of details important only to an obsessive formalism, but a curious and eloquent way of talking about this and that, while addressing the great issues of intellect. Now, as I shall presently explain, two issues that were deemed inextricable, the nature of mixtures and the resolution of doubt, predominate in Mishnaic discourse. How these issues are treated then shows us the way in which, for their part, the authorship of the Mishnah chose to address matters of common concern to intellectuals of their time and place. In this chapter we shall see expositions of three basic issues: mixtures, resolution of matters of doubt, and the interplay between distinct but interrelated rules or principles of metaphysics. In the next chapter we shall address in greater detail the problem of mixtures, a standard concern of philosophy, and show how the authorship of the Mishnah makes its statement, well within the framework of the Stoic philosophy of physics, about mixtures. We first establish the basic fact that the details of the Mishnah's discourse really do concern principles of general interest and intelligibility — mixtures, resolving doubts, interrelating separate sets of abstract facts in a single unifying grid. Only then shall we turn to a very specific demonstration of the close ties between Mishnaic and Stoic discourse on physics.

In following my claim that the Mishnah's authorship talked about pots and pans so as to make an intellectually well-crafted statement about enduring issues of mind, readers will want to judge for themselves from cases and sources, rather than merely relying upon my report of what is at hand. Accordingly, we shall work our way slowly and in painstaking detail through the underbrush of Mishnaic discourse, reading texts as they should be read, and working out, from their details, the main points under discussion. Then and only then, in the direct encounter with the sources, readers can judge whether or not I have accurately portrayed the intellectual issues and characteristics of Mishnaic discourse. For if, as I hold, we deal with philosophy in a very particular idiom, then any judgment that we have in hand the mere detritus of a collectivity of obsessive formalists will fall by the wayside, not because it is (merely) wrong, but because it is uncomprehending and ignorant of what is at hand. Accordingly, the debate underway concerns the meaning of sources, and those who wish to follow the argument will have to take responsibility to judge for themselves concerning the character and conscience of those sources.

I claim that an important issue in the Mishnah concerns the nature of mixtures and how these are to be sorted out. My first piece of evidence shows that that issue occurs. It deals with a mixture of felons of various classifications and how they are to be put to death among the four modes of execution. The particular details of the case then tell us that we have the problem of sorting out a particular confusion among data that fall within four classifications.

MISHNAH-TRACTATE SANHEDRIN 9:3-4

A. A murderer who was mixed up with others – all of them are exempt.

B. R. Judah says, "They put them all in prison."

C. All those who are liable to death who were mixed up with one another are judged [to be punished] by the more lenient mode of execution.

D. [If] those to be stoned were confused with those to be burned –

E. R. Simeon says, "They are judged [to be executed] by stoning, for burning is the more severed of the two modes of execution."

F. And sages say, "They are adjudged [to be executed] by burning, for stoning is the more severe mode of execution of the two."

G. Said to them R. Simeon, "If burning were not the more severe, it would not have been assigned to the daughter of a priest who committed adultery."

H. They said to him, "If stoning were not the more severe of the two, it would not have been assigned to the blasphemer and to the one who performs an act of service for idolatry."

I. Those who are to be decapitated who were confused with those who are to be strangled –

J. R. Simeon says, "They are killed with the sword."

K. And sages say, "They are killed by strangling."

M. 9:3

A.   He who is declared liable to be put to death through two different modes of execution at the hands of a court is judged [to be executed] by the more severe.

B.   [If] he committed a transgression, which is subject to the death penalty on two separate counts, he is judged on account of the more severe.

C.   R. Yosé says, "He is judged by the penalty which first applies to what he has done."

M. 9:4

A-B introduce the problem of C, which sets the stage for the two disputes, D-F + G-H and I-J. M. bears its own ample exegesis, and the whole restates M. 7:1. The point of concurrence at M. 9:3C is repeated. The important point is not at A, but at B. Once more, we find ourselves engaged in the exposition of the materials of Chapter Seven, now M. 7:4K-R, the sages' view that there may be two counts of culpability on the basis of a single transgression. A's point is that if one has intercourse with a married woman and is liable for strangulation, and afterward he has sexual relations with his mother-in-law and is liable for burning, he is judged on the cont of burning. If his mother-in-law had been married, we should have the problem of B. He then would be tried on the cont of the mother-in-law, which produces the execution by burning, rather than on the count of the married woman, which produces the penalty of strangulation.

Yosé's clarification requires that the woman have passed through several relationships to the lover. First she was a widow, whose daughter he had married, and so she was his mother-in-law. Afterward she was married. He had sexual relations with her. He is tried for having had sexual relations with his mother-in-law, thus for burning, since that was the first aspect in which the woman was prohibited to him. If the story were reversed, he would be tried under the count of strangulation for his sexual relations with a married woman.

Let me give another example of the interest in dealing with mixtures, in this case, how a single unitary action may encompass a variety of classifications. The interest in the correct classification of things, recognition that one thing may fall into several categories now come to expression, for the authorship of the Mishnah, in diverse ways. One of the interesting ones is the analysis of the several taxa into which a single action may fall, with an account of the multiple consequences, e.g., as to sanctions that are called into play, for a single action. I offer this instance as evidence of a prevailing concern for the right taxonomy of persons, actions, and things.

Mishnah-tractate Keritot 3:9

A.   There is one who ploughs a single furrow and is liable on eight counts of violating a negative commandment:

B.   [specifically, it is] he who (1) ploughs with an ox and an ass [Deut. 22:10], which are (2,3) both Holy Things, in the case of (4) [ploughing] Mixed Seeds in a vineyard [Deut. 22:9], (5) in the Seventh Year [Lev. 25:4], (6) on a festival [Lev. 23:7] and who was both a (7) priest [Lev. 21:1] and (8) a Nazirite [Num. 6:6] [ploughing] in a graveyard.

C.   Hanania b. Hakhinai says, "Also: He is [ploughing while] wearing a garment of diverse kinds" [Lev. 19:19, Deut. 22:11).

D.   They said to him, "This is not within the same class."

E.   He said to them, "Also the Nazir [B8] is not within the same class [as the other transgressions]."

M. 3:9

Here is a case in which more than a single set of flogging is called for. B's felon is liable to 312 stripes, on the listed counts. The ox is sanctified to the altar, the ass to the upkeep of the house (B2,3). Hanania's contribution is rejected since it has nothing to do with ploughing, and sages' position is equally flawed. The main point, for our inquiry, is simple. The one action draws in its wake multiple consequences. Classifying a single thing as a mixture of many things then forms a part of the larger intellectual address to the nature of mixtures.

My further allegation is that, when dealing with problems of mixtures, the authorship of the Mishnah further investigates the resolution of cases of doubt. For such cases, in general terms, encompass the proper classification of what is not readily subjected to taxonomy. The following sustained discussion of matters of doubt shows how, in detail, the framers address the resolution of doubt, that is to say, the sorting out of what is confused, which, I hold, forms the genus of which the issue of mixtures and how they are dealt with constitutes a subset.

MISHNAH-TRACTATE KERITOT 4:1

	A.	It is a matter of doubt whether or not one has eaten forbidden fat,
	B.	And even if he ate it, it is a matter of doubt whether or not it contains the requisite volume –
I	C.	Forbidden fat and permitted fat are before him,
	D.	he ate one of them but is not certain which one of them he ate –
II	E.	his wife and his sister are with him in the house
	F.	he inadvertently transgressed with one of them and is not certain with which of them he transgressed –
III	G.	The Sabbath and an ordinary day –
	H.	he did an act of labor on one of them and is not certain on which of them he did it –

I.   he brings [in all the foregoing circumstances] a suspensive guilt-offering.

M. 4:1

The formal traits of M. 4:1 are of principal interest, because the point, I, is self-evident. The reason A-B are distinguished from C-D, E-F, and G-H, is that the opening statement expresses its second clause with the same language as the first, namely, SPQ...SPQ..., while the triplet uses W'YN YDW'...I see no substantive difference between the two formulations.

MISHNAH-TRACTATE KERITOT 4:2-3

A.   Just as, *if he ate forbidden fat and [again ate] forbidden fat in a single spell of inadvertence, he is liable for only a single sin-offering* [M. 3:2A],

B.   so in connection with a situation of uncertainty involving them, he is liable to bring only a single guilt-offering.

C.   If there was a clarification in the meantime,

D.   just as he brings a single sin-offering for each and every transgression, so he brings a suspensive guilt-offering for each and every [possible] transgression.

E.   Just as, *if he ate forbidden fat, and blood, and remnant, and refuse, in a single spell of inadvertence, he is liable for each and every one* [M. 3:2B],

F.   so in connection with a situation of uncertainty involving them, he brings a suspensive guilt-offering for each and every one.

I   G.   Forbidden fat and remnant are before him –

H.   he ate one of them but is not certain which one of them he ate [M. 4:1C-D] –

II   I.   His wife, who is menstruating, and his sister are with him in the house –

J.   he inadvertently transgressed with one of them but is not certain with which one of them he has transgressed [M. 4:1E-F] –

III   K.   The Sabbath and the Day of Atonement –

L.   he did an act of labor at twilight, but is not certain on which one of them he did the act of labor [M. 4:1G-H] –

M.   R. Eliezer declares him liable to a sin-offering.

N.   And R. Joshua exempts him.

O.   Said R. Yosé, "They did not dispute about the case [K-L] of him who performs an act of labor at twilight, that he is exempt.

P.   – "For I say, 'Part of the work did he do while it was still this day, and part of it on the next.'

Q.   "Concerning what did they dispute?

R.   "Concerning one who does work wholly on one of the two days but does not know for certain whether he did it on the Sabbath of whether he did it on the Day of Atonement.

S.   "Or concerning him who does an act of labor but is not certain what sort of act of labor he has done –

T.   "R. Eliezer declare liable to a sin-offering.

U.   "And R. Joshua exempts him."

V.   Said R. Judah, "R. Joshua did declare him exempt even from the requirement to bring a suspensive guilt-offering.

M. 4:2

A.   R. Simeon Shezuri and R. Simeon say, "They did not dispute about something which is subject to a single category, that he is liable.

B.   "And concerning what did they dispute?

C.   "Concerning something which is subject to two distinct categories.

D.   "For R. Eliezer declares liable for a sin-offering.

E.   "And R. Joshua exempts."

F.   Said R. Judah, "Even if he intended to gather figs but gathered grapes, grapes but gathered figs,

G.   "black ones but gathered white ones, white ones but gathered black ones –

H.   "R. Eliezer declared liable to a sin-offering.

I.   "And R. Joshua exempts."

J.   Said R. Judah, "I should be surprised if R. Joshua declared him wholly exempt. If so, Why is it said, '*In which he has sinned* (Lev. $:23)?

K.   "To exclude him who was occupied [with some other matter and entirely unintentionally committed a transgressions]."

M. 4:3

M. 4:2A-F complete the opening unit, linking the whole to M. 3:2, which is explicitly cited, as indicated in italics. The point is clear. If we have a single spell of inadvertence, then, when we are certain what the man has done, he brings a sin-offering, and when we are not certain, he brings a guilt-offering. Further, if in the intervals the man becomes aware of what he has done, e.g., between eating the first olive's bulk and the second, he becomes aware that he has eaten something which may be forbidden fat, he brings a suspensive guilt-offering, D, for each and every transgression. E-F are clear as given. M. 4:2G-V, continued by M. 4:3, return us to M. 4:1, which is why I regard M. 4:1-3 as a single extended pericope. We systematically cite the triplet of M. 4:1. But there is this difference: while at M. 4:1 we have a possibility that the man has not sinned at all, when we restate the cases, G, I, and K, we make clear that there is no way that the man has *not* sinned.

He does not know for sure which sin he has committed, that is, under what category of transgression his sin-offering is brought. Eliezer declared him liable, since, if it is not for one sin, it is for the other (B. Ker. 19a). Joshua exempts, since, in line with Lev. 4:23, he insists that the man who brings a sin-offering know precisely *why* he must do so, that is, for what specific sin or category of sin.

We then have tow restatement of the same version of what is subject to dispute, O-U + V and M. 4:3A-I + J. Yosé corrects the statement of K-L, because, P, there is a possibility that the man did not sin at all, since liability must be for an act of competed labor. R, glossed by S which contributes nothing), then restates the matter essentially in line with the conception of M. 4:2G-N. Judah differs from Yosé, because, in Yosé's view, while the man does know for sure that he has sinned, he does not know what category of sin he has done. But, in Judah's version of Joshua's view, the suspensive guilt-offering is brought only when a man is not sure that he has sinned at all. Accordingly, *declared exempt* means *of any offering at all.* The final version presents a dispute between the two Simeons and Judah, M. 4:3A-E, F-I. The two Simeons go over the ground of Yosé and M. 4:2G-N. The disputants agree that the man is liable who has done a sin which is in a single category, e.g., inadvertently gathering on the Sabbath, with the uncertainty being whether he has gathered figs or grapes. In such a situation, Joshua concedes the man knows that he has committed the sin of gathering on the Sabbath and must bring a sin-offering. But if he has done something which may fall into two different categories, such as the cases given at M. 4:2G-N, eating either forbidden fat or remnant, which are subject to distinct prohibitions, or having intercourse with his wife who is a menstruant, as against having intercourse with his sister, again subject to two distinctive consideration, then we have the state dispute. Accordingly, the anonymous authority of M. 4:2G-N, Yosé, and the two Simeons, concur. It is Judah who differs even on the definition of the dispute. At M. 4:3F-I, he states the difference. Even if the man is sure he has done an action subject to a single category of prohibition, but is not certain as to the details of the action, F-G, we have the stated dispute. Judah's second gloss, J, then explains the situation which, in Judah's conception of Joshua's view, leaves the man wholly exempt from an offering. It is one in which the man in no way intended to do something prohibited. But in the case Judah himself gives at F-G, Judah's Joshua will require a suspensive guilt-offering, in contrast to Judah at M. 4:2V.

Thus far, in what is a protracted account of how, specifically, our authorship carries on its philosophical discourse about philosophical issues, I have shown that issues of mixtures occur, on the one side, and that these form a subset of the question of resolving cases of doubt, e.g., as to the classification of an action, a person, or a thing. A further claim of mine in my characterization of the modes of philosophical thought of the authorship of the Mishnah is that these intellectuals concern themselves with the operation of holiness in the materials of this world. They maintain that holiness or sanctification affects the nature of things. What is holy is treated differently, in accord with different rules, from what is ordinary and secular. Since that position is not distinctive to our authorship, being held, for example, by the authorship of the Priestly Code, we forthwith proceed to the next important characterization, on my part, of these same modes of thought and, consequently, of the issues that are dealt with. I maintain that the attitude of the individual person directly affects the standing and classification of material things, which is to say, what an Israelite thinks about an object, for instance, food or drink, affects the standing and classification of that food and drink. To join these two propositions: if an Israelite regards food or drink as holy, whatever the origin and prior disposition of that food or drink (in the Temple? in the home?), then that food or drink is subjected to the rules that govern what is holy. Accordingly, we have a picture of how attitude and intentionality affect the natural world.

Now these propositions of mine, which bespeak a religion not of pots and pans, but of will, attitude, and both affective and effective intentionality, emerge in a complex and fundamental discussion, at Mishnah-tractate Tohorot 2:2-8. I shall now present in full and awesome detail that sustained discussion. What we shall see, in the details of the several positions unfolding here, is how the attitude of a person toward food and drink changes the standing and classification of that food and drink, so that the food and drink must be dealt with in accord with different rules from those that would have prevailed had that person not taken the view of the food and drink that he has taken. Specifically, if you think that a piece of bread is in the standing of food assigned to the priesthood (in accord with the rules of Leviticus 21-22), then that bread must be deemed analogous to priestly rations and treated as such. If you form the intention of treating your bread as though it were a share of the show-bread given to the priests from the altar and therefore in the standing of Holy Things of the altar, the rules that govern the handling of that bread are analogous to the rules that governing the treatment of the altar's show-bread.

Not only so, but the discussion we shall now examine involves what are called "removes of uncleanness," and before we commence our slow reading of the passage, we had best consider these as well. The operative conception sees a sequence of contacts beginning with a principal source of uncleanness. One who or a thing that touches a source of uncleanness is held to be unclean in the first remove from that source; one who touches that person or thing is unclean in the second remove; one who touches that person or thing is unclean in the third remove. Now there is going to be a correlation between removes of uncleanness and levels of sanctification. The principle we shall see is that what is more holy is also more capable of being affected by uncleanness, which means, will be affected by uncleanness transmitted at a further remove from the original source of uncleanness, than what is less holy. Food that is ordinary and unconsecrated will be affected at fewer removes from the original source; food that is designated as priestly rations ("heave-offering" in what follows) is affected at more removes; food that is in the standing of Holy Things will be affected at still more removes.

These several principles are brought together in a grid, so that we can map out the entire interplay of sanctification, that is, the several stages of holiness into which food may fall, with the layers of uncleanness, unfolding from the original source of uncleanness outward to the third and fourth removes therefrom. And the mapping of that grid, like Ptolemy's map of the world by grids, allows a single and sustained picture of the two realities, holiness and uncleanness, to be superimposed upon one another. Clearly, we deal with a high level of utterly abstract thought, in which, through the issues of pots and pans, dead creeping things and bits of bread, we express the immaterial relationships among unseen givens: a world of uncleanness, a realm of the sacred. True, if we do not comprehend the stakes before us, we are going to see it all as a set of extraordinarily dull and incomprehensible rules about the ancient Israelite counterpart to stepping on the cracks in the sidewalks. But when we do see what is at stake, we understand once more how we deal with philosophers who sustain discourse in an odd and subtle idiom indeed. Now to the issue of removes from uncleanness in relationship to levels of sanctification — which is to say, establish a grid between two sets of rules, another principal interest of philosophers.

MISHNAH-TRACTATE TOHOROT 2:2

A. R. Eliezer says, "(1) He who eats food unclean in the first remove is unclean in the second remove; "(2) [he who eats] food unclean in the second remove is unclean in the second remove; "(3) [he who eats] food unclean in the third remove is unclean in the third remove."

B. R. Joshua says, "(1) He who eats food unclean in the first remove and food unclean in the second remove is unclean in the second remove. "(2) [He who eats food] unclean in the third remove is unclean in the second remove so far as Holy Things are concerned, "(3) and is not unclean in the second remove so far as heave-offering is concerned.

C. "[We speak of] the case of unconsecrated food

D. "which is prepared in conditions appropriate to heave offering."

MISHNAH-TRACTATE TOHOROT 2:3

A. *Unconsecrated food:* in the first remove is unclean and renders unclean;

B. in the second remove is unfit, but does not convey uncleanness;

C. and in the third remove is eaten in the pottage of heave-offering.

MISHNAH-TRACTATE TOHOROT 2:4

A. *Heave-offering:*
in the first and in the second remove is unclean and renders unclean;
B. in the third remove is unfit and does not convey uncleanness;
C. and in the fourth remove is eaten in a pottage of Holy Things.

MISHNAH-TRACTATE TOHOROT 2:5

A. *Holy Things:* in the first and the second and the third removes are susceptible to uncleanness and render unclean;
B. and in the fourth remove are unfit and do not convey uncleanness;
C. and in the fifth remove are eaten in a pottage of Holy Things.

MISHNAH-TRACTATE TOHOROT 2:6

A. *Unconsecrated food:* in the second remove renders unconsecrated liquid unclean and renders food of heave-offering unfit.
B. *Heave-offering:* in the third remove renders unclean [the] liquid of Holy Things, and renders foods of Holy Things unfit,
C. if it [the heave-offering] was prepared in the condition of cleanness pertaining to Holy Things.
D. But if it was prepared in conditions pertaining to heave-offering, it renders unclean at two removes and renders unfit at one remove in reference to Holy Things.

MISHNAH-TRACTATE TOHOROT 2:7

A. R. Eleazar says, "The three of them are equal:
B. *"Holy Things and heave-offering, and unconsecrated food:* "which are at the first remove of uncleanness render unclean at two removes and unfit at one [further] remove in respect to Holy Things; "render unclean at one remove and spoil at one [further] remove in respect to heave-offering; "and spoil unconsecrated food.
C. "That which is unclean in the second remove in all of them renders unclean at one remove and unfit at one [further] remove in respect to Holy Things; "and renders liquid of unconsecrated food unclean; "and spoils foods of heave-offering.
D. "The third remove of uncleanness in all of them renders liquids of Holy Things unclean, "and spoils food of Holy Things."

Mishnah-Tractate Tohorot 2:2-7 presupposes knowledge of the Mishnaic system of ritual purity, to which we now turn. A review of some of its essential elements is necessary for an understanding of the arguments and analyses that follow.

In the system, ritual impurity is acquired by contact with either a primary or a secondary source of uncleanness, called a "Father" or a "Child" or "Offspring" of uncleanness, respectively. In the first category are contact with a corpse, a person suffering a flux, a leper, and the like. Objects made of metal, wood, leather, bone, cloth, or sacking become Fathers of uncleanness if they touch a corpse. Foodstuffs and liquids are susceptible to uncleanness, but will not render other foodstuffs unclean in the same degree or remove of uncleanness that they themselves suffer. Foodstuffs furthermore will not make vessels or utensils unclean. But liquids made unclean by a Father of uncleanness will do so if they touch the inner side of the vessel. That is, if they fall into the contained space of an earthenware vessel, they make the whole vessel unclean.

Food or liquid that touches a Father of uncleanness becomes unclean in the *first* remove. If food touches a person or vessel made unclean by a primary cause of uncleanness, it is unclean in the *second* remove. Food that touches *second—remove* uncleanness incurs *third-remove* uncleanness, and food that touches *third-remove* uncleanness incurs *fourth-remove* uncleanness, and so on. But liquids touching either a primary source of uncleanness (Father) or something unclean in the first or second remove (Offspring) are regarded as unclean in the first remove. They are able to make something else unclean. If, for example, the other side of a vessel is made unclean by a liquid – thus unclean in the second remove – and another liquid touches the outer side, the other liquid incurs not second, but first degree uncleanness.

Heave-offering (food raised up for priestly use only) unclean in the third remove of uncleanness, and Holy Things (that is, things belonging to the cult) unclean in the fourth remove, do not make other things, whether liquids or foods, unclean. The difference among removes of uncleanness is important. First degree uncleanness in common food will convey uncleanness. But, although food unclean in the second remove will be unacceptable, it will not convey uncleanness, that is, third degree uncleanness. But it will render heave-offering *unfit*. Further considerations apply to heave-offering and Holy Things. Heave-offering can be made unfit and unclean by a first, and unfit by a second, degree of uncleanness. If it touches something unclean in the third remove, it is made unfit, but itself will not impart fourth degree uncleanness. A Holy Thing that suffers uncleanness in the first, second, or third remove is unclean and conveys uncleanness. If it is unclean in the fourth remove, it is invalid for the cult but does not convey uncleanness. It is much more susceptible than are non-cultic things. Thus, common food that suffers second degree uncleanness will render heave-offering invalid. We already know that it makes liquid unclean in the first remove. Likewise, heave-offering unclean in the third remove will make Holy Things invalid and put them into a fourth remove of uncleanness.

With these data firmly in hand, let us turn to a general discussion of M. Mishnah-Tractate Tohorot 2:2-7. Mishnah-Tractate Tohorot 2:2 introduces the removes of uncleanness. Our interest is in the contaminating effect, upon a person, of eating unclean food. Does the food make the person unclean in the same remove of uncleanness as is borne by the food itself? Thus if one eats food unclean in the first remove, is he unclean in that same remove? This is the view of Eliezer. Joshua says he is unclean in the second remove. The dispute, Mishnah-Tractate Tohorot 2:2A-B, at Mishnah-Tractate Tohorot 2:2C-D is significantly glossed. The further consideration is introduced as to the sort of food under discussion. Joshua is made to say that there is a difference between the contaminating effects upon the one who eats heave-offering, on the one side, and unconsecrated food prepared in conditions of heave-offering, on the other. This matter, the status of unconsecrated food prepared as if it were heave-offering, or as if it were Holy Things, and heave-offering prepared as if it were Holy Things, forms a substratum of our chapter, added to several primary items and complicating the exegesis. Tosefta-Tractate Tohorot 2:1 confirms, however, that primary to the dispute between Eliezer and Joshua is simply the matter of the effects of food unclean in the first remove upon the person who eats such food. The gloss, Mishnah-Tractate Tohorot 2:2C-D, forms a redactional-thematic link between Joshua's opinion and the large construction of Mishnah-Tractate Tohorot 2:3-7. Mishnah-Tractate Tohorot 2.3:5, expanded and glossed by Mishnah-Tractate Tohorot 2:6, follow a single and rather tight form. The sequence differentiates unconsecrated food, heave-offering, and Holy Things each at the several removes from the original source of uncleanness.

Eleazar, Mishnah-Tractate Tohorot 2:7, insists that, at a given remove, all three are subject to the *same* rule. The contrary view, Mishnah-Tractate Tohorot 2:3-6, is that unconsecrated food in the first remove makes heave-offering unclean and at the second remove spoils heave-offering; it does not enter a third remove and therefore has no effect upon Holy Things. Heave-offering at the first two removes may produce contaminating effects, and at the third remove spoils Holy Things, but is of no effect at the fourth. Holy Things in the first three removes produce uncleanness, and at the fourth impart unfitness to other Holy Things. Mishnah-Tractate Tohorot 2:6 then goes over the ground of unconsecrated food at the second remove, and heave-offering at the third. The explanation of Mishnah-Tractate Tohorot 2:6C is various; the simplest view is that the clause glosses Mishnah-Tractate Tohorot 2:6B by insisting that the heave-offering to which we refer is prepared as if it were Holy Things, on which account, at the third remove, it can spoil Holy Things. At Mishnah-Tractate Tohorot 2:7 Eleazar restates matters, treating all three – Holy Things, heave-offering, and unconsecrated food – as equivalent to one another at the first, second, and third removes, with the necessary qualification for unconsecrated food that it is like the other, consecrated foods in producing effects at the second and even the third removes. Commentators read *Eliezer.* They set the pericope up against Joshua's view at Mishnah-Tractate Tohorot 2:2, assigning to Joshua Mishnah-Tractate Tohorot 2:3ff. as well. My picture of the matter is significantly different from the established exegesis. To state the upshot simply:

So far as Eleazar is concerned, what is important is not the source of contamination – the unclean foods – but that which is contaminated, the unconsecrated food, heave-offering, and Holy Things. He could not state matters more clearly than he does when he says that the three of them are exactly equivalent. And they are, because the differentiations will emerge in the food affected, or contaminated, by the three. So at the root of the dispute is whether we gauge the contamination in accord with the source – unconsecrated food, or unconsecrated food prepared as if it were heave-offering, and so on – or whether the criterion is the food which is contaminated. Mishnah-Tractate Tohorot 2:3-5 are all wrong, Eleazar states explicitly at Mishnah-Tractate Tohorot 2:7A, because they differentiate among uncleanness imparted by unclean unconsecrated food, unclean heave-offering, and unclean Holy Things, and do not differentiate among the three sorts of food *to which* contamination is imparted. It is surely a logical position, for the three sorts of food do exhibit differentiated capacities to receive uncleanness; one sort *is* more contaminable than another.

And so too is the contrary view logical: *what is more sensitive to uncleanness also will have a greater capacity to impart uncleanness.* The subtle debate before us clearly is unknown to Eliezer and Joshua at Mishnah-Tractate Tohorot 2:2. To them the operative categories are something unclean in first, second, or third *removes,* without distinction as to the relative sensitivities of the several types of food which may be unclean. The unfolding of the issue may be set forth very briefly by way of conclusion: the sequence thus begins with Eliezer and Joshua, who ask about the contaminating power of that which is unclean in the first and second removes, without regard to whether it is unconsecrated food, heave-offering, or Holy things. To them, the distinction between the capacity to impart contamination, or to receive contamination, of the several sorts of food is unknown. Once, however, their question is raised — in such general terms — it will become natural to ask the next logical question, one which makes distinctions not only among the several removes of uncleanness, but also among the several sorts of food involved in the processes of contamination. The grid that is set forth here has allowed the philosophers to speculate about the interrelationship between distinct but intersecting principles, the one concerning removes of uncleanness, the other involving levels of sanctification.

I have established beyond all doubt that the issues of detail encompassed principles of broad interest and general intelligibility. These involve three fundamental problems of thought: how to deal with mixtures, how to confront cases of doubt, and how to show the interplay of abstract and immaterial rules, comparable in their framework to discrete and also intersecting laws of geometry, for instance. My next task, in demonstrating that in matters of detail, fundamental statements of a philosophical (or, in context, theological) character emerged, is to show a point-by-point counterpart, in the Mishnah, to a particular problem of philosophy. For that purpose I return to the issues of mixtures, which in ancient philosophy were classified as problems in physics. I shall show a point-for-point correspondence between the Mishnah's authorships classification of types of mixtures, expressed, as a matter of fact, in the context of pots and pans, with Stoic philosophers' classifications of types of mixtures.

5

Why and How Religion Speaks
through Politics

The Case of Classical Judaism

I.
RELIGION AND THE POLITICAL MYTH

A religious system sets forth a theory of the social order, encompassing three main components: a world-view, a way of life, and an account of the character of the social entity that realizes the way of life and explains that way of life through the specified world view. That religious statement of the social order then presents a theory of how the social group embodies an account of cosmic reality and through its everyday affairs embodies that reality. In theory, religious systems may well utilize every available medium to make their statement, utilizing music and art, theology and myth, gesture, dance and song, rules of clothing, food, sexual relationships, modes of building buildings and organizing cities, rationalizing time and space, family nurture, economic action — every mode and possibility of human action and express will serve. Through all things, systems will say the same thing. But as a matter of fact, religious systems will lay stress on some few media, even while exploiting the expressive potentialities of them all. To state matters in a crude but current way, Judaism is hung up about food, Catholicism about sex, so that piety in the one religion comes to expression at the dining table, and the other, at what happens, or does not happen, in bed.

When religious system-framers seek appropriate media for the expression of the system they propose to put forth, politics and the framing of public policy present themselves as candidates — but no more than that. For some religious systems find urgent the expression of their systemic statement through political media — political symbols, political institutions, the formation of public policy — and others do not. Or, at a given period, for particular circumstances, politics will appear irrelevant, while at another period, under different conditions, political action will take on critical importance and central expressive potentiality. Christianity for its first three centuries framed no vision of the political order, but in the fourth century confronted a new reality and formulated a theory of politics that made space for both church and state, with the Christian theory of the social order fully exposed through a large account of the interplay of religious and political institutions and the tasks of each. One result familiar to all of us is the profound reflection of Augustine on the city of God, in which the political metaphor served to convey a deeply supernatural theory of the social order.

Now, as a matter of fact, we in the West have long ago formulated a theory of the social order that distinguishes religion from politics, church or synagogue or mosque from institutions of state. We define politics in an acutely secular way as the theory of the legitimate exercise of violence, and reserve for the state the power of physical force, assigning to religion the moral force of persuasion. This is expressed in a clear way by Brian Mitchell, when he says:

> "In the West, the rightful employment of coercion is generally reserved for political powers, the civil and military authorities at their various levels. Persuasion, on the other hand, is generally left to the social powers, consisting of the many voluntary associations that influence individual behavior (church, family, community, etc.). Primitive tribes...recognize no distinction between the social and the political. The tribe functions as an extended family, organized in a strictly hierarchical fashion...Everyone has his place in the pyramid, and every social subgroup is a subordinate part of the whole. Some societies have maintained a unified, hierarchical, and essentially tribal structure...Most Western nations are still political societies, with a political system easily distinguishable from the rest of society, and a political hierarchy representing just one way in which the society is organized..."[1]

Mitchell underscores that in the West, political power is limited, and the social powers stand on their own: "Christianity...confirmed the distinction between political rule and social life, providing Western civilization with both a cosmological basis for the distinction and a powerful new social order to counterbalance the political order." One may speculate that the first three centuries of Christian history, with the Church confronting a hostile state, introduced the distinction between the Church as an autonomous social entity and the empire: "It claimed for itself the right to function free of government interference and made itself responsible for

---

[1] Brian Mitchell, "The Distinction of Powers: How Church and State Divide Us," *Religion and Public Life* 1995, 29:2.

many matters of public welfare and moral, at the same time leaving the use of coercion to civil authorities alone." The theory of the two masters conveys that distinction. The systemic message of earliest Christianity appropriated a politics of division, perhaps turning necessity into the occasion for a restatement of the systemic perspective on the coming of God's kingdom under Christ.

Now it is easy for us to miss the extreme and radical character of that theory of distinction between church and state, religion and politics, for that distinction is not only familiar in the politics of our own country but also a given of the Christian civilization that defines Western civilization. As a result, we in this country find exceedingly difficult the task of understanding a different utilization of politics from the Christian and Western, secular one, with its critical distinctions, as Mitchell has expressed them in most current form. And that difficulty persists even though the foundation-document of Christianity, the Old Testament, portrays politics as integral to the religious structure of ancient Israel, with the prophet, Moses, portrayed also as the king of Israel, law-giver and head of state. The Pentateuchal books are so set forth as to formulate the systemic statements that they wish to make through an acutely political account of the social order. Moses rules as God's prophet but also as God's political agent, and Israel takes shape as God's people: a kingdom of priests and a holy people. When by contrast, the Gospel of John portrays Jesus as king and prophet, or the Gospel of Matthew sets Jesus on the mountain forth as Moses at Sinai, the clear distinction between king and prophet, Caesar and Christ, forms the premise of all discourse.

The upshot of the character of Western Christian and secular politics, with its critical distinction between and among power in various modes, political from prophetic, for instance, is simple: we find exceedingly difficult the task of making sense of a politics that serves for systemic purposes in religious systems. We have no theory that encompasses a politics embedded in the religious theory of the social order, shaped by that theory, given legitimacy and purpose through that theory. Hence we cannot hear the religious messages that politics, when embedded in an encompassing, religious theory of the social order, wishes to set forth. And we miss the deep congruences between those messages when stated politically and the same, identical messages when stated gastronomically or sexually, to revert to the Judaic and Catholic matters to which I alluded earlier.

We are unable to make sense not only of those enormous portions of the world in which politics and religion cohere and deliver a single, uniform and cogent statement. We also cannot formulate in our own context a theory that will explain to us the political aspirations of religious societies, with the result that important components of the political order in this country, on both right and left (the Christian Coalition, the National Council of Churches, for example) come to the public square with pronouncements on public policy that invoke theological principles and express them. Consequently, religious groups appear to speak a kind of gibberish, intelligible only to themselves, when in fact they mean to make a statement not only to, but about, the social order that encompasses us all. They address the definition of what it means to be a human being, what God wants of us, how we are to relate to one another and assume public responsibilities — deeply religious categories of thought. But the rest of us hear, and fear, yet another pressure group, but an illegitimate one.

If, as I maintain, the reason we cannot understand religious discourse within the political structures of society, it is because we have no model, deriving from Western Christian and secular life, of how political discourse may convey a principal part of that same religious systemic statement that theological or mythical or liturgical discourse conveys. We do not grasp that what religions may say about the political order they say about every other dimension of human existence, and we have no useful examples of how such a global discourse takes place. My contribution to the solution to the problem at hand — one of trying to understand a kind of thinking about politics that proves alien at its deepest premises to the one that predominates among us — is then to show how in a particular case the theory of politics will itself form a statement of a religious theory of the social order, not to be distinguished from all other statements of that same theory of the social order, in whatever media they are made, under whatever circumstances they reach concrete expression and produce practical consequences.

I speak in particular of the politics of a particular Judaism, the one set forth in the Mishnah, a second-century A.D. law code that expresses a coherent philosophical program. Like the Pentateuchal Judaism, this was a Judaic system that found it necessary to utilize matters of politics and public policy in the full formulation of its systemic message.[2]

II.
POLITICS WITHIN THE JUDAIC MYTH

The principal structural components of this Judaism's politics are easily defined. Just as a systemic myth expresses the teleology of a world-view, telling people why things are the way they are, a political myth expresses that element of a social entity's world-view that instructs people why coercive power is legitimate in forcing people to do what they are supposed to do. It presents the narrative equivalent of legitimate violence, because it means through the force of its teleological apologia to coerce conformity with the social order and its norms. The political institutions envisaged by a politics convey details of the way of life of the same entity that, in theory at least, exercises the coercive power to secure compliance with the rules. Finally, the management of politics delineates, within the social entity's on-going affairs, how the institutions secure suitable and capable

---

[2] What follows reviews some of my findings in *Rabbinic Political Theory: Religion and Politics in the Mishnah.* Chicago, 1991: The University of Chicago Press.

staff to carry out their public tasks. Politics defines the concrete and material component of the conception of a social system, and the theory of politics, defining both how things should be and also how they should be done, forms the critical element in a religious system.

The task undertaken by the political myth of the Judaism set forth in the Mishnah is not only to make power specific and particular to cases. It is especially a labor of differentiation of power, indicating what agency or person has the power to precipitate the working of politics as legitimate violence at all.[3] When, therefore, we understand the differentiating force of myth that imparts to politics its activity and dynamism, we shall grasp what everywhere animates the structures of the politics and propels the system. In the case of the politics of Judaism, we shall work our way downward, into the depths of the system, toward a myth of taxonomy of power. Appealing to a myth of taxonomy, the system accomplishes its tasks by explaining why this, not that, by telling as its foundation story a myth of classification for the application of legitimate violence. The myth appeals in the end to the critical bases for the taxonomy, among institutions, of a generalized power to coerce. Let me make these somewhat abstract remarks more concrete.

Specifically, in this presentation we analyze the mythic foundations of sanctions. And when we move from sanctions to the myth expressed and implicit in the application and legitimation of those sanctions, we see a complex but cogent politics sustained by a simple myth. This somewhat protracted survey of sanctions and their implications had best commence with a clear statement of what we shall now uncover.

The encompassing framework of rules, institutions and sanctions is explained and validated by appeal to the myth of God's shared rule. That dominion, exercised by God and his surrogates on earth, is focused partly in the royal palace, partly in the Temple, and partly in the court. For us, the issue here is the differentiation of power, which is to say, which part falls where and why? Helpfully, the political myth of Judaism explains who exercises legitimate violence and under what conditions, and furthermore specifies the source for differentiation. The myth consequently serves a particular purpose—which is to answer that particular question. Indeed, the Judaic political myth comes to expression in its details of differentiation, which permit us to identify, and of course to answer, the generative question of politics.

Moving from the application of power to the explanation thereof, we find that the system focuses upon finding answers to the question of who imposes which sanction, and why. And those answers contain the myth, nowhere expressed, everywhere in full operation. So we begin with cases and end with cases, only in the mid-stages of analysis uncovering the narrative premises for our diverse cases

---

[3] A fundamental premise of my mode of systemic analysis is that where a system differentiates, there it lays its heaviest emphasis and stress. That is how we may identify what particular questions elicit urgent concern, and what other questions are treated as null.

that, when seen together, form the myth of politics in the initial structure of post-Temple Judaism. Through the examination of sanctions, we identify the foci of power. At that point we ask how power is differentiated.

How, exactly, do I propose to identify the political myth of Judaism? And precisely what data are supposed to attest to that myth? Institutions of political persuasion and coercion dominate not only through physical but also through mental force, through psychological coercion or appeal to good will. So my inquiry's premise is not far to seek. I take as a given that a political myth animates the structure of a politics. But the authorship of the Mishnah has chosen other media for thought and expression than narrative and teleological ones. It is a philosophical, not a historical (fictive) account; it is conveyed through masses of detailed rules about small things. While the Mishnah through its cases amply informs us on the institutions of politics, the mythic framework within which persuasion and inner compliance are supposed to bring about submission to legitimate power scarcely emerges, remaining only implicit throughout.[4] But it is readily discerned when we ask the right questions. If we were to bring to the authorship of the Mishnah such questions as "who tells whom what to do?" they would point to the politics' imaginary king and its equally fictive high priest, with associated authorities. Here, they would tell us, are the institutions of politics—represented in personal rather than abstract form, to be sure. But if we were to say to them, "And tell us the story (in our language: the myth) that explains on what basis you persuade people to conform," they would find considerable difficulty in bringing to the fore the explicit mythic statements made by their writing.

How then are we to identify, on the basis of what the Mishnah does tell us, the generative myths to which the system is supposed to appeal? The answer derives from the definition of politics that governs in general. A myth, we recall, explains the exercise of legitimate power. Now, we know, power comes to brutal expression when the state kills or maims someone or deprives a person of property through the imposition of legal sanctions for crime or sin.[5] In the absence of a myth of power, we therefore begin with power itself. We shall work our way back from the facts of power to the intimations, within the record of legitimately violent sanctions, of the intellectual and even mythic sources of legitimation for the exercise and use of that legitimate violence. For it is at the point of imposing sanctions, of

---

[4] Given the authority of Scripture and the character of the Pentateuch as a design of a holy state, on holy land, made up of holy people, living a holy life, we should not be surprised by silence, on the surface at least, about the reason why. People everywhere acknowledge and confess God's rule and the politics of the Torah, in its written form as the Pentateuch, claiming legitimacy attained through conformity to the law and politics. But we cannot take for granted that Scripture has supplied a myth.

[5] I do not distinguish crime from sin, since I do not think the system does. At the same time our own world does make such a distinction, and it would be confusing not to preserve it. That accounts for the usage throughout.

killing, injuring, denying property, excluding from society, that power operates in its naked form. Then how these legitimate exercises of violence are validated will set before us such concrete evidence of the myth. And, so far as there is such evidence, that will identify the political myth of Judaism.[6]

Since the analysis of sources will prove somewhat abstruse, let me signal in advance the main line of argument. Analyzing myth by explaining sanctions draws our attention to the modes of legitimate violence that the system identifies. There we find four types of sanctions, each deriving from a distinct institution of political power, each bearing its own mythic explanation. The first comprises what God and the Heavenly court can do to people. The second comprises what the earthly court can do to people. That type of sanction embodies the legitimate application of the worldly and physical kinds of violence of which political theory ordinarily speaks. The third comprises what the cult can do to the people. The cult through its requirements can deprive people of their property as legitimately as can a court. The fourth comprises conformity with consensus—self-imposed sanctions. Here the issue is, whose consensus, and defined by whom? Across these four types of sanction, four types of coercion are in play. They depend on violence of various kinds—psychological and social as much as physical. Clearly, then, the sanctions that are exercised by other than judicial-political agencies prove violent and legitimately coercive, even though the violence and coercion are not the same as those carried out by courts.

On this basis we can differentiate among types of sanctions — and hence trace evidences of how the differentiation is explained. Since our data focus upon who does what to whom, the myth of politics must explain why various types of sanctions are put into effect by diverse political agencies or institutions. The exercise of power, invariably and undifferentiatedly in the name and by the authority of God in Heaven to be sure, is kept distinct. And the distinctions in this case signal important differences which, then, require explanation. Concrete application of legitimate violence by [1] Heaven covers different matters from parts of the political and social world governed by the policy and coercion of [2] the this-worldly political classes. And both sorts of violence have to be kept distinct from the sanction effected by [3] the community through the weight of attitude and public opinion. Here, again, we find a distinct set of penalties applied to a particular range of actions. When we have seen the several separate kinds of sanction and where they apply, we shall have a full account of the workings of politics as the application of power, and from that concrete picture we may, I think, identify the range of power and the mythic framework that has to have accommodated and legitimated diverse kinds of power.

---

[6] It goes without saying that appeal to Scripture at this point is irrelevant. People used Scripture in building their system; they did not begin their system-building by perusing Scripture. But when our analysis of the application of power invites attention to Scripture, we surely are justified in seeing what we find there.

Our task therefore is to figure out on the basis of sanctions' distinct realms, Heaven, earth, and the mediating range of the Temple and sacrifice, which party imposes sanctions for (in modern parlance) what crimes or sins. Where Heaven intervenes, do other authorities participate, and if so, what tells me which party takes charge and imposes its sanction? Is the system differentiated so that where earth is in charge, there is no pretense of appeal to Heaven? Or do we find cooperation in coextensive jurisdiction, such that one party penalizes an act under one circumstance, the other the same act under a different circumstance? A survey of the sanctions enables us to differentiate the components of the power-structure before us. So we wonder whether each of these three estates that enjoy power and inflict sanctions of one kind or another — Heaven, earth, Temple in-between — governs its own affairs, without the intervention of the others, or whether, working together, each takes charge in collaboration with the other, so that power is parcelled out and institutions simultaneously differentiate themselves from one another and also intersect. The survey of sanctions will allow us to answer these questions and so identify the myth of politics and the exercise of power that Judaism promulgated through the Mishnah.

What has been said about the relationship of the Mishnah to Scripture — the system makes its own choices within the available revelation — imposes the first task. We must address this obvious question: can we not simply open the Hebrew Scriptures and choose, therein, the operative political myth? No, we cannot. Why? First, the system-builders choose what they find useful and ignore what they do not. Second, Scripture presents for a political myth pretty much everything and its opposite; it allows for government by the prophet (Moses), the king (David), the priest (Ezra). So if we are to appeal to Scripture in our search for myth, we can do so only by showing that, in the very context of the concrete exercise of power, the framers of the Mishnah turn to Scripture. They then will tell us where to look and why. In fact, our authorship does represent the entire system as the realization of God's dominion over Israel. And this representation is specific and detailed. It thus justifies an inquiry, once we have identified the questions the myth must answer, into how, in Scripture, we find responses to just those questions.

Here, then, is one instance of the way in which Scripture provides a detail of a myth accompanying a detail of legitimate coercion. The following lists the number of law-violations that one commits by making a profit, which is to say, collecting interest:

> Those who participate in a loan on interest violate a negative commandment: these are the lender, borrower, guarantor, and witnesses.
> Sages say, "Also the scribe."
> They violate the negative commandment, "You will not give him your money upon usury" (Lev. 25:37); "You will not take usury from him" (Lev. 25:36); "You shall not be a creditor to him" (Ex. 22:25); "Nor shall you lay upon him usury" (Ex. 22:25); and they violate the negative command, "You

shall not put a stumbling block before the blind, but you shall fear your God. I am the Lord" (Lev. 19:14)

M. Baba Mesia. 5:11

We appeal to the Torah to justify law-obedience and to impose sanction for disobedience. But where is the myth that sustains obedience? Let me explain this question, which is critical to all that follows. On the basis of the passage just cited, we do not know what actually happens to me if I do participate in a loan on interest and so violate various rules of the Torah. More to the point, we do not know who that penalty or effects it. That is to say, the generalized appeal to the law of the Torah and the assumed premise that one should obey that law and not violate it hardly tell me the morphology of the political myth at hand. They assume a myth that is not set forth, and they conceal those details in which the myth gains its sustaining vitality and power.

Clearly, simply knowing that everything is in accord with the Torah and that God wants Israel to keep the laws of the Torah does not reveal the systemically active component of the political myth. On the one hand, the propositions are too general; on the other hand, they do not address the critical question. The sequence of self-evident premises that runs [1] God revealed the Torah, [2] the political institutions and rules carry out the Torah, and therefore [3] people should conform, hardly sustains a concrete theory of *just* where and how God's authority serves the systemic construction at hand. The appeal to Scripture, therefore, reveals no incisive information about the Mishnah's validating myth.

This conclusion is reinforced by the references we find here and there to "the kingdom of Heaven"[7] that appeal to God's rule in an everyday framework. These form a mere allegation that, in general, what the political authorities tell people to do is what God wants them to do illuminates not at all. For example, at M. Ber. 2:5, to Gamaliel is attributed the statement, "I cannot heed you to suspend from myself the kingdom of Heaven even for one hour." Now as a matter of fact that is not a political context[8] — there is no threat of legitimate violence, for instance

---

[7] In line with the Mishnah's usage, I refer to God and God's heavenly court with the euphemism of "Heaven," and the capital H expresses the simple fact that "Heaven" always refers to God and God's court on high. The Mishnah is not clear on whether its authorship thinks God personally intervenes throughout, but there is a well-established belief in divine agents, e.g., angels or messengers, so in speaking of Heaven or Heaven's intervention, we take account of the possibility that God's agents are meant.

[8] I am puzzled by the fact that in the Mishnah "kingdom of Heaven" never occurs in what we should call a political context, rather, it occurs in the context of personal piety. My sense is that this usage should help illuminate the Gospels' presentation of sayings assigned to Jesus concerning "the kingdom," "my kingdom," "the kingdom of God," and the like. Since the Mishnah presents a highly specific politics, the selection of vocabulary bears systemic weight and meaning (something I have shown in virtually every analytical study I have carried on); these are in context technical usages.

— for the saying has to do with reciting the *shema.* No political conclusions are drawn from that allegation. Quite to the contrary, Gamaliel, head of the collegium of sages, is not thereby represented as relinquishing power to Heaven, only as expressing his obedience to divine rule even when he does not have to. Indeed, "the kingdom of Heaven" does not form a political category, even though in the politics of Judaism, all power flows from God's will and law, expressed in the Torah. In this Judaism the manipulation and application of power, allowing the impositions of drastic sanctions in support of the law for instance, invariably flow through institutions, on earth and in Heaven, of a quite concrete and material character. "The kingdom of Heaven" may be within, but violate the law deliberately and wantonly and God will kill you sooner than you should otherwise have had to die. And, as a matter of fact, the Mishnah's framers rarely appeal in the context of politics and the legitimate exercise of violence to "the kingdom of Heaven," which, in this setting, does not form a political institution at all.

Indeed, from the Pentateuchal writings, we can hardly construct the *particular* politics, including the mythic component thereof, that operates in the Mishnah's (or any other) Judaism. First of all, the Pentateuch does not prepare us to make sense of the institutions that the politics of Judaism for its part designs — government by king and high priest, rather than, as in the Pentateuch, prophet. Second, and concomitantly, the Pentateuchal myth that legitimates coercion — rule by God's prophet, governance through explicitly revealed laws that God has dictated — plays no active and systemic role whatsoever in the formulation and presentation of the Mishnah's politics of Judaism. Rather, of the types of political authority contained within the scriptural repertoire, the Mishnah's philosophers reject prophetic and charismatic authority and deem critical authority exercised by the sage's disciple who has been carefully nurtured in rules, not in gifts of the spirit. The authority of sages in the politics of Judaism does not derive from charisma, (revelation by God to the sage who makes a ruling in a given case, or even from general access to God for the sage). The myth we shall presently explore in no way falls into the classification of a charismatic myth of politics.

Is God's direct intervention (e.g., as portrayed in Scripture) represented as a preferred or even available sanction? Yes and no, but mostly no. For in our system what is important is that the myth of God's intervention on an *ad hoc* and episodic basis in the life of the community hardly serves to explain obedience to the law in the here and now. What sort of evidence would indicate that God intervenes in such wise as to explain the obedience to the law on an everyday basis? Invoking God's immediate presence, a word said, a miracle performed, would suffice. But in the entirety of the more than five hundred chapters of the Mishnah, no one ever prays to have God supply a decision in a particular case. More to the point, no judge appeals to God to put to death a convicted felon. If the judge wants the felon killed, he kills him. When God intervenes, it is on the jurisdiction assigned to God, not the court. And then the penalty is a different one from execution.

It follows that an undifferentiated myth explaining the working of undifferentiated power by appeal to God's will, while relevant, is not exact and does not explain this system in its rich detail. How the available mythic materials explain the principles of differentiation now requires attention. The explanation must be both general and specific. That is to say, while the court orders and carries out the execution, the politics works in such a way that all three political institutions, God, the court and the Temple, the three agencies with the power to bestow or take away life and property and to inflict physical pain and suffering, work together in a single continuum and in important ways cooperate to deal with the same crimes or sins. The data to which we now turn will tell us who does what to whom and why, and, in the reason why, we shall uncover the political myth we seek.

Predictably, when we work our way through sanctions to recover the mythic premises thereof, we begin with God's place in the institutionalization and execution of legitimate violence. Of course, the repertoire of sanctions does encompass God's direct intervention, but that is hardly a preferred alternative or a common one. Still, God does commonly intervene when oaths are violated, for oaths are held to involve the person who invokes God's name and God. Further, whereas when faced with an insufficiency of valid evidence under strict rules of testimony, the earthly court cannot penalize serious crime, the Heavenly court can and does impose a penalty. Clearly, then, God serves to justify the politics and account for its origin. Although God is never asked to join in making specific decisions and effecting policy in the everyday politics of the state, deliberate violation of certain rules provokes God's or the Heavenly court's direct intervention. Thus obedience to the law clearly represents submission to God in Heaven. Further, forms of Heavenly coercion such as we shall presently survey suggest a complex mythic situation, with more subtle nuance than the claim that, overall, God rules, would indicate. A politics of rules and regulations cannot admit God's *ad hoc* participation, and this system did not do so. God joined in the system in a regular and routine way, and the rules took for granted God's part in the politics of Judaism.

Precisely how does the intervention of God into the system come to concrete expression? By appeal to the rules handed down at Sinai as an ultimate reference in legal questions, for instance. This is the case in the story about R. Simeon of Mispah, who sowed his field with two types of wheat. Simeon's problem is that he may have violated the law against sowing mixed seeds in a single patch. When the matter came before Rabban Gamaliel, the passage states:

C.   They went up to the Chamber of Hewn Stone and asked [about the law regarding sowing two types of wheat in one field].

D.   Said Nahum the Scribe, "I have received [the following ruling] from R. Miasha, who received it from his father, *who received [it] from the pairs, who received [it] from the prophets, [who received] the*

law [given] to Moses on Sinai, regarding one who sows his field with
two types of wheat...."

M. Peah. 2:6 (my emphases)

Here, the law's legitimacy clearly depends on its descent by tradition from Sinai.
But that general principle of descent from Sinai was invoked only rarely. Indeed,
R. Simeon's case undermines the Mishnah's relation to God's intervention. R.
Simeon's problem is minor. Nothing important requires so drastic a claim to be
made explicit. That is to say, it is a mere commonplace that the system appeals to
Sinai.

But this is not a politics of revelation, for a politics of revelation
consistently and immediately appeals to the myth that God works in the here and
now, all the time, in concrete cases. That appeal is not common in the Mishnah's
statement of its system, and, consequently, that appeal to the myth of revelation
does not bear important political tasks and is not implicit here. Indeed I do not
think it was present at all, except where Scripture made it so (e.g., with the ordeal
inflicted on the wife accused of adultery). Why the persistent interest in legitimation
other than through the revelation of the Torah for the immediate case? The answer
to that question draws upon the traits of philosophers, who are interested in the
prevailing rule governing all cases and the explanation for the exceptions, rather
than upon those of historian-prophets, who are engaged by the exceptional case
which is then represented as paradigmatic.[9] Our philosophers appeal to a myth to
explain what is routine and orderly, and what they wish to explain is what is ordinary
and everyday: institutions and rules, not cases and *ad hoc* decisions yielding no
rule at all.

The traits of the politics of Judaism then emerge in the silences as much
as in the acts of speech, in the characteristics of the myth as much as in its contents.
The politics of Judaism appeals not to a charismatic but to a routine myth, in which
is explained the orderly life of institutions and an administration, and by which are
validated the rules and the workings of a political structure and system. True, as I
have repeatedly emphasized, all of them are deemed to have been founded on
revelation. But what kind of revelation? The answer derives from the fact that
none of the political institutions appeal in the here and the now to God's irregular
("miraculous") intervention. Treatment of the rebellious elder and the false prophet
tells us quite the opposite. The political institutions not only did not invoke
miraculous intervention to account for the imposition of sanctions, they would not
and did not tolerate the claim that such could take place.

It is the regularity and order of God's participation in the politics that the
character of the myth of the politics of Judaism maintains we have to understand
and account for. Mere allegations in general that the law originates with God's

---

[9] A fine distinction, perhaps, but a critical one, and the distinction between charisma and
routine is not a fine one at all.

revelation to Moses at Sinai do not serve to identify that middle-range myth that accounts for the structure and the system. If God is not sitting at the shoulder of the judge and telling the judge what to do (as the writers of Exodus 21ff. seem to suppose), then what legitimacy attaches to the judge's decision to give Mr. Smith's field over, or back, to Mr. Jones? And why (within the imaginary state at hand) should people support, sustain, and submit to authority? Sages' abstract language contains no answers to these questions. And yet sages' system presupposes routine and everyday obedience to power, not merely the utilization of legitimate violence to secure conformity. That is partly because the systemic statement to begin with tells very few stories. Matters that the Pentateuchal writers expressed through narrating a very specific story about how God said thus and so to Moses in this particular case, rewarding the ones who obeyed and punishing those who did not, in the Mishnah come to expression in language of an allusive and philosophical, generalizing character.

Here, too, we discern the character of the myth even before we determine its contents. While we scarcely expect that this sort of writing is apt to spell out a myth, even though a myth infuses the system, we certainly can identify the components of the philosophical and theological explanation of the state that have taken mythic form.

Even here, to be sure, the evidence proves sparse. First, of course, in the mythic structure comes God, who commands and creates, laying out what humanity is to do, exercising the power to form the social world in which humanity is to obey. God then takes care of God's particular concerns, and these focus upon *deliberate* violation of God's wishes. If a sin or crime is inadvertent, the penalties are of one order, if deliberate, of a different order. The most serious infraction of the law of the Torah is identified not by what is done but by the attitude of the sinner or criminal.[10] If one has deliberately violated God's rule, then God intervenes. If the violation is inadvertent, then the Temple imposes the sanction. And the difference is considerable. In the former case, God through the Heavenly court ends the felon's or sinner's life. Then a person who defies the laws—as these concern one's sexual conduct, attitude toward God, relationships within the family— will be penalized either (if necessary) by God or (if possible) by the earthly court. This means that the earthly court exercises God's power, and the myth of the system as a whole, so far as the earthly court forms the principal institutional form of the system, emerges not merely in a generality but in all its specificity. These particular judges, here and now, stand for God and exercise the power of God. In the latter case, the Temple takes over jurisdiction; a particular offering is called for, as the book of Leviticus specifies. But there is no need for God or the earthly court in God's name to take a position.

---

[10] The distinction between secular felony and religious sin obviously bears no meaning in the system, useful as it is to us. I generally will speak of "felon or sinner," so as not to take a position on a matter unimportant in my inquiry.

Now come the data of real power, the sanctions. We may divide sanctions just as the authorship of the Mishnah did, by simply reviewing the range of penalties for law-infraction as they occur. These penalties, as we mentioned above, fall into four classifications: what Heaven does, what political institutions do, what religious institutions do, and what is left to the coercion of public opinion, that is, consensus, with special attention to the definition of that "public" that has effective opinion to begin with. The final realm of power, conferring or withholding approval, proves constricted and, in this context, not very consequential.

Let us begin with the familiar, with sanctions exercised by the earthly court as they are fully described in Mishnah-tractates Sanhedrin and Makkot. We will review at length the imposition of sanctions as it is represented by the earthly court, the Temple, the heavenly court, the sages. This review allows us to identify the actors in the system of politics—those with power to impose sanctions, and the sanctions they can inflict. Only from this perspective will the initial statement of Judaism, in its own odd idiom, be able to make its points in the way its authorship has chosen. When we take up the myth to which that statement implicitly appeals, we shall have a clear notion of the character of the evidence, in rich detail, on which our judgment of the mythic substrate of the system has been composed.

By close attention to the facts of power and by sorting out the implications of those facts. A protracted journey through details of the law of sanctions leads us to classify the sanctions and the sins or crimes to which they apply. What precisely do I think requires classification? Our project to see who does what to whom and, on the basis of the consequent perception, to propose an explanation for that composition. For from these sanctions of state, that is, the legitimate exercise of coercion, including violence, we may work our way back to the reasons adduced for the legitimacy of the exercise of coercion, which is to say, the political myth. The reason is that such a classification will permit us to see how in detail the foci of power are supposed to intersect or to relate: autonomous powers, connected and related ones, or utterly continuous ones, joining Heaven to earth, for instance, in the person of this institutional representative or that one. What we shall see is a system that treats Heaven, earth, and the mediating institution, the Temple, as interrelated, thus, connected, but that insists, in vast detail, upon the distinct responsibilities and jurisdiction accorded to each. Once we have perceived that fundamental fact, we may compose for ourselves the myth, or, at least the point and propositions of the myth, that accounted for the political structures of Judaism and persuaded people to obey or conform even when there was no immediate threat of penalty.

A survey of [1] types of sanctions, [2] the classifications of crimes or sins to which they apply, and [3] who imposes them, now yields these results. First come the death-penalty on earth and its counterpart, which is extirpation (death before one's allotted time) imposed by Heaven:

HEAVEN	EARTH	TEMPLE	COMMUNITY
EXTIRPATION	*DEATH-PENALTY*	*DEATH-PENALTY*	
for deliberate actions			
sexual crimes	*sexual crimes:*		
incest violating sex taboos (bestiality, homosexuality)	in improper relationships: incest		
religious crimes against God	*religious crimes against God:*		
blasphemy idolatry magic sorcery profaning Sabbath	blasphemy idolatry magic sorcery profaning Sabbath		
	religious sins against family:		
	cursing parents		
	social crimes:		
	murder communal apostasy kidnapping		
	social sins:		
	public defiance of the court false prophecy		

*religious
sins,deliberately
committed,
against
God*

unclean person
who ate a Holy
Thing
uncleanness in
sanctuary
violating food
taboos
making offering
outside of Temple
violating
taboos of
holy seasons
replicating Temple
incense or oil outside

Next we deal with court-inflicted sanctions carried out against property or person (e.g., fines against property, flogging or other social or physical violence short of death for the felon or sinner):

HEAVEN	EARTH	TEMPLE	COMMUNITY
	flogging	*obligatory*	*shunning*
	exile	*offering*	*or approbation*
		and/or flogging	
		for inadvertent	
		action	
	manslaughter	uncleanness	repay moral
	incest	eating Temple	obligation (debt
	violation of	food in violation	cancelled by
	menstrual	of the law	sabbatical year)
	taboo		
	marriage in	replicating	stubbornly
	violation of	Temple oil,	rejecting
	caste rules	incense outside	majority view
		violating	opposing
		Temple food	majority will
		taboos	

	opposing
violating taboos	patriarch
of holy days	
(Passover,	obedience to
atonement	majority
	or patriarch
	uncleanness
	(Zab, mesora, etc.)
	Nazirite
violating food	sex with bondwoman
taboos	unclean Nazirite
	false oath of testimony
removing dam	false oath of deposit
with offspring	
violating negative	
commandments	

The operative distinction between inflicting a flogging and requiring a sacrifice (Temple sanctions against person or property), and the sanction of extirpation (Heavenly death-penalty), is made explicit as follows: "For those [transgressions] are people liable, for deliberately doing them, to the punishment of extirpation, and for accidentally doing them, to the bringing of a sin-offering, and for not being certain of whether or not one has done them, to a suspensive guilt-offering."

This summary yields a simple and clear fact, and on the basis of that simple fact we may now reconstruct the entire political myth on which the politics of Judaism rested. Let me emphasize: *some of the same crimes or sins for which the Heavenly court imposes the penalty of extirpation are those that, under appropriate circumstances (e. g., sufficient evidence admissible in court) the earthly court imposes the death-penalty.* That is, the Heavenly court and the earthly court impose precisely the same sanctions for the same crimes or sins. The earthly court therefore forms down here the exact replica and counterpart, within a single system of power, of the Heavenly court up there. This no longer looms as an empty generalization; it is a concrete and systemically active and indicative detail, and the system speaks through its details.

But this is not the entire story. There is a second fact, equally indicative for our recovery of the substrate of myth. We note that there are crimes for which the earthly court imposes penalties, but for which the Heavenly court does not, as well vice versa. The earthly and Heavenly courts share jurisdiction over sexual crimes and over what I classify as serious religious crimes against God. The Heavenly court penalizes with its form of the death-penalty religious sins against God, in which instances a person deliberately violates the taboos of sanctification.

And that fact calls our attention to a third partner in the distribution and application of power, the Temple with its system of sanctions that cover precisely the same acts subject to the jurisdiction of the Heavenly and earthly courts. The counterpart on earth is now not the earthly court but the Temple. This is the institution that, in theory, automatically receives the appropriate offering from the person who inadvertently violates these same taboos of sanctification. But this is an odd choice for the Mishnah, since there is now no Temple on earth. The juxtaposition appears then to involve courts and Temple, and the upshot is that both are equally matters of theory. In the theory at hand, then, the earthly court, for its part, penalizes social crimes against the community that the Heavenly court, on the one side, and the Temple rites, on the other, do not take into account at all. These are murder, apostasy, kidnapping, public defiance of the court, and false prophecy. The earthly court further imposes sanctions on matters of particular concern to the Heavenly court, with special reference to taboos of sanctification (e.g., negative commandments). These three institutions, therefore, exercise concrete and material power, utilizing legitimate violence to kill someone, exacting penalties against property, and inflicting pain. The sages' modes of power, by contrast, stand quite apart, apply mainly to their own circle, and work through the intangible though no less effective means of inflicting shame or paying honor.

The facts we have in hand draw us back to the analysis of our differentiation of applied and practical power. In the nature of the facts before us, that differentiation tells us precisely for what the systemic myth will have to give its account. Power flows through three distinct but intersecting dominions, each with its own concern, all sharing some interests in common. The Heavenly court attends to deliberate defiance of Heaven, the Temple to inadvertent defiance of Heaven. The earthly court attends to matters subject to its jurisdiction by reason of sufficient evidence, proper witnesses, and the like, and these same matters will come under Heavenly jurisdiction when the earthly court finds itself unable to act. Accordingly, we have a tripartite system of sanctions—Heaven cooperating with the Temple in some matters, with the court in others, and, as noted, each bearing its own distinct media of enforcing the law as well. What then can we say concerning the systemic myth of politics? The forms of power and the modes of mediating legitimate violence draw our attention to a single political myth, one that we first confronted, if merely as a generality and commonplace to be sure, at the very outset. The unity of that myth is underlined by the simple fact that the earthly court enters into the process right along side the Heavenly court and the Temple; as to blasphemy, idolatry, and magic, its jurisdiction prevails. So, as I have stressed, a single myth must serve all three correlated institutions.

It is the myth of God's authority infusing the institutions of Heaven and earth alike, an authority diffused among three principle foci or circles of power, Heaven's court, the earthly court, and the Temple in-between. Each focus of power has its own jurisdiction and responsibility, Heaven above, earth beneath, the Temple in the position of mediation—transmitting as it does from earth to Heaven the penalties handed over as required. And all media of power in the matter of sanctions intersect at some points as well: a tripartite politics, a single myth drawing each component into relationship with a single source and origin of power, God's law set forth in the Torah. But the myth has not performed its task until it answers not only the question of why, but also the question of how. Specifically, the details of myth must address questions of the details of power. Who then tells whom to do what? And how are the relationships of dominion and dominance to compliance and obedience made permanent through myth?

We did not require this sustained survey to ascertain that God through the Torah has set forth laws and concerns. That generality now may be made quite specific, for it is where power is differentiated and parceled out that we see the workings of the political myth. So we ask, how do we know who tells whom to do, or suffer, what sanction or penalty? It is the power of myth to differentiate that defines the generative question. The key lies in the criterion by which each mode of power, earthly, mediating, and Heavenly, identifies the cases over which it exercises jurisdiction. The criterion lies in the attitude of the human being who has done what he or she should not: did he act deliberately or unintentionally?

I state the upshot with heavy emphasis: *the point of differentiation within the political structures, supernatural and natural alike, lies in the attitude and intention of a human being.* We differentiate among the application of power by reference to the attitude of the person who comes into relationship with that power. A person who comes into conflict with the system, rejecting the authority claimed by the powers that be, does so deliberately or inadvertently. The myth accounts in the end for the following hierarchization of action and penalty, infraction and sanction: [1] If the deed is deliberate, then one set of institutions exercises jurisdiction and utilizes supernatural power. [2] If the deed is inadvertent, another institution exercises jurisdiction and utilizes the power made available by that same supernatural being.

A sinner or criminal who has deliberately violated the law has by his or her action challenged the politics of Judaism. Consequently, God or God's surrogate imposes sanctions—extirpation (by the court on high), or death or other appropriate penalty (by the court on earth). A sinner or criminal who has inadvertently violated the law is penalized by the imposition of Temple sanctions, losing valued goods. People obey because God wants them to and has told them what to do, and when they do not obey, a differentiated political structure appeals to that single hierarchizing myth. The components of the myth are two: first, God's will, expressed in the law of the Torah, second, the human being's will, carried out in obedience to the law of the Torah or in defiance of that law.

Have we come so far and not yet told the story that the myth contains? I have now to explain and spell out the story that conveys the myth of politics in Judaism. It is not in the Mishnah at all. Do I find the mythic foundation in Scripture, which accounts for the uses and differentiation of power that the Mishnah's system portrays? Indeed I do, for, as we realize, the political myth of Judaism has to explain the differentiation of sins or crimes, with their associated penalties or punishments, and so sanctions of power. And in Scripture there is a very precise answer to the question of how to differentiate among sins or crimes and why to do so. Given the position of the system of the Mishnah, the point of differentiation must rest with one's attitude or intentionality And, indeed, I do have two stories of how the power of God conflicts with the power of humanity in such wise as to invoke the penalties and sanctions in precisely the differentiated modes we have before us. Where do I find such stories of the conflict of wills, God's and humanity's?

The first such story of power differentiated by the will of the human being in communion or conflict with the word of the commanding God comes to us from the Garden of Eden.[11] We cannot too often reread the following astonishing words:

> The Lord God took the man and placed him in the garden of Eden...and the Lord God commanded the man, saying, "Of every tree of the garden you are free to eat; but as for the tree of knowledge of good and bad, you must not eat of it; for as soon as you eat of it, you shall die."
>
> ...When the woman saw that the tree was good for eating and a delight to the eyes, and that the tree was desirable as a source of wisdom, she took of its fruit and ate; she also gave some to her husband, and he ate...
>
> The Lord God called out to the man and said to him, "Where are you?"
>
> He replied, "I heard the sound of You in the garden, and I was afraid, because I was naked, so I hid."
>
> Then He asked, "Who told you that you were naked? Did you eat of the tree from which I had forbidden you to eat?"
>
> ...And the Lord God said to the woman, "What is this you have done!"
>
> So the Lord God banished him from the garden of Eden...

Now a reprise of the exchange between God, Adam, and Eve, tells us that at stake was responsibility: who has violated the law, but who bears responsibility for deliberately violating the law:

---

[11] This is not to suggest that the distinction behind the system's differentiation is important only in the myth of Eden. Quite to the contrary, the authorship of the laws of Leviticus and Deuteronomy repeatedly appeals to that same distinction in speaking of the "Israel" that they wish to bring into existence — an Israel in the Eden of the Land of Israel. But our interest is in myth, and I find in the myth of Eden the explanation for the point of differentiation that the political myth of Judaism invokes at every point. So, as I have said, the sanctions lead to the systemic question that requires mythic response, and once we know the question, we can turn to Scripture for the myth (as much as we can find in Scripture ample expansion, in law, of that same myth).

"The woman You put at my side — she gave me of the tree, and I ate."
"The serpent duped me, and I ate."
Then the Lord God said to the serpent, "because you did this...."

The ultimate responsibility lies with the one who acted deliberately, not under constraint or on account of deception or misinformation, as did Adam and Eve Then the sanction applies most severely to the one who by intention and an act of will has violated God's intention and will.

Adducing this story by itself poses several problems. First, the story-teller does not allege that Adam intended to violate the commandment; he followed his wife. Second, the penalty is not extirpation but banishment. That is why to establish what I conceive to be the generative myth, I turn to a second story of disobedience and its consequences, the tale of Moses's hitting the rock:

> The community was without water, and they joined against Moses and Aaron...Moses and Aaron came away from the congregation to the entrance of the Tent of Meeting and fell on their faces. The Presence of the Lord appeared to them, and the Lord spoke to Moses, saying, "You and your brother Aaron take the rod and assemble the community, and before their very eyes order the rock to yield its water. Thus you shall produce water for them from the rock and provide drink for the congregation and their beasts."
>
> Moses took the rod from before the Lord as He had commanded him. Moses and Aaron assembled the congregation in front of the rock; and he said to them, "Listen, you rebels, shall we get water for you out of this rock?" And Moses raised his hand and struck the rock twice with his rod. Out came copious water, and the community and their beasts drank.
>
> But the Lord said to Moses and Aaron, "Because you did not trust me enough to affirm My sanctity in the sight of the Israelite people, therefore you shall not lead this congregation into the land that I have given them."
>
> Those are the waters of Meribah, meaning that the Israelites quarrelled with the Lord — through which He affirmed His sanctity.
>
> Numbers 20:1-13

Here we have not only intentional disobedience, but also the penalty of extirpation. Both this myth and the myth of the fall make the same point. They direct attention to the generative conception that at stake in power is the will of God over against the will of the human being, and in particular, the Israelite human being.

The political myth of Judaism now emerges in the Mishnah in all of its tedious detail as a reprise—in now-consequential and necessary, stunning detail—of the story of God's commandment, humanity's disobedience, God's sanction for the sin or crime, and humanity's atonement and reconciliation. The Mishnah omits all explicit reference to myths that explain power and sanctions, but invokes in its rich corpus of details the absolute given of the story of the distinction between what is deliberate and what is mitigated by an attitude that is not culpable, a distinction set forth in the tragedy of Adam and Eve, in the failure of Moses and Aaron, and in countless other passages in the Pentateuch, Prophetic Books, and Writings. Then the Mishnah's is a politics of life after Eden and outside of Eden. The upshot of the matter is that the political myth of Judaism sets forth the constraints of freedom, the human will brought to full and unfettered expression, imposed by the constraints of revelation, God's will made known.

Since it is the freedom of humanity to make decisions and frame intentions that forms the point of differentiation among the political media of power, we are required, in my view, to return to the paradigmatic exercise of that same freedom, that is, to Eden, to the moment when Adam and Eve exercise their own will and defy God. Since the operative criterion in the differentiation of sanction—that is, the exercise of legitimate violence by Heaven or by earth or by the Temple—is the human attitude and intention in carrying out a culpable action, we must recognize the politics before us rehearses the myth of Adam and Eve in Eden—it finds its dynamic in the correspondence between God's will and humanity's freedom to act however it chooses, thus freely incurring the risk of penalty or sanction for the wrong exercise of freedom.

At stake is what Adam and Eve, Moses and Aaron, and numerous others intend, propose, plan, for that is the point at which the politics intervenes, making its points of differentiation between and among its sanctions and the authorities that impose those penalties. For that power to explain difference, which is to say, the capacity to represent and account for hierarchy, we are required, in my opinion, to turn to the story of the fall of Adam and Eve from Eden and to counterpart stories. The reason is that the political myth derives from that same myth of origins its points of differentiation and explains by reference to the principal components of that myth — God's and humanity's will and power— the dynamics of the political system at hand. God commands, but humanity does what it then chooses, and in the interplay of those two protean forces, each power in its own right, the sanctions and penalties of the system apply.

Power comes from two conflicting forces, the commanding will of God and the free will of the human being. Power expressed in immediate sanctions is also mediated through these same forces, Heaven above, human beings below, with the Temple mediating between the two. Power works its way in the interplay between what God has set forth in the law of the Torah and what human beings do, whether intentionally, whether inadvertently, whether obediently, whether defiantly. That is why the politics of Judaism is a politics of Eden. And that further explains why sages' systemic statement turned to politics as the necessary medium for its full formulation. Quite how matters were to be phrased as this Judaism crossed the frontier from the realm of theory and theology to practical issues of public policy is not to be predicted on the basis of the systemic statement we have examined, which, we now see, in no way made provision for the complexities of an ordinary, diverse society. But, then, systems never do.

6

Why Does Judaism Have an Economics? How through Halakhah the Mishnah Sets Forth its Political Economy

Let me begin with a simple piece of evidence that the ancient sages of Judaism recognized cycles of abundance and scarcity, if they did not call them business cycles. [1]Sages most certainly understood the principles of market economics as they affected the market mechanism and manipulated those principles to achieve their own goals, as the following story indicates:

> A pair of birds in Jerusalem went up in price to a gold denar.
> Said Rabban Simeon b. Gamaliel, "By this sanctuary! I shall not rest tonight until they shall be sold at silver denars."
> He entered the court and taught, "The woman who is subject to five confirmed miscarriages or five confirmed fluxes brings only a single offering, and she eats animal sacrifices, and the rest of the offerings do not remain as an obligation for her."
> And pairs of birds stood on that very day at a quarter-denar each, [one hundredth of the former price, the demand having been drastically reduced].
> (M. Keritot 1:7K-Q)

The story shows that sages recognized the affect upon prices of diminished demand and were prepared to intervene in the market. Now to the more general question at hand: what is an economics, and does Judaism have one, and, if so, why?

---

[1] The Inaugural Saul Reinfeld Lecture in Judaic Studies at Connecticut College, New London, Connecticut, on Wednesday, April 13, 1988.

An economics is a theory about the rational disposition of scarce resources. The key word is "rational," of course, since what is reasonable in one setting or culture is incomprehensible in another, and in due course I shall explain the rational of the economics of Judaism. But so far as a social entity knows how and why scarce resources are assigned to, or end up in the hands of, one person, rather than some other, or one institution or class or other social organization, rather than some other, that social entity has an economics. A religion, such as Judaism (defined presently), need not have an economics, and most religions do not have an economic theory at all. Christianity prior to the Middle Ages, for example, had no economics, even though it had by then developed a rich and complex politics. And sayings relevant to an economics, answering questions concerning the definition of wealth, property, production and the unit of production, ownership, the determination of price and value and the like, – sayings relevant to economics in general may take shape within a religion, without that religion's setting forth an economics at all. For opinions on this and that, sayings about mercy to the poor, recommendations of right action, fairness, honesty, and the like – all these components of economics do not by themselves add up to an economics.

Only a sustained and systematic, internally coherent theory that over all and in an encompassing way explains why this, not that, defines market in relationship to ownership, production in relationship to price, above all, constitutes an economics. In the case of a religion, moreover, the presence of a theory on wealth and ownership, production and consumption, requires explanation. What we want to know, in particular, is what a particular religion wishes to express through its statements within the realm of economics, and why it is through economics in particular that the religion finds it necessary to make those statements. When, therefore, I ask, why does Judaism have an economics? I mean to answer that particular question: why does Judaism make its statement, in part, by discussing in a systematic and cogent way and within an encompassing theory the matter of the rational disposition of scarce resources?

Economics from Aristotle to Quesnay and Riqueti, in the eighteenth century, dealt with not the science of wealth but rather "the management of the social household, first the city, then the state."[2] Economics disembedded from politics developed only in the eighteenth century. Prior to that time, it formed a principal part of the study of political economy. That is to say, economics formed a component of the larger sociopolitical order and dealt with the organization and management of the household (*oikos*). The city (*polis*) was conceived as comprising a set of households. Political economy, therefore, presented the theory of the construction of society, the village, town, or city, out of households, a neat and

---

[2] Elizabeth Fox-Genovese, *The Origins of Physiocracy. Economic Revolution and Social Order in Eighteenth-Century France* (Ithaca and London: Cornell University Press), p. 9. See also Karl Polanyi, *The Lifelihood of Man*. Edited by Harry W. Pearson (New York, San Francisco, and London, 1977: Academic Press), p. 7.

orderly, intensely classical and, of course, utterly fictive conception. One part of that larger political economy confronted issues of the household and its definition as the principal unit of economic production, the market and its function within the larger political structure, and the nature and definition of wealth. And the reason that one important Judaism had an economics was that that Judaism proposed to tell the Jews how to build an ideal society, a holy society, and in order to make its statement, that Judaism appealed to the correct, hence, the rational distribution of scarce resources: to distributive, rather than to market, economics, as we shall see. It was only through appeal to ancient principles of distributive economics, resting on the Temple, priesthood, and cult, that the Judaism at hand found it possible to say what it wished to say in politic economy.

I. THE ECONOMICS OF JUDAISM
WHICH JUDAISM? WHICH ECONOMICS?

The Judaism the economics of which is under study is the one that rested on the myth of Moses' receiving the Torah at Sinai in two media, written and oral. The written one corresponded to the Hebrew Bible or Old Testament. The oral one was ultimately written down by the sages of Judaism in late antiquity, beginning with the composition of the Mishnah, the Mishnah, a utopian system expressed in the form of a law code, closed at ca. A.D. 200. The initial statement of that Judaism is represented by the Mishnah. The Judaism of the Dual Torah, bearing the adjectives normative, talmudic, rabbinic, classical, and the like, unfolded through the exegesis of the two Torahs, written and oral, Scripture and Mishnah, through the first seven centuries of the Common Era (=A.D.) and yielded as its authoritative document the Talmud of Babylonia or Bavli. But only the initial and fundamental document of that Judaism forms the object of study here. My purpose here is to describe the economics of (a) Judaism in the context of in systemic context, to offer an account of economics in the foundation document of the canon of the Judaism of the Dual Torah.

When we place the economics, or, more really, the political economics of the Mishnah into the context of Graeco-Roman economic thought, we gain a clearer picture of the power of economics to serve in the expression and detailed exposition of a utopian design for society. For, as Robert Lekachman states, "We see the economics of Plato and Aristotle somewhat differently when we realize that what they were discussing above all was the good life, the just state, and the happy man."[3] They sought a unified science of society. And that serves as a suitable definition, also, for the program of the framers of the Mishnah. The authorship of the Mishnah covered every important problem that any treatise on economics, covering not only the rules of household management covered in an *oikonomikos*, but also the law of money-making, found it necessary to discuss, and on that basis,

---

[3] Robert Lekachman, *History of Economic Ideas* (New York, 1959: Harper & Bros.), p. 4.

I claim to describe in some modest detail what I conceive to have been the economics of Judaism as the Mishnah's authorship defined Judaism and as the ancient world understood the science of economics, or, in its context, political economy. But let me start from the beginning, and that means, turn to the familiar definition of our subject.

The Mishnah, the initial statement of the Judaism of the Dual Torah, not only encompasses but integrates economics within its larger system. That particular Judaism, indeed, makes its statement, also, through the exquisite details of rules and regulations governing the householder, the market, and wealth. The Mishnah's remarkably successful capacity to make its systemic statement, also, through the concerns of economics, its capacity to accomplish the detailed exegesis of economics within its larger social vision and system – these lack a significant counterpart in the generality of philosophy and theology in ancient times. Only in Aristotle do we find a great system builder who encompassed, within his systemic statement, economic theory. Plato forms no important counterpart, and, as to Christianity, down to the end of late antiquity, in the seventh century, economics as a matter of theory enjoyed no position whatsoever. In theologies of Christianity, for one example, we find slight interest in, or use of, theories on the household, markets, and wealth, in the framing of the Christian statement, which bears no judgment that we may identify as a statement upon, or of, economics. Only when we turn to Aristotle do we find a counterpart to the truly remarkable accomplishment of the authorship of the Mishnah in engaging economics in the service of its larger systemic statement. Indeed, as the Mishnah's authorship's power of the extraordinarily detailed exegesis of economics as a systemic component becomes clear to us, we shall conclude that, among the social theorists of antiquity, the framers of the Mishnah take first place in the sophistication and profundity of their thought within political economy.[4]

But the fact that both Aristotle and the authorship of the Mishnah appealed to economic theory in spelling out their ideas by itself does not require us to bring into juxtaposition, for purposes of comparison and contrast, the economic thought of the two writings, Aristotle's and the Mishnaic sages'. What requires that work is the simple fact that the Mishnah came forth in the age of the Second Sophistic, and, in diverse ways, adheres to the attitudes and agenda of that movement. Not only so, but when we do read Aristotle's thought on economic theory, we find clear and detailed propositions in common between him and our authorship. But there is yet a third reason. Both Aristotle and the sages of the Mishnah thought deeply and sustainedly about economic issues. The power of economics as framed by Aristotle, the only economic theorist of antiquity worthy of the name was to develop the relationship between the economy to society as a whole.[5] And the framers of the Mishnah did precisely that: they incorporated issues of economics, even at a

---

[4] That considerable claim of mine forms the *leitmotif* of this lecture.

[5] Polanyi, op. cit., "Aristotle Discovers the Economy," p. 79.

profound theoretical level, into the system of society as a whole, as they proposed to construct society. That is why to paraphrase Polanyi's judgment of Aristotle, the authorship of the Mishnah will be seen as attacking the problem of man's livelihood within a system of sanctification of a holy people with a radicalism of which no later religious thinkers about utopias were capable. None has ever penetrated deeper into the material organization of man's life under the aspect of God's rule. In effect, they posed, in all its breadth, the question of the critical, indeed definitive place occupied by the economy in society under God's rule. That is what we shall see in the remarkable statement, within an even more subtle idiom, of the economics of Judaism as the framers of the Mishnah defined that economics.

Just as through economics, Aristotle made the larger point that animated his system as a whole, so through economics did the framers of the Mishnah. The theory of both, moreover, falls into the same classification of economic theory, namely, the theory of distributive economics, familiar in the Near and Middle East from Sumerian times down to, but not including, the age of Aristotle himself. Before proceeding, let me define market and distributive economics since these form the two economic theories at issue in antiquity, and, among them, the far more ancient, the distributive, shaped the economic thought of the two important systems of antiquity that made their statement, also, through economics, those of Aristotle and the Mishnah. In market economics merchants transfer goods from place to place in response to the working of the market mechanism, which is expressed in price. In distributive economics, by contrast, traders move goods from point to point in response to political commands. In market economics, merchants make the market work by calculations of profit and loss. In distributive economics, there is no risk of loss on a transaction.[6] In market economics, money forms an arbitrary measure of value, a unit of account. In distributive economics, money gives way to barter and bears only intrinsic value, as do the goods for which it is exchanged. It is understood as "something that people accept not for its inherent value in use but because of what it will buy."[7] The idea of money requires the transaction to be complete in the exchange not of goods but of coins. The alternative is the barter transaction, in which, in theory at least, the exchange takes place when goods change hands. Clearly, therefore, in the Mishnah's conception of the market and of wealth, distributive, not market, economics shapes details of all transactions. In distributive economics money is an instrument of direct exchange between buyers and sellers, not the basic resource in the process of production and distribution that it is in market economics.

---

[6] Davisson and Harper, *European Economic History,* p. 130.
[7] Ibid., p. 131.

II. THE DISTRIBUTIVE ECONOMICS OF THE JUDAISM OF THE DUAL TORAH

That distributive mode of economics, rationalized within theology and also fully realized in the detail of law, will not have astonished the framers of social systems from ancient Sumerian times, three thousand years before the time of the Mishnah, onward. For from the beginning of recorded time, temples or governments imposed the economics of distribution, and market economics, where feasible at all, competed with the economics of politics, organization, and administration. From remote antiquity onward, a market economy coexisted with a distributive economy.[8] Distributive economic theory characteristic of ancient temples and governments, which served as the storage points for an economy conceived to be self-supporting and self-sustaining, involved something other than a simultaneous exchange of legally recognized rights in property and its use; one party gave up scarce goods, the other party did not do so, but received those goods for other than market considerations. Free disposition of property, in distributive economics, found limitations in rules of an other-than-market character, for example, taboos with no bearing upon the rational utilization of resources and individual decisions on the disposition of assets.

If, for example, the private person who possesses property may not sell that property to anyone of his choice, or may not sell it permanently, then the possessor of the property does not exercise fully free choice in response to market conditions.[9] The reason is that he cannot gain the optimum price for the land at a given moment, set by considerations of supply and demand for land or (more really) for the produce of land of a particular character. Another, a co-owner, in addition to the householder in possession of a piece of property, has a say. The decisions of that other owner are not governed solely (or at all) by market considerations. In the case of temple communities or god-kings, land ownership and control fall into the hands of an entity other than the private person, whether we call it the temple,

---

[8] See Morris Silver, *Economic Structures of the Ancient Near East* (London and Sydney: Croom Helm, 1985), and J. Wansbrough's review of that book in *Bulletin of the London School of Oriental and African Studies* 1987: 50-361-2. In this and prior studies Silver has successfully refuted the thesis of Polanyi that "there were not and could not be circumstances conducive to a market economy" (Wansbrough, p. 362). But the distinction between distributive and market economics has no bearing whatsoever upon whether or not, in remote antiquity, there was no such thing as a market in an economic sense, as Polanyi maintained. My argument focuses only upon economic theory. But, as is clear, I take for granted that Silver and those he represents have established as fact the coexistence of market and distributive economics, such as I claim to discern, also, in the system of the Mishnah.

[9] Presently we shall note the integral relationship of a theory of ownership of property, specifically, a conception of property being private, and a theory of market economics. A mark of a distributive economics will be systemic intervention into not only the rationing (distribution) of resources but also of the means of production.

priesthood, the government, the gild, or even the poor(!). Then, with private property and its use placed under limitations and constraints of an other-than-market origin, market trading is not possible: "While there could be a considerable development of governmental status distribution and some marginal barter, there could not develop a price-making market."[10] Private property in land, not merely in control of production, was required for the formation of a market economics in the conditions of antiquity, when ownership of production derived from ownership of land.

A further mark of the distributive economy is that transactions take the form of commodities of real value, that is, barter, and not of symbolic value, that is, money. In ancient Mesopotamia, with its distributive economics, while silver was the medium of exchange, it was used in ingots and required weighing at each transfer.[11] That conception dominates in the Mishnah. Finally, in distributive economics, profit is a subordinate consideration, and, in the hands of so sophisticated a mind as Aristotle's and as the Mishnah's authorship's, profit is treated as unnatural. Competing with market economics in the Mishnah is a fully developed and amply instantiated, if never articulated, distributive economics. The Mishnah's authorship took over the economics of the Priestly Code, itself a restatement, in the idiom of the Israelite priesthood, of the distributive economics of temples and kings beginning with the Sumerians and Egyptians and coming down to the Greeks. Market economics was an innovation, its economics not fully understood, at the time of the Priestly Code, and, for reasons of their own, the framers of the Mishnah fully adopted and exhaustively spelled out that distributive economics, even while setting forth a plan for the economic life of "Israel" in a market economy.

That old and well-established theory of economics, in the received Scriptures, is accurately represented by the Priestly Code, spelled out in the rules of the biblical books of Leviticus and Numbers, upon which the Mishnah's authorship drew very heavily. The economic program of the Mishnah, as a matter of fact, derived its values and also its details from the Priestly Code and other priestly writings within the Pentateuchal mosaic. Indeed, at point after point, that authorship clearly intended merely to spin out details of the rules set forth in Scripture in general, and, in economic issues such as the rational use of scarce resources, the Priestly Code in particular. The Priestly Code assigned portions of the crop to the priesthood and Levites as well as to the caste comprising the poor; it intervened in the market processes affecting real estate by insisting that land could not be permanently alienated but reverted to its "original" ownership every fifty years; it treated some produce as unmarketable even though it was entirely fit; it exacted for the Temple a share of the crop; it imposed regulations on the labor force that were not shaped by market considerations but by religious taboos,

---

[10] Davisson and Harper, op. cit., p. 125.

[11] A. Leo Oppenheim, *Ancient Mesopotamia. Portrait of a Dead Civilization* (Chicago & London, 1972: The University of Chicago Press), p. 87.

for example, days on which work might not be performed, or might be performed only in a diminished capacity.

In these and numerous other details, the Priestly Code stated in the Israelite-priestly idiom and in matters of detail the long-established principles of distributive economics and so conformed to thousands of years of that distributive economics that treated private property as stipulative and merely conditional and the market as subordinate and subject to close political supervision. Market economics came into being in Greece in the very period – the sixth century B.C. – in which the Priestly Code was composed. Aristotle theorized about an economics entirely beyond anyone's ken and stated as principle the values of an economics (and a social system, too) long since transcended. Market economics, moreover, had been conveyed in practice to the Middle East a century and a half or so later by Alexander. By the time of the Mishnah, seven centuries after the Pentateuch was closed, market economics was well-established as the economics of the world economy in which, as a matter of fact, the land of Israel and Israel, that is, the Jews of Palestine, had been fully incorporated. Theories of fixed value, distribution of scarce resources by appeal to other than the rationality of the market – these represented anachronisms. But, as the Mishnah's sages' prohibition against profit, which they called "usury" and their odd conception of a true value inherent in a commodity shows us, the framers of the Mishnah developed a dual economics, partly market, partly distributive. That is the fact that permits us to treat as matters of economic theory a range of rules that, in market economics, can have no point of entry whatsoever.

Only when we have grasped the general terms within which those concrete rules are worked out shall we understand the mixed economics characteristic of the Judaism of the Mishnah. A distributive economics, we now realize full well, is one that substitutes for the market as the price-fixing mechanism for the distribution of goods the instrumentality of the state or some other central organization, in the case of Scripture's economics in the Priestly Code of ca. A.D. 500, the Temple. In such an economics, in the words of Davisson and Harper,

Such an organization will involve people's giving and receiving, producing and consuming, according to their status.[12] Substituting for the market as a rationing device, the distributive economy dealt with "the actual things that are distributed," while in markets, "purchases and sales are usually made for money, not directly for other commodities or services."[13]

The definition of market economics calls to our attention the contrary traits of distributive economics, in particular, the intervention of authority other than the market in controlling both production and distribution of scarce goods. In the case of the Mishnah, the Temple requires the recognition of the status of certain individual participants – in addition to the householder – in the transaction of

---

[12] Davisson and Harper, op. cit., p. 115.
[13] Ibid., p. 123.

distributing the material goods of the economy, in particular, portions of the crop. Priests, Levites, and the poor have a claim on the crop independent of their role in the production of the crop, for example, in labor, in land-ownership, in investment of seed and the like. Not only so, but the market is not the sole point of transfer of value. For material goods of the economy are directed to the Temple – so in the theory of the Mishnah – without any regard for the working of the market. When it comes to the claim of the Temple and priesthood upon the productive economy, there is no consideration of the exchange of material value for material value, let alone of the intervention of considerations of supply and demand, the worth of the goods as against the worth of the services supplied by the Temple, and the like.[14] Davisson and Harper state of the market, "Even politically powerful interests and corporations must agree to accept the market decisions whether or not the outcome of a particular market transaction favors a person of high status."[15] But in the Mishnah, that simply is not so. And, we shall further observe, the Temple taboos imposed upon the productive economy considerations of a nonmarket, nonproductive character, in consequence of which the maximization of productivity forms only one among several competing considerations, and not the most important one, in the planning of production.

This brings us to the fundamental and necessary trait of market economics, private property. Davisson and Harper further state,

> Private ownership of property...is an essential condition of the market, but its existence does not guarantee that a market will exist or that contractual exchanges will occur [that can reach a conclusion with a simultaneous exchange of legally recognized rights in property and its use]. To be sure, in the absence of private property in the ancient Near East and early medieval Europe, we find a distributive economic order. Is there, then, some relation of cause and effect between private property and the operation of a market? It seems that insofar as there is monolithic ownership and control of property (as in the Sumerian temple communities or with the god-king pharaoh of Egypt) there can be no development of a market. Where private property was so limited, there could be no market trading. While there could be a considerable development of governmental status distribution and some marginal barter, there could not develop a price-making market.[16]

That statement again draws our attention to the datum of the Mishnah, which informs, by the way, its economics as well: that God owns the land and that the

---

[14] True, the ideology of the Priestly Code insisted that payment of the Temple taxes insured that God would "bless" the country with ample harvests, large herds, big families, and the like. But these factors in shaping of public opinion, therefore of considerations of demand, on their own do not – and cannot – fall into the classification of economic facts.

[15] Davisson and Harper, op. cit., p. 123.

[16] Ibid., pp. 124-125

household holds the land in joint tenancy with God. Private ownership does not extend to the land at all.[17] That simple fact imposes upon the Mishnah's economic theory the principles of distributive economics, even while the framers of that theory address a world of market economics. It accounts for the mixed economics – market, distributive – of the Mishnah. Not only so, but as we just noted, the mortal owner-partner with God in the management of the household is not free to make decisions based solely on maximizing productivity; other considerations as to the use of land, as much as to the disposition of the crop, intervened.

Both Aristotle and the framers of the Mishnah addressed economic theory not only within the framework of distributive economics. They also acknowledged the facts of market economics, even while reaffirming (each party in its own terms and context) the higher (Aristotle: "natural," thus more natural, Mishnah authorship: "holy" and hence holier) value associated with distributive economics. For Aristotle, therefore, the criterion of correct economic action derived from a larger concern to uncover natural, as against unnatural, ways of conducting affairs, and for the sages of the Mishnah, the counterpart criterion appealed to the theology of the Priestly Code, with its conception of the magical character of the land the Jews held as their own, which they called (and still call) "the land of Israel." This land was subject to particular requirements, because God owned this land in particular and through the Temple and the priesthood constituted the joint-owner, along with the Israelite householder, of every acre.

III. WHY DOES JUDAISM HAVE AN ECONOMICS?

The Mishnah is a document of political economy, in which the two critical classifications are the village, *polis*, and the household, *oikos*. Since, however, the Mishnah's framers conceived of the world as God's possession and handiwork, theirs was the design of a university in which God's and humanity's realms flowed together. Their statement bears comparison, therefore, to Plato's *Republic* and Aristotle's *Politics* as a utopian program (*Staatsroman*) of a society as a political entity, encompassing, also, its economics; but pertinent to the comparison also is Augustine's conception of a city of God and a city of man. In the Mishnah we find thinkers attempting, in acute detail, to think through how God and humanity form a single *polis* and a single *oikos*, a shared political economy, one village and one household on earth as it is in heaven.[18]

---

[17] But God does not lay claim to joint ownership of other goods and services of the economy, apart from the land and its produce, with the result that private ownership of the commercial and manufacturing economy assuredly prevailed, one of the reasons I refer to the Mishnah's economic theory as a mixed one.

[18] That is why I conceive the more profound inquiry to address the politics of Judaism, as the Mishnah presents that politics: the city of God which is the city of humanity, unlike the distinct cities conceived by Augustine. The matter is neatly expressed in numerous specific

The Mishnah's sages placed economics, both market and distributive, in the center of their system, devoting two of their six divisions to it (the first and the fourth, for distributive and market economics, respectively), and succeeded in making their statement through economics in a sustained and detailed way far beyond the merely generalizing manner in which Aristotle did. And no one in antiquity came near Aristotle, as I said. It was with remarkable success that the sages of Judaism presented an economics wholly coordinated in a systemic way with a politics. The framers of the Mishnah joined together the premises of two distinct economic theories, market economics. And these two distinct theories, moreover, coexisted on the foundations of an economics of reciprocity, joining heaven to earth.[19] The conception of God's enjoying standing and power within the domain of economic life formed not a theological but an economic fact, on the basis of which decisions on the allocation of scarce resources and on the nature of wealth and ownership were reached and carried out in law. That simple fact constitutes the single indicative trait of the Judaism of the Mishnah, its power to translate theological conviction into exquisitely detailed rules for everyday life. Let me spell out how, in economics, the sages of the Mishnah made their theological statement.

IV. THE DISTRIBUTIVE ECONOMICS OF JUDAISM AND THE THEOLOGY OF JUDAISM

The economic data with which the Mishnah's framers made their statement came to them from the Priestly Code. On the face of matters, therefore, the authorship of the document appealed to an economic theory that derived from an ancient age (we would say it was seven hundred years old, back to ca. 500 B.C., but they would say it was fourteen hundred years old, back to Sinai, which would bear a date of ca. 1200 B.C.). The truly anachronistic character of the Mishnah's

---

rules. See for example Roger Brooks, *Support for the Poor in the Mishnaic Law of Agriculture: Tractate Peah* (Chico, 1983: Scholars Press for Brown Judaic Studies), p. 49 to Mishnah-tractate Peah 1:4-5: "The Mishnah's framers regard the Land as the exclusive property of God. When Israelite farmers claim it as their own and grow food on it, they must pay for using God's earth. Householders thus must leave a portion of the yield unharvested as *peah* and give this food over to God's chosen representatives, the poor. The underlying theory is that householders are tenant farmers who pay taxes to their landlord, God." In this concrete way the interpenetration of the realms of God and humanity is expressed. That conception of the household and the village made up of households, the *oikos* and the *polis,* yields not only an economics, but also a politics. And the politics is the foundation for the economics, as we shall repeatedly observe.

[19] But it seems to me not productive to pursue as an issue of theoretical economics the notion of an exchange between heaven and earth, that is, between God and Israel. That conception leads us deep into territory beyond the substance of economics, into intangibles that we cannot grasp, measure, or weigh. Accordingly, I leave out of this account any notion of an

distributive economics[20] becomes clear, however, when we realize that by the fourth century B.C., the Middle East received and used the legacy of Greece, brought by Alexander, in which a type of private property, prerequisite to the development of the market and available for the free use of the holder of that property independent of the priesthood or other government intervention, had developed.[21] For the theory of the Mishnah both the market and the distributive systems form one system and represent two components of one system. So we deal with a single theory, holding together two distinct economics. What we shall now see is how the distributive component of the Mishnah's economic theory reshapes the three principal categories that have occupied our attention, the household, the market, and wealth. But we ask, first of all, why the system of the Mishnah appealed to economics to begin with, and the answer to that question comes to us from theology, not economics. What the Mishnah's authorship wished to say, we shall now see, they could express only by utilizing the principal categories of economics under study here.

At the center of the Mishnah's economics is the disposition of resources with unremitting regard to the status of recipients in the transaction. In no way does the economics of Judaism in its initial statement conform to the definition of market economics just now cited. Our task therefore is how to understand in detail the foundation of the principles of distribution that define the theory of economics within the larger system of the Mishnah. In this way we grasp how profoundly the economics of the system has been shaped by the larger systemic statement and message.[22] The Mishnah's distributive economics derives from the theory that the Temple and its scheduled castes on earth exercise God's claim to the ownership of the holy land. It is, in fact, a theology that comes to expression in the details of material transactions. The theology derives from the conviction expressed in the

---

economics of reciprocity and deal only with (re)distribution and market exchange. I also omit reference to "householding" as too vague; no one imagines that Israel's economy in its land was a subsistence economy, certainly not at any point, from the sixth century B.C. forward, covered by the Pentateuchal law codes or their successors. So I see no point of interest in householding, because it is irrelevant, nor can I cope with "reciprocity," because it is a category covering economic relations between units that are not this-worldly (to put it mildly).

[20] For an account of archaizing tendency of the Second Sophistic in general, that is to say, the age of philosophy in which the Mishnah's authors did their work, see E. L. Bowie, "Greeks and Their Past in the Second Sophistic," in M. I. Finley, ed., *Studies in Ancient Society* (London and Boston, 1974: Routledge & Kegan Paul), pp. 166-209. Bowie shows that "the archaism of language and style known as Atticism is only part of a wider tendency, a tendency that prevails in literature not only in style but also in choice of theme and treatment, and that equally affects other areas of cultural activity." I shall address this matter more systematically in my coming study of the Mishnah in the context of the philosophy of the Second Sophistic.

[21] Davisson and Harper, p. 125.

[22] Whether or not other economic theories express broader systemic values or are simply disembedded from systems and structures is not at issue in this account. It seems to me

Psalm, "The earth is the Lord's." That conviction is a statement of ownership in a literal sense. God owns the earth. But the particular earth that God owns is the land of Israel, and, within that land, the particular earth is land in the land of Israel that is owned by an Israelite. With that Israelite, a land-owner in the land of Israel, God is co-owner.

From that theological principle, spun out of the notion that when Israelites occupy the land that God has given to the Israelites, namely, the land of Israel, that land is transformed, and so too are the principles of ownership and distribution of the land, all else flows. The economics of the Judaism rests upon the theory of the ownership of a designated piece of real estate, ownership that is shared between God and partners of a certain genus of humanity whose occupancy of that designated piece of real estate, but no other, affects the character of the dirt in question. The theology consists in an account of what happens when ground of a certain locale is subject to the residency and ownership of persons of a certain genus of humanity. The generative conception of the theology involves a theory of the affect – the enchantment and transformation – that results from the intersection of "being Israel:" land, people, individual person alike. But let us turn directly to the economics of it all.

Since God owns the land of Israel, God – represented by, or embodied through, the Temple and priesthood and other scheduled castes – joins each householder who also owns land in the land of Israel as an active partner, indeed, as senior partner, in possession of the landed domain. God not only demands a share of the crop, hence comprises a householder. God also dictates rules and conditions concerning production, therefore controls the householder's utilization of the means of production. Furthermore, it goes without saying, God additionally has provided as a lasting inheritance to Israel, the people, the enduring wealth of the country, which is to remain stable and stationary and not to change hands in such wise that one grows richer, the other poorer. Every detail of the distributive economics therefore restates that single point: *the earth is the Lord's*. That explains why the householder is partner of the Lord in ownership of the land, so that the Lord takes his share of the crop at the exact moment at which the householder asserts his ownership of his portion.[23]

---

clear that all expositions of Aristotle's economics find it possible to show the coherence of his economics with his larger systemic, philosophical concerns. But why Aristotelian economics, read in light of Scripture, much like the economics of the Judaism of the Mishnah, formed out of the marriage of Aristotle and Scripture, should have served Latin Christianity so long (and so well) as it did, I do not know.

[23] It is not only at the exact moment, but, as a matter of fact, in response to the householder's own decision and intention that God takes an interest in the crop. Before the householder exercises his ownership of the land through disposing of the crop, God does not exercise his ownership, except passively, by dictating the conduct of the means of production. What this means is that, within the anthropology of the Mishnaic system, God responds to man's emotions, attitudes, and intentions, and so reveals what I believe we may call anthropopathism.

But the ongoing partnership between God and Israel in the sanctification and possession of the land is not a narrowly secular arrangement. Both parties share in the process of the sanctification of the land, which accounts for, and justifies, Israel's very possession of the land. The Israelite landowner has a particular role in effecting the sanctification of the land, in that, land is holy and subject to the rules of God only when the Israelite landowner owns land in the land of Israel. Once more, land located elsewhere owned by Israelites, and land located in the land of Israel but not owned by Israelites, has no material relationship to the processes of sanctification, in utilization and in the disposition of the products of the land, that are at the heart of the distributive economics at hand. That fact is demonstrated by the conception about the character of the land, and of God's relationship to it, that the longer Israel has lived in the land of Israel, the holier that part of the land. Israel's dwelling in the land makes it holy. "Areas in which Israelites have lived for longer periods of time are holier and are subject to more rigorous restrictions,"[24] than those in which Israel has lived for a shorter period. The laws of the sabbatical year apply more strictly to the territories in which Israel lived before and after 586. Areas occupied only before but not after, or vice versa, are subject to fewer restrictions. This has an important implication for the nature of God's ownership of the land. Newman comments, "In Leviticus the land is sanctified by God alone, who dwells in it and who has given it to Israel, his people. The Mishnah's framers by contrast, claim that Israelites also play an active part in sanctifying the land."[25] Accordingly, in the Mishnah's system, the partnership of Israel, represented by the householder, with God in ownership of the land affects the very character of the land itself, making it different from other land, imparting to it the status of sanctification through the presence of the two sources of sanctification, God and the Israelite, the Israelite householder in particular.

That explains why, in the case of the conception of ownership of wealth set forth by the authorship of the Mishnah, a conception informed by the rules of Leviticus, God's joint ownership and tenancy with the farmer imposed a dual economics, the one, a distributive economic order, the other, a market system pure and simple. The one partner, God, had no strong interest in the market system; the other partner, the householder, was assumed to have only such an interest in the

---

The conception of God as emotionally consubstantial with man therefore is embedded, even, in the economics. In this connection, Abraham J. Heschel, *The Prophets* (Philadelphia: Jewish Publication Society of America) explores the anthropological theology of prophetic writings along the same lines. But I know no study of the emotional correspondences between God and man other than my *Incarnation of God. The Character of Divinity in Formative Judaism* (Philadelphia, 1988: Fortress Press), in which the matter plays no central role.

[24] Louis E. Newman, *The Sanctity of the Seventh Year: A Study of Mishnah-Tractate Shebiit* (Chico, 1983: Scholars Press for Brown Judaic Studies), p. 19.
[25] Ibid., p. 19.

rational utilization and increase of scarce resources, land and crops, herds and chattels. God's share was to be distributed in accord with God's rules, the farmer keeping the rest. That is what I mean by a mixed system, one partner framing policy in line with a system of distributive economics, the other in market economics. The authorship of the Mishnah thus effected and realized in a systematic way rules governing land use, placement of diverse types of crops, rights of ownership, alongside provision of part of the crop to those whom God had designated as recipients of his share of the produce. That explains why that authorship could not imagine a market economy at all, and why the administered market (which, as we noted, is no market at all) in which government – priests' government – supposedly distributed status and sustained economic relationships of barter took the place of the market. What falls into the system of sanctification is what grows from the land through the householder's own labor ("cultivated"), is useful to the householder for sustaining life ("food"). God owns the land, the householder is the sharecropper, and the wealth of the householder therefore is the land that God allows for the householder's share and use. Wealth consists of land and what land produces, crops and cattle, as well as a large labor force, comprising the children of a growing population.

At the end we have to listen not only to what the authorship of the Mishnah says, but also to what it does not treat. What are the scarce resources that the economics of Judaism ignores? The economics of the system expresses in tacit omissions a judgment concerning the dimensions of the economy that to begin with falls subject to the enchantment of sanctification expressed in glorious triviality by our authorship. For matching the explicit rules are the authorship's ominous silences. Its land-centeredness permits its economics to have no bearing not only upon the economy comprising Jews who were not householders, but also Jews who lived overseas. The Mishnah's distributive economics is for the "Israel" of "the land of Israel" to which the Mishnah speaks. There is no address to the economics of "Israel" outside of the land. For distributive economics governs only agricultural produce of the land of Israel, and, it follows, market economics, everything else, and everywhere else. No wonder, then, that the framers of the Talmud of Babylonia, addressing, as they did, Jews who did not live on holy or sanctified dirt, took no interest whatsoever in the Mishnah-tractates upon which we have focused here, the ones that state in rich detail the theory of a distributive economics of God as owner, scheduled caste as surrogate, Temple as focus, and enlandisement as rationale, for an utterly fictive system.

Strictly speaking, the economics of the Mishnah is not an economics at all. The reason is that in the Mishnah's system, economics is embedded in an encompassing structure, to which economic considerations are subordinated, forming merely instrumental components of a statement made not in response to, but merely through, economics. And economics can emerge as an autonomous and governing theory only when disembedded from politics and society.[26] Economic institutions, such as the market, the wage system, a theory of private ownership, and the like, in no way can have served the system of the Mishnah, not because in their moral or ethical value they proved less, or more, suitable than competing institutions, such as the sacerdotal system of production and distribution, a theory of divine-human joint tenancy, and a system made up of both wages for labor and also fees for correct genealogy, that the Mishnah's framers adopted. Economics viewed in its own terms cannot have served the system of the Mishnah because the system-builders viewed nothing in its own terms, but all things in the framework of the social system they proposed to construct. I earlier observed that Christian theologians for the first seven centuries simply ignored economics, having no theory to contribute to economic thought and no sustained interest in the subject. But when we realize the character and function of economics in the system of the Mishnah, we realize that the same reason accounts for the presence of an economics as for its absence.

V. Conclusion

Not all Judaic religious systems – statements of a world view and a way of life addressed to a well-defined social entity – have made judgments upon precisely those issues that conventionally comprise economics.[27] The priestly code

---

[26] That interest in whether or not economics is "embedded" or "disembedded" explains, once more, why I have tried to avoid those components of Polanyi's interpretation that have come under interesting criticism. I find especially suggestive the comments of Sally Humphreys, "Thus, what disturbed the philosophers of the fourth century was not, as Polanyi thought, an increase in profit-making on price differentials, but the disembedding or structural differentiation of the economy, leading to the application of 'economic' criteria and standards of behavior in a wide range of situations recognized as economic above all by the fact that money was involved; the old civic virtues of generosity and self-sufficiency were being replaced by the market attitudes of the traders." See Sally C. Humphreys, "History, Economics, and Anthropology: The Work of Karl Polanyi," *History & Theory* 1969, 8:165-212, p. 211. Note also Otto Erb, *Wirtschaft und Gesellschaft im Denken der hellenischen Antike* (Berlin, 1939), cited by her. Humphreys asks an interesting question: "Would a decrease in the importance of market institutions in a society which had reached this level of differentiation produce a revival of the attitudes whose loss Aristotle and Polanyi deplored? In the Roman Empire the state increasingly had to take over the functions of the market system in order to ensure an adequate supply and distribution of food to the city population. This change was accompanied by an increase in private redistribution....The process of bureaucratization of the economy and the rise under the influence of Christianity of new attitudes to economic matters has never really been studied."

[27] See Barry Gordon, "Biblical and Early Judeo-Christian Thought: Genesis to Augustine," in S. Todd Lowry, ed., *Pre-Classical Economic Thought. From the Greeks to the Scottish*

did. We look in vain, in the counterpart rules of a priestly community, the Essenes at Qumran, for an interest in the same questions. The authorship of the Priestly Code concerned itself with distributive economics, true value, the reversion of property to its "original" owner, and other fundamental conceptions that everything belonged in place, and that there was a given order that constituted the right arrangement and disposition of material wealth. So too, as we shall see, did the authorship of the Mishnah. But I find slight equivalent interest in the law codes of the Essenes of Qumran in these same matters, and there is no counterpart to the sustained and detailed attention to them accorded by the authorship of the Mishnah. For the whole of antiquity, we recognize, Christian theologians and jurisprudents (after Constantine) managed to say practically nothing about matters of economic

Enlightenment (Boston, Dordrecht, Lancaster: Kluwer Academic Publishers), pp. 43-67, and the commentary by Roman A. Ohrenstein, "Some Socioeconomic Aspects of Judaic Thought," *ibid.*, pp. 68-76. Note also the following items, among many:

R. Barraclough, *Economic Structures in the Bible* (Canberra, 1980: Zadok Centre).

Roland de Vaux, *Ancient Israel* (London, 1978: Darton, Longman and Todd).

Barry Gordon, *Economic Analysis before Adam Smith: Hesiod to Lessius* (London, 1975: MacMillan).

Idem., "Lending at Interest: Some Jewish, Greek, and Christian Approaches, 800 B.C.– A.D.. 100," *History of Political Economy*, 1982. 14:406-26.

Frederick C. Grant, The Economic Background of the Gospels (New York, 1973: Russell and Russell) (Repr. of 1926 ed.).

B. J. Meislin and M. L. Cohen, "Backgrounds of the Biblical Law against Usury," *Comparative Studies in Society and History,* 1963-4. p. 6.

Ben Nelson, *The Idea of Usury* (Chicago and London, 1969: University of Chicago Press).

E. Neufeld, "Socio-Economic Background of Yobel and Shemitta," *Rivista degli studi orientali,* 1958, 33-53, 124.

Robert North, *Sociology of the Biblical Jubilee* (Rome, 1954: Pontifical Biblical Institute).

Roman A. Ohrenstein, "Economic Thought in Talmudic Literature in the Light of Modern Economics," *American Journal of Economics and Sociology,* 1968. 27:185-96.

Idem., "Economic Self-Interest and Social Progress in Talmudic Literature," *American Journal of Economics and Sociology,* 1970. 29:59-70.

Idem., "Economic Aspects of Organized Religion in Perspective: The Early Phase," *The Nassau Review,* 1970, 27-43.

Idem., "Economic Analysis in Talmudic Literature: Some Ancient Studies of Value," *American Journal of Economics and Sociology,* 1979. 38.

Idem., "Some Studies of Value in Talmudic Literature in the Light of Modern Economics," *The Nassau Review,* 1981. 4:48-70.

Morris Silver, *Prophets and Markets: The Political Economy of Ancient Israel* (Boston, 1983: Kluwer-Nijhoff).

J. Viner, "The Economic Doctrines of the Christian Fathers," *History of Political Economy,* 1978: 10:9-45.

theory. Only with the advent of Aristotle in the life of the Christian intellect in the West do we find a counterpart interest to that of the authorship of the Mishnah. That authorship made a choice, and we can explain why this, not that, when we realize that the requirements of the system of the Mishnah encompasses, also, the task of framing an economic theory as a medium for the statement of the system's main points concerning sanctification.

What I have shown is that the Mishnah is a document of political economy, in which the two critical classifications are the village, *polis*, and the household, *oikos*. Since, however, the Mishnah's framers conceived of the world as God's possession and handiwork, theirs was the design of a universe in which the God's and humanity's realms flowed together. The result is a distributive economics, familiar from most ancient times onward, but a distributive economics that, in the same system, coexisted with a kind of market economics.[28]

The Mishnah's sages placed economics, both market (for civil transactions) and distributive (for sacred transactions, for example, with scheduled castes and the Temple), in the center of their system, devoting two of their six divisions to it (the first and the fourth, for the distributive and the market economics, respectively), and succeeded in making their statement through economics in a sustained and detailed way far beyond the manner in which Aristotle did. And no one in antiquity came near Aristotle, as I said. It was with remarkable success that the sages of Judaism presented an economics wholly coordinated in a systemic way with a politics. In this proposed kind of study of religion and economics, therefore, we find ourselves on the border between sociology and economics, following how the sociology of economics – and therefore this kind of inquiry concerning religious materials places us squarely into the middle of discourse on political economy. Compared to the work of Plato and Aristotle, the Mishnah's system presents the single most successful political economy accomplished in antiquity.

---

[28] I explain this matter in my *Economics of Judaism. The Initial Statement* (Chicago, 1989: The University of Chicago Press).

APPENDIX
JEWS IN ECONOMIES AND THE ECONOMICS OF JUDAISM
THE CASE OF SALO W. BARON

The economics of Judaism, as the economics of the Jews, is hardly an unexplored field of inquiry.[29] Indeed, any study of pertinent topics, whether of the Jews' economics or of the Jews' own economy, of the Jews in economic life or of the economics of Judaism, takes its place in a long, if somewhat irregular and uneven, line of works on the subject. The most important and best known statement on the economics of Judaism purports to account, by appeal to the economics of Judaism and the economic behavior of Jews, for the origins of modern capitalism. Werner Sombart, *The Jews and Modern Capitalism*,[30] in 1911 set the issues of the economics of Judaism within a racist framework, maintaining that Jews exhibited an aptitude for modern capitalism, and that aptitude derives in part from the Jewish religion, in part from the Jews' national characteristics. Jewish intellectuality, teleological mode of thought, energy, mobility, adaptability, Jews' affinity for liberalism and capitalism – all of these accounted for the role of Jews in the creation of the economics of capitalism, which dominated. Sombart appealed, in particular, to the anthropology of the Jew, maintaining that the Jews comprise a distinct anthropological group. Jewish qualities persist throughout their history: "constancy in the attitude of the Jews to the peoples among whom they dwelt, hatred of the Jews, Jewish elasticity." "The economic activities of the Jew also show a remarkable constancy." Sombart even found the knowledge of economics among the rabbis of the Talmud to be remarkable. In the end Sombart appealed to the fact that the Jews constitute a "Southern people transplanted among Northern peoples." The Jews exhibited a nomadic spirit through their history. Sombart contrasted "the cold North and the warm South" and held that "Jewish characteristics are due to a peculiar environment." So he appealed to what he found to be the correlation between Jewish intellectuality and desert life, Jewish adaptability and nomad life, and wrote

---

[29] For an introduction to the economic study of talmudic literature, see Roman A. Ohrenstein, "Economic Thought in Talmudic Literature in the Light of Modern Economics," *The American Journal of Economics and Sociology,* 1968, 27:185-96, who cites earlier writings on the subject, cf. p. 185, n. 3. Ohrenstein's "Economic Self-Interest and Social Progress in Talmudic Literature: A Further Study of Ancient Economic Thought and its Modern Significance," *American Journal of Economics and Sociology,* 1970, 29:59-70, typifies the perfectly dreadful work in hand in that field. I do not here treat Tamari's work on Jewish ethics vis-à-vis economics, because that seems to me a methodologically still more primitive work than any under discussion here.

[30] The edition I consulted is Werner Sombart, *The Jews and Modern Capitalism.* With a new introduction by Samuel Z. Klausner. Translated by M. Epstein (New Brunswick and London, 1982: Transaction Books).

about "Jewish energy and their Southern origin," "'Sylvanism' and Feudalism compared with 'Saharaism' and Capitalism," and ended, of course, with the theme of the Jews and money and the Jews and the Ghetto.

The romantic and racist view of the Jews as a single continuing people with innate characteristics which scientific scholarship can identify and explain of course formed the premise for Sombart's particular interest, in the economic characteristics of the Jew and the relationship of this racial trait to the Jews' origin in the desert. While thoroughly discredited, these views have nonetheless generated a long sequence of books on Jews' economic behavior. Today people continue to conceive "Jewish economic history" as a cogent subject that follows not only synchronic and determinate, but also diachronic and indeterminate lines and dimensions. Such books have taken and now take as the generative category the Jews' constituting a distinct economy, or their formation of a social unit of internally consistent economic action and therefore thought, the possibility of describing, analyzing, and interpreting the Jews within the science of economics. But that category and its premise themselves still await definition and demonstration, and these to this day are yet lacking. Consequently, while a considerable literature on "the Jews' economic history" takes for granted that there is a single, economically cogent group, the Jews, which has had a single ("an") economic history, and which, therefore, forms a distinctive unit of economic action and thought, the foundations for that literature remain somewhat infirm.[31]

The conception of Jews' having an economic history, part of the larger, indeed encompassing, notion of the Jews' have had a single history as a people, one people, has outlived the demise of the racist rendition of the matter by Sombart. But what happens when we take seriously the problems of conception and method that render fictive and merely imposed a diachronic history of the Jews, unitary, harmonious, and continuous, and when we realize that the secondary and derivative conception of a diachronic economics of the Jews is equally dubious? Whether or not it is racist, that unitary conception of the Jews as a single, distinctive, ongoing historical entity, a social group forming also a cogent unit of economic action, is surely romantic. Whatever the salubrious ideological consequences, such an economics bypasses every fundamental question of definition and method. If the Jews do not form a distinct economy, then how can we speak of the Jews in particular in an account of economic history? If, moreover, the Jews do not form a distinct component of a larger economy, then what do we learn about economics when we

---

[31] I hasten to state at the outset that Jews' role in diverse economies, so far as that role is distinctive, surely permits us to appeal as an independent variable to the fact that certain economic actors are Jews. But what trait or quality about those actors as Jews explains the distinctive traits of Jews as a group – if any does – requires careful analysis in a comparative framework, e.g., Jews as a distinct component of a variety of economies. None of these entirely valid and intellectually rigorous inquires is under discussion here.

know that (some) Jews do this, others, that? And if Jews, in a given place and circumstance, constitute a distinct economic unit within a larger economy, then how study Jews' economic action out of the larger economic context which they help define and of which they form a component? The upshot of these questions is simple: how shall we address those questions concerning rational action with regard to scarcity that do, after all, draw our attention when we contemplate, among other entities, the social entities that Jews have formed, and now form, in the world? And this brings us to the work of Salo W. Baron in social and economic history of the Jews, since in Baron's definition of the matter we are able to see precisely how this kind of study should not be done – and why.

Salo W. Baron[32] claims to know about economic trends among Jews in the second, third, and fourth centuries. As evidence he cites episodic statements of rabbis, as in the following:

> In those days R. Simon ben Laqish coined that portentous homily which, for generations after, was to be quoted in endless variations: "'You shall not cut yourselves,' this means you shall not divide yourselves into separate groups...." Before the battle for ethnic-religious survival, the inner class struggle receded.
>
> Age-old antagonisms, to be sure, did not disappear overnight. The conflict between the scholarly class and "the people of the land" continued for several generations....
>
> Class differences as such likewise receded into the background as the extremes of wealth and poverty were leveled down by the unrelenting pressure of Roman exploitation. Rarely do we now hear descriptions of such reckless display of wealth as characterized the generation of Martha, daughter of Boethos, before the fall of Jerusalem. Even the consciously exaggerated reports of the wealth of the patriarchal house in the days of Judah I fell far short of what we know about the conspicuous consumption of the Herodian court and aristocracy.[33]

It would be difficult to find a better example of over-interpretation of evidence to begin with irrelevant to the point than Baron's concluding sentence of the opening paragraph of this abstract. Not having shown that there was an inner class struggle

---

[32] *A Social and Religious History of the Jews* (New York, 1952: Columbia University Press) II. *Ancient Times,* Part II, pp. 241-260. Compare my "Why No Science in Judaism?" in *From Description to Conviction* (Atlanta, 1987: Scholars Press for Brown Judaic Studies), on the counterpart problems of intellect exhibited by Saul Lieberman, Baron's contemporary. I place the matter into a still broader context in: *Paradigms in Passage: Patterns of Change in the Contemporary Study of Judaism.* Lanham, 1988: University Press of America. Studies in Judaism Series.

[33] Baron, op. cit., p. 241.

or even spelled out what he means by class struggle, how he knows the category applies, let alone the evidence for social stratification on which such judgments rest, Baron leaps into his explanation for why the class struggle receded. That is not the only evidence of what can only be regarded as indifference to critical issues characteristic of writing on Jews' economies, but it is probative. The rest of the passage shows how on the basis of no sustained argument whatsoever, Baron invokes a variety of categories of economic history and analysis of his time, for example, conspicuous consumption, class struggle ("inner" presumably different from "outer"), and on and on.

When discussing economic policies, which draw us closer to the subject of this book, Baron presents a discussion some may deem fatuous.[34] Precisely how he frames the issues of economic theory will show why:

> Economic Policies: Here too we may observe the tremendous influence of talmudic legislation upon Jewish economy.

The premise that there was (a) Jewish economy, and that talmudic legislation affected economic action, is simply unsubstantiated. How Baron knows that people did what rabbis said they should, or that Jews formed an economy in which people could make decisions in accord with sages' instructions, he does not say. The premise of all that follows, then, is vacant. More to the point of our interest in matters of economic theory, we turn to Baron's program of discourse on what he has called "policies:"

> The rabbis constantly tried to maintain interclass equilibrium. They did not denounce riches, as some early Christians did, but they emphasized the merely relative value of great fortunes....The persistent accentuation of collective economic responsibility made the Jewish system of public welfare highly effective. While there was much poverty among the Jews, the community, through its numerous charitable institutions, took more or less adequate care of the needy.
>
> Man's right, as well as duty, to earn a living and his freedom of disposing of property were safeguarded by rabbinic law and ethics only in so far as they did not conflict with the common weal....
>
> Private ownership, too, was hedged with many legal restrictions and moral injunctions in favor of over-all communal control....
>
> Rabbinic law also extended unusual protection to neighbors....
>
> Nor did the individual enjoy complete mastery over testamentary dispositions....
>
> Apart from favoring discriminatory treatment of apostates, who were supposed to be dead to their families, the rabbis evinced great concern for the claims of minor children to support from their fathers' estate....

---

[34] Ibid., pp. 251-255.

In a period of economic scarcity social interest demanded also communal control over wasteful practices even with one's own possessions....

How this mélange of this and that – something akin to economic policy, some odd observations on public priority over private interest that sounds suspiciously contemporary (to 1952), counsel about not throwing away bread crumbs – adds up to "economic policies" I cannot say. But the data deserve a still closer scrutiny, since Baron represents the state of economic analysis of Judaism and so exemplifies precisely the problem I propose to solve in a different way. Here is his "man's right" paragraph:

Man's right, as well as duty, to earn a living and his freedom of disposing of property were safeguarded by rabbinic law and ethics only in so far as they did not conflict with the common weal. Extremists like R. Simon ben Yohai insisted that the biblical injunction, "This book of the law shall not depart out of thy mouth, but thou shalt meditate therein day and night," postulated wholehearted devotion to the study of Torah at the expense of all economic endeavors. But R. Ishmael effectively countered by quoting the equally scriptural blessing, "That thou mayest gather in thy corn and thy wine and thine oil." Two centuries later, the Babylonian Abbaye, who had started as a poor man and through hard labor and night work in the fields had amassed some wealth, observed tersely, "Many have followed the way of R. Ishmael and succeeded; others did as R. Simeon ben Yohai and failed." Sheer romanticism induced their compeer, R. Judah bar Ila'i, to contend that in olden times people had made the study of the law a full-time occupation, and devoted only little effort to earning a living, and hence had proved successful in both....R. Simeon ben Yohai himself conceded, however, that day and night meditation had been possible only to a generation living on Mannah or to priestly recipients of heave-offerings....In practice the rabbis could at best secure, as we shall see, certain economic privileges for a minority of students, relying upon the overwhelming majority of the population to supply society's needs to economically productive work.

From the right to earn a living being limited by the common weal, we jump to study of the Torah as the alternative to productive labor. That move of Baron's I cannot myself claim to interpret. I see no connection between the balance between "freedom of disposing of property" and "conflict with the common weal," on the one side, and " the issue of work as against study, on the other. The rest of the discussion concerns only that latter matter, and the paragraph falls to pieces by the end in a sequence of unconnected sayings joined by a pseudo-narrative ("two centuries later...") and an equally meretricious pretense of sustained argument "...himself conceded"), all resting on the belief that the sayings assigned to various sages really were said by them.

This reading by Baron of how "the Jews'" policies and behavior in economics are to be studied should not be set aside as idiosyncratic. The obvious flaws of historical method, the clear limitations in even so simple a matter as the competent construction of a paragraph – these should not obscure the fact that Baron's construction of the Jewish economy and Jewish economic policy is representative and not at all idiosyncratic. The received conception first of all imputes to the Jews a single economic history, which can be traced diachronically. Proof lies in works in both English and Hebrew. Take for example the book entitled, *Economic History of the Jews*, assigned to Salo W. Baron, Arcadius Kahan, and others, edited by Nachum Gross.[35] Baron wrote Chapters One through Seven, Kahan, Eight through Ten, of Part One, "general survey," and the titles of these sequential chapters follow: "the first temple period, exile and restoration, the second temple period, the talmudic era, the Muslim Middle Ages, medieval Christendom, economic doctrines, the early modern period, the transition period, the modern period." That, I contend, is a program of diachronic economic history. These chapters can have been composed and presented in the sequence before us only if the author assumed that a single group, with a continuous, linear history, formed also a cogent and distinct economic entity, with its own, continuous, linear, economic history.

"Economic doctrines" as Baron expounds them are amply familiar to us: bits and pieces of this and that. The remainder of the book covers these topics: agriculture, industry, services. Each part is subdivided, for example, under services: "banking and bankers, brokers, contractors, court Jews, department stores, Jewish autonomous finances, market days and fairs, mintmasters and moneyers, moneylending, peddling, secondhand goods, slave trade, spice trade, stock exchanges." Here again, we may be sure, data on department stores derive from one time and place, those on slave trade, from another. But laid forth sequentially, the chapter titles indicate a conception of a single unitary and continuous economic history, in which any fact concerning any Jew at any time or place connects with any fact concerning any other Jew at any other time or place, the whole forming a cogent economy. Nor should work in Hebrew be expected to exhibit a more critical definition of what is subject to discourse. The same Nachum Gross edited *Jews in Economic Life. Collected Essays In Memory of Arcadius Kahan (1920-1982)*.[36] Here is the portrait of a field, as sequential essays outline that field:

The Economic Activities of the Jews
The Cardinal Elements of the Economy of Palestine during the Herodian
    Period
The Economy of Jewish Communities in the Golan in the Mishnah and Talmud
    Period

---

[35] New York, 1975: Schocken.
[36] Jerusalem, 1985: The Zalman Shazar Center for the Furtherance of the Study of Jewish History.

The Itinerant Peddler in Roman Palestine

The German Economy in the 13th-14th Centuries: The Framework and
Conditions for the Economic Activity of the Jews

On the Participation of Jewish Businessmen in the Production and Marketing
of Salt in Sixteenth Century Poland and Lithuania

Economic Activities of Jews in the Caribbean in Colonial Times

Jewish Guilds in Turkey in the Sixteenth to Nineteenth Centuries

and on and on. Nor do I exaggerate the utter confusion generated by the conception
of "the Jews" as an economic entity, continuous from beginning to the present.
The juxtaposition of these two papers seems to me to make the point rather sharply:

Jewish Population and Occupations in Sherifian Morocco

On the Economic Activities of the Moldavian Jews in the second half of the
18th and the first half of the 19th centuries

There is no need to ask what one thing has to do with the other. We just take for
granted that Jews are Jews wherever they lived, whenever they thrived, and whatever
Jews' occupations were in Sherifian Morocco bears a self-evident relationship to
whatever Moldavian Jews did for a living half a world and a whole civilization
distant. Having cited the juxtaposition of titles, with justified confidence I simply
rest my case.

7

How the Mishnah Expresses Theology:
The Mishnah's Theology of History

The framers of the Mishnah present us with a kind of historical thinking quite different from the one that they, along with all Israel, had inherited in Scripture. The legacy of prophecy, apocalypse, and mythic-history handed on by the writers of the books of the Hebrew Scriptures of ancient Israel, for instance, Jeremiah, Daniel, and Genesis, Exodus, and Deuteronomy, respectively, exhibits a single and quite familiar conception of history. First of all, history refers to events seen whole. Events bear meaning, form a pattern, and, therefore, deliver God's message and judgment. The upshot is that every event, each one seen on its own, must be interpreted in its own terms, not as part of a pattern but as significant in itself. What happens is singular, therefore an event to be noted and points toward lessons to be drawn for where things are heading and why.

If things do not happen at random, they also do not form indifferent patterns of merely secular, social facts. What happens is important because of the meaning contained therein. That meaning is to be discovered and revealed through the narrative of what has happened. So for all Judaisms until the Mishnah, the writing of history serves as a form or medium of prophecy. Just as prophecy takes up the interpretation of historical events, so historians retell these events in the frame of prophetic theses. And out of the two — historiography as a mode of mythic reflection, prophecy as a means of mythic construction — emerges a picture of future history, that is, what is going to happen. That picture, framed in terms of visions and supernatural symbols, in the end focuses, as much as do prophecy and history-writing, upon the here and now.

The upshot is simple. History consists of a sequence of one-time events, each of them singular, all of them meaningful. These events move from a beginning somewhere to an end at a foreordained goal. History moves toward eschatology, the end of history. The teleology of Israel's life finds its definition in eschatological fulfillment. Eschatology therefore constitutes not a choice *within* teleology, but the definition *of* teleology. That is to say, a theory of the goal and purpose of things (teleology) is shaped solely by appeal to the account of the end of times (eschatology). History done in this way then sits enthroned as the queen of theological science. Events do not conform to patterns. They form patterns. What happens matters because events bear meaning, constitute history. Now, as is clear, such a conception of mythic and apocalyptic history comes to realization in the writing of history in the prophetic pattern or in the apocalyptic framework, both of them mythic modes of organizing events. We have every right to expect such a view of matters to lead people to write books of a certain sort, rather than of some other. In the case of Judaism, obviously, we should expect people to write history books that teach lessons or apocalyptic books that through pregnant imagery predict the future and record the direction and end of time. And in antiquity that kind of writing proves commonplace among all kinds of groups and characteristic of all sorts of Judaisms but one. And that is the Judaism of the Mishnah. Here we have a Judaism that does not appeal to history as a sequence of one-time events, each of which bears meaning on its own. What the Mishnah has to say about history is quite different, and, consequently, the Mishnah does not conform in any way to the scriptural pattern of representing, and sorting out, events: history, myth, apocalypse.

The first difference appears right at the surface. The Mishnah contains no sustained narrative whatsoever, a very few tales, and no large-scale conception of history. It organizes its system in non-historical and socially unspecific terms. That is to say, there is no effort at setting into a historical context, e.g., a particular time, place, a circumstance defined by important events, any of the laws of the Mishnah. The Mishnah's system is set forth out of all historical framework, as we observed in Chapter One. That is a medium for the presentation of a system that has no precedent in prior systems of Judaism or in prior kinds of Judaic literature. The law codes of Exodus and Deuteronomy, for example, are set forth in a narrative framework, and the priestly code of Leviticus, for its part, appeals to God's revelation to Moses and Aaron, at specific times and places. In the Mishnah we have neither narrative nor setting for the representation of law.

Instead of narrative which, as in Exodus, spills over into case-law, the Mishnah gives description of how things are done in general and universally, that is, descriptive laws. Instead of reflection on the meaning and end of history, it constructs a world in which history plays little part. Instead of narratives full of didactic meaning, the Mishnah's authorship as we shall see in a moment provides lists of events so as to expose the traits that they share and thus the rules to which they conform. The definitive components of a historical-eschatological system of

Judaism — description of events as one time happenings, analysis of the meaning and end of events, and interpretation of the end and future of singular events — none of these commonplace constituents of all other systems of Judaism (including nascent Christianity) of ancient times finds a place in the Mishnah's system of Judaism. So the Mishnah finds no precedent in prior Israelite writings for its mode of dealing with things that happen. The Mishnah's way of identifying happenings as consequential and describing them, its way of analyzing those events it chooses as bearing meaning, its interpretation of the future to which significant events point — all those in context were unique. In form the Mishnah represents its system outside of all historical framework.

Yet to say that the Mishnah's system is ahistorical could not be more wrong. The Mishnah presents a different kind of history. Its authorship revises the inherited conception of history and reshapes that conception to fit into its own system. When we consider the power of the biblical myth, the force of its eschatological and messianic interpretation of history, the effect of apocalypse, we must find astonishing the capacity of the Mishnah's framers to think in a different way about the same things. As teleology constructed outside the eschatological mode of thought in the setting of the biblical world of ancient Israel proves amazing. By "history," as the opening discussion makes clear, I mean not merely events, but how events are so organized and narrated as to teach (for them, theological, for us, religions-historical or social) lessons, reveal patterns, tell us what we must do and why, what will happen to us tomorrow. In that context, some events contain richer lessons than others; the destruction of the Temple of Jerusalem teaches more than a crop failure, being kidnapped into slavery more than stubbing one's toe. Furthermore, lessons taught by events — "history" in the didactic sense — follow a progression from trivial and private to consequential and public.

The framers of the Mishnah explicitly refer to very few events, treating those they do mention within a focus quite separate from what happened — the unfolding of the events themselves. They rarely create or use narratives. More probative still, historical events do not supply organizing categories or taxonomic classifications. We find no tractate devoted to the destruction of the Temple, no complete chapter detailing the events of Bar Kokhba, nor even a sustained celebration of the events of the sages' own historical life. When things that have happened are mentioned, it is neither in order to narrate, nor to interpret and draw lessons from, the event. It is either to illustrate a point of law or to pose a problem of the law — always *en passant*, never in a pointed way. So when sages refer to what has happened, this is casual and tangential to the main thrust of discourse. Famous events, of enduring meaning, such as the return to Zion from Babylonia in the time of Ezra and Nehemiah, gain entry into the Mishnah's discourse only because of the genealogical divisions of Israelite society into castes among the immigrants (M. Qiddushin 4:1). Where the Mishnah provides little tales or narratives, moreover, they more often treat how things in the cult are done in general than what, in particular, happened on some one day. It is sufficient to refer casually to well-known incidents. Narrative, in the Mishnah's limited rhetorical repertoire, is reserved for the narrow framework of what priests and others do on recurrent occasions and around the Temple. In all, that staple of history, stories about dramatic events and important deeds, in the minds of the Mishnah's jurisprudents provide little nourishment. Events, if they appear at all, are treated as trivial. They may be well-known, but are consequential in some way other than is revealed in the detailed account of what actually happened. Let me now show some of the principal texts that contain and convey this other conception of how events become history and how history teaches lessons.

Sages' treatment of events determines what in the Mishnah is important about what happens. Since the greatest event in the century and a half, from ca. 50 to ca. 200, in which the Mishnah's materials came into being, was the destruction of the Temple in 70, we must expect the Mishnah's treatment of that incident to illustrate the document's larger theory of history: what is important and unimportant about what happens. The treatment of the destruction occurs in two ways. First, the destruction of the Temple constitutes a noteworthy fact in the history of the law. Why? Because various laws about rite and cult had to undergo revision on account of the destruction. The following provides a stunningly apt example of how the Mishnah's philosophers regard what actually happened as being simply changes in the law. We begin with Mishnah-tractate Rosh Hashanah Chapter Four.

ROSH HASHANAH CHAPTER FOUR

4:1-3

A.   The festival day of the New Year which coincided with the Sabbath –

B.   in the Temple they would sound the *shofar*.

C.   But not in the provinces.

D.   When the Temple was destroyed, Rabban Yohanan ben Zakkai made the rule that they should sound the *shofar* in every locale in which there was a court.

E.   Said R. Eleazar, "Rabban Yohanan b. Zakkai made that rule only in the case of Yabneh alone."

F.   They said to him, "All the same are Yabneh and every locale in which there is a court.

M. Rosh Hashanah 4:1

A.   And in this regard also was Jerusalem ahead of Yabneh:

B.   in every town which is within sight and sound [of Jerusalem], and nearby and able to come up to Jerusalem, they sound the *shofar*.

C.   But as to Yabneh, they sound the *shofar* only in the court alone.

M. Rosh Hashanah 4:2

A.   In olden times the *lulab* was taken up in the Temple for seven days, and in the provinces, for one day.

B.   When the Temple was destroyed, Rabban Yohanan ben Zakkai made the rule that in the provinces the *lulab* should be taken up for seven days, as a memorial to the Temple;

C.   and that the day [the sixteenth of Nisan] on which the *omer* is waved should be wholly prohibited [in regard to the eating of new produce] [M. Suk. 3:12].

M. Rosh Hashanah 4:3

First, let us examine the passage in its own terms, and then point to its consequence for the argument about history. The rules of sounding the *shofar* run to the special case of the New Year which coincides with the Sabbath, M. 4:1A-C. Clearly, we have some diverse materials here since M. 4:1A-D (+ E-F), are formally different from M. 4:3. The point of difference, however, is clear, since M. 4:3A has no counterpart at M. 4:1A-C, and this is for redactional reasons. That is, to connect his materials with what has gone before, the redactor could not introduce the issue of M. 4:1A-C with the formulary, *In olden times... When the Temple was destroyed....* Consequently, he has used the more common, mild apocopation to announce his topic, and then reverted to the expected formulary pattern, which, I think, characterized M. 4:1A-C as much as M. 4:3. M. 4:2A assumes a different antecedent construction from the one we have, a formulary which lists points in which Jerusalem is ahead of Yabneh, and, perhaps, points in which Yabneh is ahead of Jerusalem. But M. 4:2 clearly responds to M. 4:1E's view. The meaning of the several entries is clear and requires no comment.

But the point as to the use and meaning of history does. What we see is that the destruction of the Temple is recognized and treated as consequential — but only for the organization of rules. The event forms division between one time and some other, and, in consequence, we sort out rules pertaining to the temple and synagogue in one way rather than in another. That, sum and substance, is the conclusion drawn from the destruction of the Temple, which is to say, the use that is made of that catastrophe: an indicator in the organization of rules. What we see is the opposite of an interest in focusing upon the one-time meaning of events. Now it is the all-time significance of events in the making of rules. Events are now treated not as irregular and intrinsically consequential but as regular and merely instrumental.

4:4

A.   At first they would receive testimony about the new moon all day long.

B.   One time the witnesses came late, and the Levites consequently were mixed up as to [what] song [they should sing].

C.   They made the rule that they should receive testimony [about the new moon] only up to the afternoon offering.

D.   Then, if witnesses came after the afternoon-offering, they would treat that entire day as holy, and the next day as holy too.

E.   When the Temple was destroyed, Rabban Yohanan b. Zakkai made the rule that they should [once more] receive testimony about the new moon all day long.

F.   Said R. Joshua b. Qorha, "This rule too did Rabban Yohanan b. Zakkai make:

G.   "Even if the head of the court is located somewhere else, the witnesses should come only to the location of the council [to give testimony, and not to the location of the head of the court]."

M. Rosh Hashanah 4:4

A-C form a complete unit. E is distinctly secondary. The long antecedent narrative, A-D is formally out of phase with M. 4:3. The appendix supplied at F-G is thematically appropriate.

The passages before us leave no doubt about what sages selected as important about the destruction: it produced changes in synagogue rites. Although the sages surely mourned for the destruction and the loss of Israel's principal mode of worship, and certainly recorded the event of the ninth of Ab in the year 70, they did so in their characteristic way: they listed the event as an item in a catalogue of things that are like one another and so demand the same response. But then the destruction no longer appears as a unique event. It is absorbed into a pattern of like disasters, all exhibiting similar taxonomic traits, events to which the people, now well-schooled in tragedy, knows full well the appropriate response. So it is in demonstrating regularity that sages reveal their way of coping. Then the uniqueness of the event fades away, its mundane character is emphasized. The power of taxonomy in imposing order upon chaos once more does its healing work. The consequence was reassurance that historical events obeyed discoverable laws. Israel's ongoing life would override disruptive, one-time happenings. So catalogues of events, as much as lists of species of melons, served as brilliant apologetic by providing reassurance that nothing lies beyond the range and power of ordering system and stabilizing pattern. Here is yet another way in which the irregular was made regular and orderly, subject to rules:

MISHNAH-TRACTATE TAANIT 4:6-7

4:6   A.   Five events took place for our fathers on the seventeenth of Tammuz, and five on the ninth of Ab.

B.   On the seventeenth of Tammuz (1) the tablets [of the Torah] were broken, (2) the daily whole offering was cancelled, (3) the city wall was breached, (4) Apostemos burned the Torah, and (5) he set up an idol in the Temple.

C.   On the ninth of Ab (1) the decree was made against our forefathers that they should not enter the land, (2) the first Temple, (3) the second [Temple] were destroyed, (4) Betar was taken, (5) the city was ploughed up [after the war of Hadrian].

D.   When Ab comes, rejoicing diminishes.

M. Taanit 4:6

4:7   A.   In the week in which the ninth of Ab occurs it is prohibited to get a haircut and to wash one's clothes.

B.   But on Thursday of that week these are permitted,

C.   because of the honor due to the Sabbath.

D.   On the eve of the ninth of Ab a person should not eat two prepared dishes, nor should one eat meat or drink wine.

E.   Rabban Simeon b. Gamaliel says, "He should make some change from ordinary procedures."

F.   R. Judah declares people obligated to turn over beds.

G.   But sages did not concur with him.

M. Taanit 4:7

I include M. Taanit 4:7 to show the context in which the list of M. 4:6 stands. The stunning calamities catalogued at M. 4:6 form groups, reveal common traits, so are subject to classification. Then the laws of M. 4:7 provide regular rules for responding to, coping with, these untimely catastrophes, all (fortuitously) in a single classification. So the raw materials of history are absorbed into the ahistorical, supernatural system of the Mishnah. The process of absorption and regularization of the unique and one-time moment is illustrated in the passage at hand.

A still more striking example of the reordering of one-time events into all-time patterns derives from the effort to put together in a coherent way the rather haphazard history of the cult inherited from Scripture, with sacrifices made here and there and finally in Jerusalem. Now, the entire history of the cult, so critical in the larger system created by the Mishnah's lawyers, produced a patterned, therefore sensible and intelligible, picture. As is clear, everything that happened turned out to be susceptible of classification, once the taxonomic traits were specified. A monothetic exercise, sorting out periods and their characteristics, took the place of narrative, to explain things in its own way: first this, and then that, and, in consequence, the other. So in the neutral turf of holy ground, as much as in the trembling earth of the Temple mount, everything was absorbed into one thing, all classified in its proper place and by its appropriate rule. Indeed, so far as the lawyers proposed to write history at all, they wrote it into their picture of the long tale of the way in which Israel served God: the places in which the sacrificial labor was carried on, the people who did it, the places in which the priests ate the meat left over for their portion after God's portion was set aside and burned up. This "historical" account forthwith generated precisely that problem of locating the regular and orderly, which the philosophers loved to investigate: the intersection of conflicting by equally correct taxonomic rules, as we see at M. Zebahim 14:9, below. The passage that follows therefore is history, so far as the Mishnah's creators proposed to write history: the reduction of events to rules forming compositions of regularity, therefore meaning. We follow Mishnah-tractate Zebahim Chapter Fourteen.

14:4-8

I.   A.   Before the tabernacle was set up, (*1) the high places were permitted, and (2) [the sacrificial] service [was done by] the first born [Num. 3:12-12, 8:16-18].

B.   When the tabernacle was set up, (1) the high places were prohibited, and (2) the [sacrificial] service [was done by] priests.

C.   Most Holy Things were eaten within the veils, Lesser Holy Things [were eaten] throughout the camp of Israel.

M. Zebahim 14:4

II. A.   They came to Gilgal.

B.   The high places were prohibited.

C.   Most Holy Things were eaten within the veils, Lesser Holy Things, anywhere.

M. Zebahim 14:5

III. A.   They came to Shiloh.

B.   The high places were prohibited.

C.   (1) There was no roof-beam there, but below was a house of stone, and hangings above it, and (2) it was 'the resting place' [Deut. 12:9].

D.   Most Holy Things were eaten within the veils, Lesser Holy Things and second-tithe [were eaten] in any place within sight [of Shiloh].

M. Zebahim 14:6

IV. A.   They came to Nob and Gibeon.

B.   The high places were permitted.

C.   Most Holy Things were eaten within the veils, Lesser Holy Things, in all the towns of Israel.

M. Zebahim 14:7

V.   A.   They came to Jerusalem.

B.   The high places were prohibited.

C.   And they never again were permitted.

D.   And it was 'the inheritance' [Deut. 12:9].

E.   Most Holy Things were eaten within the veils, Lesser Holy Things and second-tithe within the wall.

M. Zebahim 4:8

Let us rapidly review the formal traits of this lovely composition, because those traits justify my insistence that we deal with a patterning of events. This set of five formally balanced items bears remarkably few glosses. The form is best revealed at M. 14:5, 7. M. 14:6C is the only significant gloss. M. 14:4 sets up a fine introduction, integral to the whole despite its interpolated and extraneous information at A2, B2. M. 14:8C is essential; D is a gloss, parallel to M. 14:6C2. The unitary construction is self-explanatory. At some points it was permitted to sacrifice on high places, at others, it was not, a neat way of harmonizing Scripture's numerous contradictions on the subject. M. 14:4B depends upon Lev. 17:5. M. 14:5 refers to Joshua 4:19ff.; M. 14:6, to Joshua 18:1. The 'resting place' of Deut. 12:9 is identified with Shiloh. At this point the obligation to separate second tithe is incurred, which accounts for the conclusion of M. 14:4D. M. 14:7 refers to I Samuel 21:2, 7, after the destruction of Shiloh, and to I Kings 3:4. M. 14:8 then identifies the 'inheritance' of Deut. 12:9 with Jerusalem. The 'veils' are familiar at M. 5:3, 5, and the walls of Jerusalem, M. 5:6-8.

14:9

A.   All the Holy Things which one sanctified at the time of the prohibition of the high places and offered at the time of the prohibition of high places outside –

B.   lo, these are subject to the transgression of a positive commandment and a negative commandment, and they are liable on their account to extirpation [for sacrificing outside the designated place, Lev. 17:8-9, M. 13:1A].

C.   [If] one sanctified them at the time of the permission of high places and offered them up at the time of the prohibition of high places,

D.   lo, these are subject to transgression of a positive commandment and to a negative commandment, but they are not liable on their account to extirpation [since if the offerings had been sacrificed when they were sanctified, there should have been no violation].

E.   [If] one sanctified them at the time of the prohibition of high places and offered them up at the time of the permission of high places,

F.   lo, these are subject to transgression of a positive commandment, but they are not subject to a negative commandment at all.

M. Zebahim 14:9

Now we see how the Mishnah's sages turn events into rules and show the orderly nature of history. The secondary expansion of M. 14:4-8 is in three parts, A-B, C and E-F, all in close verbal balance. The upshot is to cover all sorts of circumstances within a single well-composed pattern. This is easy to represent by simple symbols. We deal with two circumstances and two sets of actions: The circumstance of the prohibition of high places, (-), and that of their permission (+), and the act of sanctification of a sacrifice (A) and offering it up, (B), thus:

> A: –A –B = negative, positive, extirpation
> C: +A +B = negative, positive
> E: –A +B = positive only.

We cannot have +A +B, since there is no reason to prohibit or to punish the one who sanctifies and offers up a sacrifice on a high place when it is permitted to do so (!). Accordingly, all possible cases are dealt with. In the first case, both sanctification and offering up take place at the time that prohibition of high places applies. There is transgression of a positive commandment and a negative commandment. The negative is Deut. 12:13, the positive, Deut. 12:14. *Take heed that you do not offer your burnt-offerings at every place that you see; but at the place which the Lord will choose in one of your tribes, there you shall offer your burnt-offerings...* The mixtures, C and E, then go over the same ground. If sanctification takes place when it is permitted to sanctify animals for use in high places, but the offering up takes place when it is not allowed to do so (e.g., the former for M. 14:4, the latter, M. 14:6), extirpation does not apply (Lev. 17:5-7). When we then reverse the order (e.g., M. 14:6, M. 14:7), there is no negative (Deut. 12:13), but the positive commandment (Deut. 12:14) has been transgressed. C surely conforms to Simeon's theory, M. 14:2P, but sages, M. 14:2Q, need not differ. But matters do not stop here. The rule-making out of the raw materials of disorderly history continues unabated.

14:10

A. These are the Holy Things offered in the tabernacle [of Gilgal, Nob, and Gibeon]:

B. Holy Things which were sanctified for the tabernacle.

C. Offerings of the congregation are offered in the tabernacle.

D. Offerings of the individual [are offered] on a high place.

E. Offerings of the individual which were sanctified for the tabernacle are to be offered in the tabernacle.

F. And if one offered them up on a high place, he is free.

G. What is the difference between the high place of an individual and the high place of the community?

H. (1) Laying on of hands, and (2) slaughtering at the north [of the altar], and (3) placing [of the blood] round about [the altar], and (4) waving, and (5) bring near.

I.   R. Judah says, "there is no meal-offering on a high place [but there is in the tabernacle]" –

J.   and (1) the priestly service, and (2) the wearing of garments of ministry, and (3) the use of utensils of ministry, and (4) the sweet-smelling savor and (5) the dividing line for the [tossing of various kinds of] blood, and (6) the rule concerning the washing of hands and feet.

K.   But the matters of time, and remnant, and uncleanness are applicable both here and there [by contrast to M. 14:3F-I].

M. Zebahim 14:10

When M. 14:4-8 refer to a high place which was permitted, and refer also to the presence of veils, it is assumed that there were both a tabernacle (hence the veils) and also high places. This must mean Gilgal, M. 14:5 and Nob and Gibeon, M. 14:7. Now the issue is, if there are both a tabernacle and a high places, which sorts of offerings belong to which kind of altar? It follows that the pericope treats the situations specified at M. 14:5, 7, a secondary expansion. A is answered by B. C-F go on to work out their own interests, and cannot be constructed to answer A, because they specify *are offered in the tabernacle* as a complete apodosis, which A does not require and B clearly does not want. B tells us that even though it is permitted to offer a sacrifice on a high place, a sacrifice which is set aside for the tabernacle (obviously) is to be offered there. Then C-F work the matter out. C and D are clear as stated. Holy Things which are sanctified for the tabernacle are offerings of the congregation (C). It is taken for granted that they are meant for the tabernacle, even when not so designated as specified b B. Individuals' sacrifices are assumed to be for high places unless specified otherwise (D). Obviously, if they are sanctified for the tabernacle, E, they are sacrificed there. But there is no reason to inflict liability if they are offered on a high place, F. The whole is carefully worked out, leaving no unanswered questions.

G then asks what difference there is between the high place which serves an individual, and "the high place" – the tabernacle – which serves the congregation, that is, the ones at Gilgal, Nob, and Gibeon. H specifies five items, J, six more, and Judah brings the list up to twelve. K completes the matter. *Time* refers to the improper intention to the flesh or burn the sacrificial parts after the appropriate time, thus *refuse*. The word-choice is unexpected. The inclusion of M. Zeb. 14:9, structurally matching M. Taanit 4:7, shows us the goal of the historical composition. It is to set forth rules that intersect and produce confusion, so that we may sort out confusion and make sense of all the data. The upshot may now be stated briefly: the authorship at hand had the option of narrative, but chose the way of philosophy: generalization through classification, comparison and contrast.

The Mishnah absorbs into its encompassing system all events, small and large. With what happens the sages accomplish what they do with everything else:

a vast labor of taxonomy, an immense construction of the order and rules governing the classification of everything on earth and in Heaven. The disruptive character of history — one-time events of ineluctable significance — scarcely impresses the philosophers. They find no difficulty in showing that what appears unique and beyond classification has in fact happened before and so falls within the range of trustworthy rules and known procedures. Once history's components, one-time events, lose their distinctiveness, then history as a didactic intellectual construct, as a source of lessons and rules, also loses all pertinence. So lessons and rules come from sorting things out and classifying them, that is, from the procedures and modes of thought of the philosopher seeking regularity. To this labor of taxonomy, the historian's way of selecting data and arranging them into patterns of meaning to teach lessons, proves inconsequential. One-time events are not what matters. The world is composed of nature and supernature. The repetitious laws that count are those to be discovered in Heaven and, in Heaven's creation and counterpart, on earth. Keep those laws and things will work out. Break them, and the result is predictable: calamity of whatever sort will supervene in accordance with the rules. But just because it is predictable, a catastrophic happening testifies to what has always been and must always be, in accordance with reliable rules and within categories already discovered and well explained. That is why the lawyer-philosophers of the mid-second century produced the Mishnah — to explain how things are. Within the framework of well-classified rules, there could be messiahs, but no single Messiah.

Up to now I have contrasted "history" with "philosophy," that is, disorderly and unique events as against rules governing all events and emerging inductively from them. I therefore have framed matters in such a way that the Mishnah's system appears to have been ahistorical and anti-historical. Yet in fact the framers of the Mishnah recognized the past-ness of the past and hence, by definition, laid out a conception of the past that constitutes a historical doctrine. Theirs was not an anti-historical conception of reality but a deeply historical one, even though it is a different conception of the meaning of history from the familiar one. It was, in a single word, social scientific, not historical in the traditional sense of history-writing. Let me explain this difference, since it is fundamental to understanding the Mishnah's system as essentially philosophical and, in our terms, scientific.

To express the difference, I point out that, for modern history-writing, what is important is to describe what is unique and individual, not what is on-going and unremarkable. History is the story of change, development, movement, not of what does not change, develop, or move. For the thinkers of the Mishnah, historical patterning emerges as today scientific knowledge does, through taxonomy, the classification of the unique and individual, the organization of change and movement within unchanging categories. That is why the dichotomy between history and eternity, change and permanence, signals an unnuanced exegesis of what was, in fact, a subtle and reflective doctrine of history. That doctrine proves entirely consistent with the large perspectives of scribes, from the ones who made omen-series in ancient Babylonia to the ones who made the Mishnah.

How, then, in the Mishnah does history come to full conceptual expression? History as an account of a meaningful pattern of events, making sense of the past and giving guidance about the future, begins with the necessary conviction that events matter because they form series, one after another. And when we put a series together, we have a rule, just as when we put cases together, we can demonstrate the rule that governs them all. The Mishnah's authorship therefore treats historical events just as they sort out anything else of interest to them: correct composition of contracts, appropriate disposition of property, proper conduct on a holy day, all things imputed through specific events, formed so that we can derive out of the concrete the abstract and encompassing rule, just as I pointed out in Chapter One. What we see, therefore, is the congruence of language and thought, detail and main point, subject-matter and sheltering system.

That is why we may not find surprising the Mishnah's framers' reluctance to present us with an elaborate theory of events, a fact fully consonant with their systematic points of insistence and encompassing concern. Events do not matter, one by one. The philosopher-lawyers exhibited no theory of history either. Their conception of Israel's destiny in no way called upon historical categories of either narrative or didactic explanation to describe and account for the future. The small importance attributed to the figure of the Messiah as an historical-eschatological figure, therefore, fully accords with the larger traits of the system as a whole. Let me speak with emphasis: If what is important in Israel's existence is sanctification, an ongoing process, and not salvation, understood as a one-time event at the end, then no one will find reason to narrate history.

By this point the reader must wonder where, if at all, the Mishnah's system attends to the events of the preceding century, which, after all, changed for all time the conditions of Israel's existence. If my thesis about the meaning and uses of history in the Mishnah's Judaism is valid, then we should see a head-on confrontation with the great events of the age. And so we do, but we must be prepared for the identification of what matters. To the framers of the Mishnah, a great sage is an event, as much as a battle is noteworthy, and the destruction of the temple finds its counterpart in the death of a sage. In both instances, we shall see a pattern, and it is the same pattern. With the decline in the holiness of the Temple and the cult, changes took place, leading to disaster. With the death of the great sages (most of them second century figures, as a matter of fact), changes took place, leading to social disaster. That is the message conveyed by the details of Mishnah-tractate Sotah Chapter Nine, to which we now turn. Let us first outline the chapter in its own terms.

The concluding chapter of Mishnah-tractate Sotah takes up the rite of breaking the heifer's neck (Deut. 21:1ff.). An effort is made at M. 9:1A-B to link the matter to M. 7:1-2's interest in the use of Hebrew in the rite, but, in fact, the relevant pericope is M. 9:6, which covers the ground of the formula spoken in the rite. So the whole unit — M. 9:1-8 — is essentially autonomous of its larger setting. A fair proportion of the whole is devoted to the exegesis of the relevant Scriptures, specifically, M. 9:1, 2, 3, 5, and 6. M. 9:2-4 present what seems to be a triplet of rulings assigned to Eliezer. M. 9:7-8 provide materials more natural to Mishnah, e.g., a triplet on how we dispose of the heifer if the murderer should be found at various points in the rite (M. 9:7), and a treatment of various kinds of evidentiary situations (M. 9:8).

The chapter's second half, M. 9:9-15, carries us to our point of interest, for it proceeds in a quite different direction, providing reflections on the decline of the times in general (M. 9:9-12), the catastrophes which followed the destruction of the Temple (M. 9:12-14), and, finally, a very long potpourri of sayings on the equivalent catastrophes attendant upon the death of sages, principally of the second century (M. 9:15). The link of these materials to the coherent half of the chapter comes at the outset, M. 9:9: the rite of breaking the heifer's neck was cancelled because there were so many murders, and, still more germane to the tractate, as a whole, the rite of the bitter water was annulled because there were so many adulterers. I am inclined to think that this excellent conclusion at M. 9: 9 has been constructed to link the formally unified materials which follow, M. 9:9, 11-12, to the foregoing — both to Chapter Nine and to the tractate as a whole — and then the further pericopae, M. 9:12-15, were carried in the wake of what, if left alone, would have formed a rather deft conclusion to the work of redacting both the tractate and the chapter.

9:1

A.   The rite of the heifer whose neck is to be broken is said in the Holy Language,

B.   since it is said, *If one be found slain in the land lying in the field...*

C.   *then your elders your judges shall come forth* (Deut. 21:1-2).

D.   Three from the high court in Jerusalem went forth.

E.   R. Judah says, "Five, since is is said, *Your elders* – thus, two, and *your judges,* thus, two, and there is no such thing as a court made up of an even number of judges, so they add to their number yet one more."

M. Sotah 9:1

The pericope is in two units, A-B, and C-E. The former revert to the theme of M. 7:1-2, but it is only at M. 9:6 that what must be said in Hebrew plays a role. The cited verse, then, should be Deut. 21:7. There is no point at which the proof text begun at B serves the purposes of A. It follows that A is a superscription attached as part of the redactional work. The use of B indeed is in connection with C-E. The anonymous view is that three go forth, but Judah shows that the cites verse requires five.

9:2-4

A. [If] it was fond hidden under a heap of rocks or hanging from a tree or floating on the surface of water, they did not break the neck of a heifer,

B. since it is said, *On the ground* {Deut. 21:1] – not hidden under a pile of rock.

C. *Lying* – not hung on a tree.

D. *In the field* – not floating on the water.

E. [If] it was fond near the frontier, near a town which had a gentile majority, or near a town which had no court, they did not break a heifer's neck.

F. They measure only from a town which has a court.

I. G. "[If] it was found exactly between two such towns, then the two of them bring two heifers," the words of R. Eliezer.

H. And Jerusalem does not have to bring a heifer whose neck is to be broken.

M. Sotah 9:2

II. A. "[If] its head is found in one places and its body in another place, they bring the head to the body," the words of R. Eliezer.

B. R. Aqiba says, "They bring the body to the head."

M. Sotah 9:3

III. A. From what point did they measure?

B. R. Eliezer says, "From his belly-button."

C. R. Aqiba says, "From his nose."

D. R. Eliezer b. Jacob says, "From the place at which he was turned into a corpse – from his neck."

M. Sotah 9:4

We apparently have a triplet involving Eliezer and Aqiba, but if that is the case, then M. 9:2G is defective. The material at the beginning, M. 9:2A-F, H, is clear as given. The law is stated in Mishnah's usual way, A, then given an exegetical foundation, B-D. E does not enjoy similar exegetical support. Its apodosis may be, *They did not measure.* The opinion contrary to Eliezer's will say that there is no breaking of the heifer's neck at all. The dispute of M. 9:3 concerns where the parts of the corpse are to be buried. Eliezer has the corpse buried where the larger part is located. Aqiba wants the corpse to be buried where the head is located. Then, M. 9:4, they dispute the point at which the measuring began. The belly-button is the middle of the body. The nose is the point from which the soul exits. Eliezer b. Jacob's contribution to the dispute ignores the antecedent form and reasoning.

9:5

A.   The elders of Jerusalem took their leave and went away.

B.   The elders of that town bring *a heifer from the herd with which labor had not been done and which had not drawn the yoke* (Deut. 21:3).

C.   But a blemish does not invalidate it.

D.   They brought it down into a rugged valley (and *rugged* is meant literally, hard, but even if it is not rugged, it is valid).

E.   And they break its neck with a hatchet from behind.

F.   And its place is prohibited for sowing and for tilling, but permitted for the combing out of flax and for quarrying stones.

M. Sotah 9:5

Narrative style characterizes A-D. The Jerusalemites measure the distance between the corpse and the surrounding towns, M. 9:1. They then go home, and the elders of the town which has to carry out the rite do their duty. The place in which the rite takes place, F, cannot be used for agricultural purposes.

9:6

A.   The elders of that town wash their hands in the place in which the neck of the heifer is broken, and they say,

B.   *Our hands have not shed this blood, nor did our eyes see it* (Deut. 21:7).

C.   Now could it enter our minds that the elders of a court might be shedders of blood?

D.   But [they mean:] He did not come into our hands and we sent him away without food.

E.   And we did not see him and let him go along without an escort.

F.   And [it is] the priests [who] say, *Forgive O Lord, your people Israel, whom you have redeemed, and do not allow innocent blood in the midst of your people, Israel* (Deut. 21:8).

G.   They did not have to say, *And the blood shall be forgiven them* (Deut. 21:8).

H.   But the Holy Spirit informs them, "Whenever you do this, the blood shall be forgiven to you."

M. Sotah 9:6

The narrative concludes here, with two more legal-analytical pericopae to come. A-B, as we noticed, are the point at which M. 9:1-8 are relevant to M. 7:1-2. C-E are a secondary interpolation, making an interesting point. Then the exposition of the Scriptures is concluded. The differentiation, within the cited verse, among the several voices provokes T. to provide us with numerous examples of the same phenomenon of various voices' speaking at a single point in Scripture.

9:7

I. A. [If] the murderer was fond before the neck of the heifer was broken, it [simply] goes forth and pasture sin the herd.

II. B. [If the murderer is fond] after the neck of the heifer is broken, it is to be buried in its place.

    C. For to begin with it was brought in a matter of doubt. It has atoned for the matter of doubt on which account it was brought and which has gone its way.

III. D. [If] the neck of the heifer was broken and afterward the murderer was found, lo, this one is put to death.

M. Sotah 9:7

The triplet bears a gloss at C. Otherwise it is in excellent form. Once the heifer is killed, the place in which it was killed remains prohibited and the heifer's carcass cannot be used for any gain. The murderer in any event will be punished (Deut. 21:9).

9:8

I. A. [If] one witness says, "I saw the murderer," and one witness says, "you did not see him."

    (B. [If] one woman says, "I saw him," and one woman says, "You did not see him,")

    C. they would go through the rite of breaking the neck of the heifer.

II. D. [If] one witness says, "I saw," and two say, "You did not see," they would break the neck of the heifer.

III. E. [If] two say, "We saw," and one says to them, "You did not see," they did not break the neck of the heifer.

M. Sotah 9:8

The rite of breaking the heifer's neck is performed when there is no sound evidence as to who has killed him. Here we run a parallel to M. 6:4. At A, B, we have testimony which is cancelled out. At D the evidence is inadequate for conviction. But at E we have ample evidence for punishing the murderer.

9:9

I. A. When murderers became many, the rite of breaking the heifer's neck was cancelled.

    B. [This was] when Eleazar b. Dinai cam along, and he was also called Tehinah b. Perishah. Then they went and called him, " Son of a murderer."

II. C. When adulterers became many, the ordeal of the bitter water was cancelled.

D.   And Rabban Yohanan b. Zakkai cancelled it, since it si said, *I will not punish your daughters when they commit whoredom, nor your daughters-in-law when they commit adultery, for they themselves go apart with whores* (Hosea 4:14).

III.   E.   When Yosé b. Yoezer of Seredah and Yosé b. Yohanan of Jerusalem died, the grape-clusters were cancelled,

F.   since it is said, There is no cluster to eat, my soul desired the first ripe fig (Micah 7:1).

M. Sotah 9:9

The formal construction constituted by M. 9:9, 11, 12, is joined to the foregoing because of the obvious connection at A, the rite of breaking the heifer's neck. Once we establish the pattern of accounting for the end of one or another of the rites, then a whole sequence will follow in natural order. This pericope gives us a triplet, M. 9:9A, glossed at B, C, glossed at D, and E, bearing a proof-text at F.

A.   Yohanan, high priest, did away with the confession concerning tithe.
B.   Also: He cancelled the rite of the Awakeners and the Stunners.
C.   Until his time a hammer did strike in Jerusalem.
D.   And in his time no man had to ask concerning doubtfully-tithed produce.

M. Sotah 9:10

The general theme of accounting for the cessation of ancient rites accounts for the inclusion of this obviously irrelevant item, which ignores the established form and also is uninterested in the basic notion of the construction as a whole, which is the decline of the generations. Yohanan's time, by contrast, is represented in a positive light.

9:11-13

IV.   A.   When the Sanhedrin was cancelled, singing at wedding feats was cancelled, since it is said, *They shall not drink wine with a song* (Is. 24:9).

M. Sotah 9:11

V.   A.   When the former prophets died out, the Urim and Tummim were cancelled.

VI.   B.   When the sanctuary was destroyed, the Shamir-worm ceased and [so did] the honey of *supim*.

C.   And faithful men came to an end,

D.   since it is written, *Help, O Lord, for the godly man ceases* (Ps. 12:2).

E.   Rabban Simeon b. Gamaliel says in the name of R. Joshua, "From the day on which the Temple was destroyed, there is no day on which there is no curse, and dew has not come down as a blessing. The good taste of produce is gone."

F.   R. Yosé says, "Also: the fatness of produce is gone."

                                                                    M. Sotah 9:12

A.   R. Simeon b. Eleazar says, "[When] purity [ceased], it took away the taste and scent; [when] tithes [ceased], they took away the fatness of corn."

B.   And sages say, "Fornication and witchcraft made an end to everything."

                                                                    M. Sotah 9:13

We now revert to the established form and theme, with three more entries, M. 9:11, M. 9:12A, and M. 9:12B+C. Once the destruction of the Temple is introduced, M. 9:12B-C, we shall turn from the general theme of the decline of the generations to the specific one of the change in the world effected by the catastrophe of A.D. 70.

9:14

I.   A.   In the war against Vespasian they decreed against the wearing of wreaths by bridegrooms and against the wedding-drum.

II.   B.   In the war against Titus they decreed against the wearing of wreaths by brides.

      C.   And [they decreed] that a man should not teach Greek to his son.

III. D.   In the last war [Bar Kokhba's] they decreed that a bride should not go out in a palanquin inside the town.

      E.   But our rabbis [thereafter] permitted the bride to go out in a palanquin inside the town.

                                                                    M. Sotah 9:14

The triplet, A,B, and D, bears glosses at C and E. *Titus* had best be replaced by Quitus, in the time of Trajan, which makes better sense for our form. The decline of the generation in general and the affect, upon the public welfare, of the destruction of Jerusalem in particular now yield to the third and final theme in this unit, the decline of the generations in consequence of the passing of the great age of the sages. Now the composition makes its great point, that the destruction of the temple and the death of great sages mark the movement of time and impart to an age the general rules that govern life therein. That is the "lesson of history," and it is not drawn from a single event but from patterns exhibited by many like events, and these then are of two classifications: what happens in respect to holiness in the cult, and to holiness in the sage.

9:15

A.   When R. Meir died, makers of parables came to an end.

B.   When Ben Azzai died, diligent students came to an end.

C.   When Ben Zoma died, exegetes came to an end.

D.   When R. Joshua died, goodness went away from the world.

E.   When Rabban Simeon b. Gamaliel died, the locust came, and troubles multiplied.

F.   When Eleazar b. Azariah died, wealth went away from the sages.

G.   When R. Aqiba died, the glory of the Torah came to an end.

H.   When R. Hanina b. Dosa died, wonder-workers came to an end.

I.   When R. Yosé Qatnuta died, pietists went away.

J.   (And why was he called *Qatnuta?* Because he was the least of the pietists.)

K.   When Rabban Yohanan b. Zakkai died, the splendor of wisdom came to an end.

L.   When Rabban Gamaliel the Elder died, the glory of the Torah came to an end, and cleanness and separateness perished.

M.   When R. Ishmael b. Phabi died, the splendor of the priesthood came to an end.

N.   When Rabbi died, modesty and fear of sin came to an end.

O.   R. Pinhas b. Yair says, "When the Temple was destroyed, associates became ashamed and so did free men, and they covered their heads.

P.   "And wonder-workers became feeble. And violent men and big takers grew strong.

Q.   "And none expounds and none seeks [learning] and none asks.

I.   R.   "Upon whom shall we depend? Upon our Father in heaven."

S.   R. Eliezer the Great says, "From   day on which the Temple was destroyed, sages began to be like scribes, and scribes like ministers, and ministers like ordinary folk.

T.   "And the ordinary folk have become feeble.

U.   "And none seeks.

II.   V.   "Upon whom shall we depend? Upon our Father in heaven."

W.   With the footprints of the Messiah: presumption increases, and dearth increases.

X.   The Vine gives its fruit and wine at great cost.

Y.   And the government turns to heresy.

Z.   And there is no reproof.

AA.   The gathering place will be for prostitution.

BB.   And Galilee will be laid waste.

CC.   And the Gablan will be made desolate.

DD.   And the men of the frontier will go about from town to town, and none will take pity on them.

	EE.	And the wisdom of scribes will putrefy.
	FF.	And those who fear sin will be rejected.
	GG.	And the truth will be locked away.
	HH.	Children will shame elders, and elders will stand up before children.
	II.	*For the son dishonors the father and the daughter rises up against her mother, the daughter-in-law against her mother-in-law; a man's enemies are the men of his own house* (Mic. 7:6).
	JJ.	The face of the generation in the face of a dog.
	KK.	A son is not ashamed before his father.
III.	LL.	Upon whom shall we depend? Upon our Father in heaven.
	MM.	R. Pinhas b. Yair says, "Heedfulness leads to cleanliness, cleanliness leads to cleanness, cleanness leads to abstinence, abstinence leads to holiness, holiness leads to modesty, modesty leads to the fear of sin, the fear of sin leads to piety, piety leads to the Holy Spirit, the Holy Spirit leads to the resurrection of the dead, and the resurrection of the dead comes through Elijah, blessed be his memory, Amen."

M. Sotah 9:15

The pericope is divided into the following components: A-N, thirteen names, O-R, with its parallel at S-V, W-LL – a potpourri, joined, if at all, only by LL, and MM. It would appear, however, that W-LL yield thirteen clearcut and distinct stichs. Pinhas, MM, has ten. So perhaps there is some effort at presenting a formally interesting construction. The point of it all requires no comment in the present context.

The theology of the Mishnah encompasses history and its meaning, but, we now realize, history and the interpretation of history do not occupy a central position on the stage of Israel's life portrayed by the Mishnah. The critical categories derive from the modalities of holiness. What can become holy or what is holy? These tell us what will attract the close scrutiny of our authorship and precipitate sustained thought, expressed through very concrete and picayune cases. If I had to identify the two most important foci of holiness in the Mishnah, they would be, in the natural world, the land, but only The Holy Land, the Land of Israel, and, in the social world, the people, but only The People of Israel. In the interplay among Land, People, and God, in the matter at hand we see the inner workings of the theological vision of the sages of the Mishnah.

8

History and Purity in First-Century Judaisms

PURITY IN STASIS:
THE FOUNDATIONS OF THE MISHNAIC SYSTEM OF CLEANNESS

When we reduce to their most fundamental propositions the sayings in Mishnah-Tosefta attributed to the document's earliest-named authorities or those serving as presuppositions to such sayings, we come upon a complete system of uncleanness.[1] Each principal component of such a system – a definition first, of the sources of uncleanness; second, of the circumstances, or places, or times at which uncleanness is affective; and third, of the modes by which uncleanness is removed and purification attained – is in place by the turn of the first century A.D. This Mishnaic[2] system, I shall now explain, is in exquisite stasis, resting upon eternally recurrent natural forces, and, at its essence, is above the realm of historical event and action. What is unclean is abnormal and disruptive of the economy of nature, and what is clean is normal and constitutive of the economy and the wholeness of nature. The hermeneutic route to that conception is to be located, to begin with, in the way in which what is unclean is restored to a condition of cleanness. It is restored through the activity of nature – unimpeded by human intervention in removing the uncleanness – through the natural force of water

---

[1] This work is done in detail in my *History of the Mishnaic law of Purity,* vol. 22, *The Mishnaic System of Uncleanness: Its Content and History* (Leiden, 1977). A few of the results of the study, as they pertain to the first century A.D., are summarized here. I presented this essay as a lecture at the University of Tübingen Protestant Theological Faculty on the occasion of that University's five hundredth anniversary. I express thanks for the hospitality accorded to me at that time as well as for the Medal in Celebration of the Five Hundredth Anniversary that the University presented to me.

[2] I refer to the system as *Mishnaic* because it is ultimately preserved, with complications and expansions, in Mishnah. There is reason to claim the system to be Pharisaic in origin.

collected in its original state. Accordingly, if to be clean is normal, then it is that state of normality which is restored by natural processes themselves. It follows from the exegetical fulcrum of purification that to be unclean is abnormal and is the result of unnatural processes. The first of these is death, which disturbs the house of life by releasing, in quest of a new house, corpse uncleanness, to be defined as that which is released by death. Corpse uncleanness may be contained in a tent, which is a small enclosed space, or, as we see in later strata, in a broken utensil. Once corpse uncleanness finds that new home, its capacity for contamination ends. The second are menstrual blood, flux of blood outside of the menstrual cycle, and a flow from the penis outside of the normal reproductive process. Here too the source of the uncleanness, in the case of the Zabah and the Zab, most certainly is constituted by that which functions contrary to nature or which disrupts what is deemed to be the normal course of nature. The bed and the table are to be so preserved as to remain within the normal lines of the natural economy. It follows that cleanness of the table is to be attained and protected, with regard to both the food which is consumed thereon and to the utensils used in preparing and serving it. The former is defined, of course, along lines of what is acceptable to the cult. The latter matter is developed out of pertinent passages of Scripture and these verses are interpreted in such a way as to serve the system as a whole. Specifically, what is ordinary, useful, distinctive to a given purpose, and normal is deemed susceptible to uncleanness and must therefore be kept apart from those things which, for their own reasons, are deemed extraordinary and abnormal. If such an object then is made unclean, it must be restored to cleanness through natural processes. Food and drink, by contrast, fall outside of the system of purification; no provision is made for them.

The system takes shape, therefore, through the confluence and contrast of opposites perpetually moving from the one side to the other – from the clean to the unclean, from the unclean to the clean. It is remarkably stable and unchanging. Death happens constantly. Water flows regularly from heaven to earth. The source of menstrual uncleanness is as regular as the rain. And the similar uncleanness of the Zab and Zabah through analogy attains regularity through that same source. Meals happen day by day, and if, for the Israelite within the system, the table is a regular resort, so too is the bed. The system therefore creates an unchanging rhythm of its own. It is based on recurrent natural sources of uncleanness and perpetual sources of cleanness, and it focuses upon the loci of ordinary life in which people, whatever else they do, invariably and always are going to be engaged: nourishment and reproduction – *the sustenance of life and the creation of life.*

There is scarcely room for history, which above all is disruptive and disintegrative. Only when the symbolic perfection of the cult's perpetuity is shattered by events will a place have to be made for history. But at that point the cultic system, including uncleanness, is made subordinate to some other system and no longer serves as the principal focus and pivot of the system. Then uncleanness and all that goes with it become conditions for the expression of some further, now deeper, ontology, rather than the a priori ontological and mythopoeic reality. History, in the form of perceived disruption of the Temple. whether through destruction and cessation of the cult at Jerusalem or through the conviction of the cult's desecration by its own practitioners, transforms what is primary and uncontingent into something contingent and secondary. Some systemic element in the available symbolic repertoire other than Temple and cult, for instance, Land and People, comes to the center. The Essenes of Qumran, seeing themselves as the new Temple, accomplish a subtle shift in that their community locates itself at the center, from which the cultic metaphor flows. They are not merely *like* the Temple. Since uncleanness can effect exclusion from the community, that community itself forms the metaphorical crux. The real, this-worldly cult, including conditions for this conduct in cleanness, moves to the periphery. Then the focus of the lines of structure shifts. Uncleanness will be made to bear other meanings (for example, societal ones) and will be forced to define something other than the terms of exclusion from the concrete holy Temple. In this regard the shift comes even at Qumran, for there cleanness is definitive of admission to the commune; uncleanness, of exclusion.[3] When we ask about the role of history in the system of uncleanness at the foundation of the Mishnaic law, this fact will assume importance.

The argument, that at the core of the system is the conviction that what is normal is clean and what is abnormal or disruptive is unclean, is powerfully supported by the convictions of the Priestly Code on why Israel should keep clean and normally is clean. It is because the opposite of *unclean* is *holy*. Israel's natural condition, pertinent to the three dimensions of life – Land, people, and cult – is holiness. God's people is to be like God in order to have ultimate access to him. Accordingly, it is what causes Israel to cease to be holy, in the present context uncleanness, which is abnormal, and, to state the reverse, what is abnormal is unclean. Cleanness thus is a this-worldly expression of the mythic conception of the holiness and the set-apartness of all three – people, Land, and cult. By keeping oneself apart from what affects and afflicts other lands, peoples, and cults ("the Canaanites who were here before you"), the Israaelite attains that separateness which is expressive of holiness and reaches the holiness which is definitive also of the natural condition of Israel. The processes of nature correspond to those of supernature, restoring in this world the datum to which this world corresponds. The disruptive sources of uncleanness – unclean foods and dead creeping things, persons who depart from their natural condition in sexual and reproductive organs

---

[3] The point here is that if one disobeys the social regulations of the Essene community at Qumran, he is declared effectively unclean and excluded from the right to touch the pure things of the community. It follows that the community is now deemed *equivalent* to the cult, not merely *like* the cult (see my *Idea of Purity in Ancient Judaism* [Leiden, 1973], pp. 53-54, 67-68, 80-82).

(or, later on, in their skin condition and physical appearance), and the corpse – all of these affect Israel and necessitate restorative natural processes.

PURITY NOW AND AT THE END:
THE ESSENES' TELEOLOGICAL INTERPRETATION OF PURITY

What is the place of the system of cleanness in the larger structure of which it is part? For the Essene community at Qumran the answer is not difficult to find. The community treated cleanness as vital at its chief group activity, the meal, because it saw itself as a sacred community assembled at a meal, the cleanness of which both expressed the holiness of the group and replicated the holiness of the Temple. Of still greater interest, cleanness is a precondition of participation in the eschatological war which loomed on the community's horizon and for which it proposed to prepare carefully, in part through perpetual cultic cleanness. After the war the soldiers were to restore their status of cleanness and that of the Jerusalem Temple, presumably because of the contamination of the corpses they would make in battle. It follows that cleanness is understood as a precondition of holiness; and holiness, of the messianic eschaton. Cleanness for the Essenes therefore constitutes not an abiding status, a permanent process outside of history. It is a necessary step in the historical process itself; the condition of the eschatological war which leads to the end of history.[4]

The Essene community at Qumran, after all, conceived that a world historical event had already intruded into the realm of cleanness. Jerusalem and its Temple were hopelessly contaminated at the hands of willfully unclean people, people who had sexual relations in the Temple or the city and thereby contaminated both.[5] Accordingly, the eternal and recurrent system of cleanness *already* had been disrupted. That is, in part, why the Essene community found it necessary at a given point in time to establish a realm of holiness, and therefore of cleanness, on its own and outside of the Temple. But the original breaking of the system out of its eternal cycle once and for all time introduced into the system a historical-eschatological concern. Cleanness now is not natural to Israel but only to that segment of Israel assembled in the community. Cleanness is to be restored through the activity of that saving, pure, and purifying remnant. Provisional for now, cleanness will be made permanent only at the end of time and the conclusion of history.

---

[4] As we note in a moment, this same notion (without the concept of an eschatological war) is attributed to Pinhas b. Yair (M. Sot. 9:15). But the saying stands all by itself. I cannot find anyone else who shares his notion that cleanness leads to sanctification which leads onward and upward in the salvific ladder. As I shall point out below, one of the exceedingly difficult problems is that we have no clear notion of the role of cleanness in the eschatological theory of Pharisaism, nor, indeed, do we have a reliable picture of that theory to begin with.

[5] To the Essenes the events of A.D. 70 took place long before 70.

The endless cycle, once removed from the eternity of the holy Temple which had been desecrated, could be restored to its perfect cyclicality only when history itself could for all time be brought to a final conclusion by the anointed Messiah and the holy warriors, at which time the holiness and cleanness of the Temple would be restored. Cleanness is a precondition of the end of days, which at the table of Qumran can be foreshadowed and adumbrated. But cleanness also, for its perfection, now depends upon the coming of the end of days. It is, therefore, an accident of history, not an element of a system essentially immune to history. Once historicized, cleanness and the system of which it is part never cease to be, not subjects and actors, but objects of social and metaphysical reality. Perfection once was and once more can be attained. But those for whom the Temple had been desecrated and was as good as destroyed conceived that what should not be subject to the vagaries of historical disaster indeed had been destroyed. It is only through the introduction, into historical processes, of the sacred community that cleanness would regain the perfect locus it had lost. In the meantime, cleanness would, at best, contingently serve as a precondition of the end and as a definition of the commune aiming at the end. The unarticulated system of the Essenes, remarkably congruent in its skeletal characteristics to that of the earliest sages of Mishnah, therefore locates cleanness within the scheme of history in the interim and not as essential to an eternally recurring cycle in an unchanging natural economy.

The Mishnaic system at its origins, by contrast, hardly leaves space for change. Its cogency and capacity to function as a system depend upon the opposite of change. We refer once more to the way in which uncleanness is removed, for that is the path into the center of the system. The system itself exhibits two fixed and static dimensions which correspond to and complement one another: nature and supernature. Omitted from the system is what is not natural but man-made. The intervention of man interrupts the process of purification and renders water incapable of effecting uncleanness. By definition, water drawn by man is unsuitable. Thus, the one point when human intervention is possible is the point which explicitly secures human exclusion from the system. Man of course does not bring about the uncleanness of the sources of uncleanness. But what the Mishnaic system at the outset chooses to say about that matter is insufficiently distinctive to produce a contrary expectation. Man is the locus of uncleanness. The ways in which human beings sustain and create life define the foci and the loci of the system. But in these matters, too, human intervention is secondary. Man cannot clean food but must choose clean food and protect its cleanness. Human beings must refrain from sexual relations at certain times. Their unnatural condition with respect to their sexual organs makes them vehicles for the imposition of uncleanness on objects they use in ordinary life – beds and chairs. That means everywhere they stand or sit or lie can be made unclean by them. But, as I said, the one point at which human volition enters the system, the choice to remove uncleanness permits no role whatsoever to the human being. A person can enter the system by inadvertence. A person cannot leave it by conscious creation of means of purification. That pair of opposites is excluded.

If human action is systematically excluded, what about the complex of human actions which constitutes history? Obviously, human beings may desecrate not only themselves, but their tables and beds, and the cult and Temple as well. But, for the Pharisees, the Temple has not been desecrated. Everything we know about them suggests that, to the contrary, the cult is as it always was from the moment God ordained it: a locus of sanctity, a place of cleanness. So far as the cult defines the being of Israel, so long as the enduring conduct of its affairs in cleanness and holiness shapes the fundamental ontological situation of Israel, Israel – Land, cult, and people alike – is beyond history. Or, to put it differently, while things happen, history does not. The first destruction and the subsequent restoration of the Temple testify to the permanence of that system of permanent normality of which the center is the cult, the setting is the Land, the actors are the priests and people – all of them holy and set apart, above all, from history.

We simply do not know the place in history assigned to cleanness by the framers of the Mishnaic system. It is clear from the Essenes' thought on the subject that cleanness defines the group, on the one side, and sets the precondition of the groups' eschatological program, on the other. The evidence in our hands leaves not a hint at an equivalent conception in the earliest stratum of Mishnah.[6] If, to be sure, we identify the Pharisees with the framers of Mishnah, then we may expect to find a concern for the condition of the state and for the conduct of its affairs. For to begin with, the Pharisees are represented as a political party. It would and should follow that the replication of cultic cleanness at the table should bear deep meaning for the larger anticipation of the group for the conduct of affairs. For system are one and comprehensive, and it is not possible to suppose that all that characterizes Pharisees before 70 is an interest in tithing and purity law. The Gospels' picture is of a group engaged in political activities not only in eating clean meals. Josephus' account of the earlier Pharisees is equally explicit on their politics. Accordingly, cleanness may constitute, as Pinhas b. Yair says (M. Sot. 9:15), a way station on the path to the Messianic kingdom prior to and a condition for holiness. None of this is to be gainsaid.

To ask further about the role of history in the Mishnah's primitive system of uncleanness, we return to our observation that, for the Essenes, the lines of structure delineated by uncleanness shift, along with the point of centrality, the locus of the system's interest. At the Essene community of Qumran uncleanness served to exclude and cleanness to include, therefore defining the periphery of the commune. Cleanness performed a social and sectarian function. The center from which lines of structure go forth is reached by following those lines back to the

---

[6] To be sure, cleanness defines those who may eat together, which seems to be a fairly essential characteristic of the self-definition of Pharisaism.

locus defined by them. It thereby becomes clear that cult is replaced at the center by society, the Essene society in particular. The cult of Jerusalem has been rejected at one specific time. From that moment what happens perpetually is made contingent upon what has happened at some point. Ontological reality now is defined not in eternal, recurrent, and unchanging patterns of being. Once something has happened, then happenings, events of the life of the commune, disrupt the old eternal patterns. The community itself perceives just that and focuses its attention on what is to come in the eschaton. It follows that the vehicle, the locus, of meaning is that one thing which moves from the old mode of permanence to the new: the community itself, which in the interim, is all there is to bear the burden of the sacred. That is why, I think, the focus of uncleanness shifts from cult which is reduced to a mere metaphor, to community which is served by, and also generative of, the said metaphor.

THE TWO SYSTEMS COMPARED

If this is a sound observation, then what do we learn about Mishnah's equivalent focus of uncleanness and the point of origin of lines of structure signified thereby in the context of history? What place is there for transience and historical movement in the earliest system of uncleanness contained within Mishnah? The answer to the question of who is excluded by uncleanness and included by cleanness must lie in exactly the same datum as has just now come under discussion. What is permitted and prohibited? We begin with the negative observation that, while in IQS one is unclean who violates the norms of the community, in early and late Mishnaic law one is unclean who is made unclean only and solely by those sources of uncleanness specified in Scripture or generated by analogy to those of Scripture. The contrast of the Essene community yields the fact that the Mishnaic system at its foundations presents no element of a societal revision of the locus of uncleanness, for there is none in the definition of the sources of uncleanness. The locus remains in the cult, where it was, but the periphery is extended to include the table. Keeping clean does not define one's membership in a sect, so far as Mishnah is concerned. The very tight adherence in Mishnah's fundamental stratum to Scripture and its explicit rules, both by interpreting them literally (as was done at Qumran) and by exegetically expanding them by analogy – treating the table like the table of the Lord in the Temple and the bed like the bed which in Canaanite times polluted the land, shows that no shift whatsoever had taken place in the point from which the lines of structure, delineated by uncleanness, go forth. The Temple is uncontingent. The extension of the Temple's rules outside is secondary and contingent. The bed and table depend for meaning and significance upon the cult. Life is to be created and sustained in accord with the rules definitive of the world which is the center of life: the holy altar. Nothing has effected a shift in focus, from the enduring, real Temple of Jerusalem, either exclusively or even primarily to the community which keeps the cleanness laws and defines itself in terms of those laws. What is prohibited by uncleanness is entry into the Temple and analogous commensality at any table, anywhere. What is permitted is nurture and creation of human life everywhere. Israel remains whole, and uncleanness and cleanness do not effect social differentiation within it. If the law is not made to define a sect but to establish the rules by which common actions may be carried out, then for those who shape the world (in part) through the system under examination, nothing has happened to reshape the locus of the rules and disrupt their linear relationship to their enduring center. To state matters bluntly: for the Mishnaic system history has not (yet) happened.

The cult ordained by God goes on above, not through, time. For the Mishnaic system at its origins, no shift has taken place in the patterns of the lines of structure. The table and the bed are at the periphery and conduct at the one and in the other depends, as it always has, on the model by which rules of conduct are framed. Since the Temple in all its holiness endures, no other locus comes into view. The community formed by those who keep the laws in just the right way is not distinct from the world of those who do not, and indeed does not constitute a community at all, Israel remains Israel in all its full, old sense. The Land is wholly holy, not only that part of it consecrated by the life of the holy community thereon. Nothing has changed in the age-old ontology which defines being and discovers reality in order, permanence, recurrence, and the eternal, enduring passage of time. The sacrifice still marks and differentiates the days and months and seasons and links them into a larger pattern. Time's passage depends upon it. The cult still stands at the pivot, the spatial center of the Land, still forms the nexus between heaven and earth. The people, the whole people, still performs regular and holy actions through the priesthood which is at its center. Those who then eat their meals as if they are priests know they are not priests but aspire to the priestly sanctity. They do not claim to be the new priests or the only true and right ones.

If, as seems clear, nothing has changed, then the reason is that nothing has happened. It follows that cleanness is not a condition of the eschaton, and uncleanness is not a function of history. Cleanness is attained now where it always has been attained and uncleanness now is definitive of the locus of cleanness as it has always defined the locus of cleanness. The Temple remains, depriving of consequence what happens around and outside it. If we are unable to discern either a place for history in the uncleanness law, or a role in history for that law, the reason is apt to be that there is none.

Yet it is not wholly accurate to say that nothing has happened. True, nothing has happened to deprive the Temple of its mythopoeic power and central, pivotal position. But something must have happened to draw a small group of people to the conclusions that the sanctity of the Temple is to be extended beyond its walls, on the one hand, and that the locus of the sanctity is to be their table and bed by analogy to the cult, on the other. Obviously what could have happened is that someone responded to the Priestly Code by coming to such a conclusion, which, if not innate, at least is defensible within the exegesis of Leviticus 11-15 and 18. But that too seems unlikely simply because significant shifts have taken place and important conceptions have come to the fore, giving expression for instance to modes of purification on which the Priestly Code is ambiguous. At some point the enduring character of the Temple evoked a conception of replicating the Temple's modes of sanctification in and among Israel's Land and People, just as, at some point, the unsatisfactory character of the Temple and its priesthood provoked the group which settled at Qumran to come to the same conclusion but to effect that conclusion in a diametrically opposite way. Accordingly, the structurally and systemically analogous character of the ideas on uncleanness of the two groups – the Essene community at Qumran and the people who stand at the threshold of the development of Mishnaic law – demand the conclusion that, as for Qumran so for Mishnah, there has been an event or a personality of immense consequence. But in the latter case, that is all that we know, and it is, as I have said, only by comparison to the former.

If this theory of the character of the earliest stratum of Mishnaic thought on cleanness is sound, then over the next century from the beginning of the Mishnaic system before the first century A.D. we should find development of the given laws but no essentially new viewpoints. The generative analogy cannot shift. Creative intellectual forces can only take up and build upon what has been laid down at the outset. The point at which we should anticipate (but do not observe) major developments will be after the destruction of the Temple. Then the Pharisees' continuators in the time of Yavneh will enter into the situation of the Essenes in the age of the Temple.

I have carefully avoided specifying the time at which the Mishnaic system originated, claiming only that it is prior to the turn of the first century. It is equally important to avoid claiming to know the sort of group within which the system began. Only with grave reservations have we alluded to the Pharisees as the point of origination or even as the sect which principally stands behind the system transmitted through successive generations to the authorities of 70 and afterward. Still, I think we may specify two facts about that group within which the system as a whole takes shape.

First, like the Essene community at Qumran, the group behind Mishnah surely included a sizable number of priests. Mishnah's fundamental concerns and emphases, while different from those of the Priestly Code, fall wholly within the code's conception of what lies at the core of Israelite ontology. Moreover, the subtle and complex development of scriptural rules on transfer of uncleanness (e.g., *midras* and *maddaf*) has to have been undertaken somewhat earlier. It is likely that priests in the Temple will have had occasion to do the work more than any other group. The availability of such technical terms as *midras* surely suggests that prior to the systemic construction in which these terms and concepts are given their place, the concepts themselves had been worked out. Whether or not the group consisted mainly, or even exclusively, of priests we do not know. The probability is that it encompassed ordinary Israelites pretending to be wanting to live life as priests. But that is less clear than that it was composed of knowledgeable and experienced people, who had a clear notion of cultic law and knew how to apply it.

Second, unlike the group at Qumran, the people whose thought supplies the foundation of Mishnah's legal development did not deem the Temple to be desecrated. They probably did not regard their table as the surrogate for the Temple, but only as a locus *analogous* to its altar. The otherness of the metaphor is preserved. The table is *like* the altar. It is not conceived either *as* a new altar, or as *equivalent* in sanctity to the old one. These two simple and indubitable facts, upon which we have reflected at length, seem to me to yield a picture of a group different in social definition from the Essenes, with a different set of concerns, to be sure expressed in terms of cleanness similar to those of the Essenes, and with a different conception of the central ontological issues of cleanness and of holiness. For them the Temple stood for an ideal to be realized outside its precincts. The cult presented a transcendent aspiration to be attained beyond its gates. Accordingly, the conceptions of the Priestly Code are grasped in all of their philosophical profundity and religious depth and explored at new heights of meaning. Whether priests or lay people, whether gathered out of the common life or located within it, the people whose conceptions stand behind and generate the Mishnaic system of uncleanness pursue the sanctification of Israelite life, and set for themselves the goal of sanctifying profane things and purifying unclean ones. Scripture demands the distinction between holy and unclean. Mishnah begins with the profound conviction that that distinction is to be made so that it may be overcome. To begin with, it asserts that the common is to be surpassed, the profane to be transcended, the unclean to be made sacred.

PURITY AFTER 70: EARLY RABBINISM AND THE MISHNAIC SYSTEM OF UNCLEANNESS

After 70, the unfolding of the system proceeds without significant variation or change and follows the lines already laid out in the period before 70. Let us dwell upon the points of continuity which are many and impressive. The development of the rules on the uncleanness of menstrual blood, the Zab, and corpse uncleanness is wholly predictable on the basis of what has gone before. The principal conceptual traits carry forward established themes. For example, if we have in hand an interest in resolving matters of doubt, then, in Yavneh, further types of doubts will be investigated. Once we know that a valid birth is not accompanied by unclean blood, we ask about the definition of valid births. Yavnean rulings of corpse contamination dwell upon secondary and derivative issues. In important areas of the law the system goes ahead in a remarkably predictable path, clearly moving forward, past the destruction of the Temple, along lines laid down long before. What happens when a system, revolving about a symbolic center and perceived as a metaphorical construction, loses its concrete point of comparison, the center to which everything is deemed peripheral and comparable? What happens to the modes of thought – thinking through analogy and contrast – which give conceptual form and force to the system? The clear answer to the latter question in the case of the Mishnaic law of purities is that the modes of thought persist. New inquiries may be raised, but the ways of working them out in conceptual detail already are known and predictable; analogical and contrastive thinking about the known illuminates the unknown.

If, for example, we consider an important innovation in the law, we find ourselves able to interpret it without reference to the impact of the Temple's destruction. It would have come about had the Temple remained standing, and this is demonstratable. I refer to the innovation of Aqiba in introducing into the process of declaring "leprosy" clean or unclean an authority unknown in Scripture, namely, not a priest but a sage, who is "expert in them and in their names." The sage knows the facts of the character of the *nega'* and *O(s,)ara'at* and therefore can be relied upon to rule which is clean and which is unclean. The introduction into the system of a whole corpus of law on a source of uncleanness cannot, to be sure, be credited to the need to make a place for the sages, authorities not of the priestly caste. Scripture itself is clear on *nega' O(s,)ara'at* as a source of major uncleanness.

The Essene community at Qumran as well as the nascent Christian community likewise make provisions for the participation of a nonpriest in the system. After himself healing a leper, Jesus tells the man, "Go, show yourself to the priest" (Matt. 8:1-4, Mark 1:40-44, Luke 5:12-14). Likewise CD 13:5-7[7] provides for an informed person to instruct a priest in what to say in connection with blemishes: "But if there be a judgment regarding the law of blemishes, then the priest shall come and stand in the camp, and the overseer shall instruct him in the exact meaning of the Law. Even if he [the priest} be an imbecile, it is he who shall lock him up; for theirs is the judgment." Accordingly, provision for the role of the informed person is an aspect of the working out of relationships between the commune and the established priesthood and Temple, and in no way is the destruction of the Temple a particular and causative factor in the consideration of the problem. The sage does not heal, of course, but has the knowledge to recognize symptoms of healing or uncleanness. The role of each sort of authority is particular to the system of which he forms a part.

---

[7] C. Rabin, *The Zadokite Documents* (Oxford, 1958), p. 62.

PERFECTION AND IMPLAUSIBILITY

The destruction of the Temple cannot be presented as the principal cause of the several important shifts in the Mishnaic system of uncleanness which took place in the Yavnean period.[8] The lines of development in many important components of the system are continuous with the character of the law before 70. Whether or not the Temple was destroyed, it was inevitable that these areas would develop within the as-yet unanswered questions – the logical tensions implicit in their earliest structure. The provision of a place for the sage in the determination of uncleanness formerly reserved for the priest does not depend of the event of 70, since exactly the same consideration is revealed in CD. Any system, not only Mishnah's in which an authority other than the priest stands at the center must at some point take up the problem of how said authority related to the priest in decisions reserved by Scripture to the priesthood. The answer in CD and in Negaim is to treat the priest as an indispensable idiot, preserving for him a formal role while treating that role as a decidedly secondary formality. The profound thought of Makhshirin and Kelim on the role of man in inaugurating the working of the system responds to the conception of Miqvaot of the role of nature in bringing the process to a conclusion and restoring the economy of nature. Internal systemic considerations, imbedded in the logic of the law, account even for the transformation of what had been an undifferentiated metaphor into a fact. A single continuum now joins the table at home to the altar.[9] Cleanness of the domestic table is not merely *like* cleanness of the Temple altar but stands in a single concrete line which ascends from the former, via the cleanness of the priest's heave-offering, to the latter. What formerly was compared to something else now is placed into material relationship with that other thing.

Yet the fact remains that the Temple *was* destroyed. The legal developments under examination are given in the names of Yavneans and stand in a direct line either with rulings given in the names of authorities before 70 or with suppositions taken for granted and not subjected to controversy after 70. The evidence, both in its silence and in its full expression, strongly suggests that it was after 70 in particular that these interesting developments of the system did take place. Whether or not they would have occurred if the calamity did not happen of course is not subject to inquiry. As I have argued, they are implicit in the antecedent system and susceptible of discovery without regard to external events. Even though the role for the authority other than the priest is defined by the Essenes at a different time and in other

---

[8] Yavnean period, from Yavneh, the location of the rabbinic group after 70.

[9] I refer to the development of the notion of removes of uncleanness, first, second, third, corresponding to levels of sanctification of food, ordinary food, heave-offering, and Holy Things, for example, as exemplified at M. Tohorot 2:3-7. It would carry us far afield to lay out the sources on this complex matter. The point which is relevant is as given.

circumstances from the age and context of the calamity of 70, even though the system itself invites consideration of the role of human agency and intent in its commencement, and even though the deep thought on levels of sanctification is invited by the ambiguities of the very metaphor upon which the system is founded, the facts are what they are.

It follows that, while we cannot ask how the destruction of the Temple affected the Mishnaic system of uncleanness, we do ask how the development of the system after 70 is congruent with the effects of the Temple's destruction. The answer is obvious. First, the destruction radically revises the institutional context for the priestly government of surviving Israel. New sorts of leaders emerge, one of which is the sage, qualified because he is expert "in them and in their names." Negaim testifies to that fact and to the further and still more important fact that Aqiba in particular proposes to investigate the deep implications of the rise of the sage for a law to the working of which the priest is essential. The catastrophe raises the question of whether or not people bear responsibility for what has happened. If they do, they take on a heavy burden of guilt. If they do not, however, they face an equally paralyzing fact: their own powerlessness to shape their fate. The issue is resolved by stress upon the responsibility of Israel for its own fate, a painful conclusion made ineluctable by the whole of the scriptural heritage of Leviticus, Deuteronomy, and the prophetic literature. But Scripture is clear that those who have brought disaster by their deeds also can overcome it. Reversion to the right way will produce inexorable redemption. If people are not helpless, then their deeds and their intentions matter very much. The catastrophe provides an occasion for reflection on the interplay between action and intention, in the established supposition that what people propose to do and actually do are their own responsibility. And, as we have seen, the central issue – the fate and focus of the sacred – is faced head-on.

The Mishnaic system of uncleanness at Yavneh contains within itself developments remarkably congruent to the institutional, psychological, and metaphysical crisis precipitated by the destruction of the Temple. Its message is clear. The sages will lead Israel to the restoration of the world destroyed by Israel's own deeds. They will do so through the reformation of attitudes and motives, which will lead to right action with the result that, even now, the remnants of holiness may be protected from the power of uncleanness. The holy priesthood and people, which endure and which are all that endure after the cultic holocaust of 70, form the last, if diminished, sanctuary of the sacred. In domestic life, at table, the processes of life are nurtured and so shaped as to preserve and express that remnant of the sacred which remains in this world. The net result of the Yavnean stage is the law's unfolding is that history – the world-shattering events of the day – is kept at a distance from the center of life. The system of sustaining life shaped essentially within an ahistorical, indeed anti-historical, ontology goes forward in its own path, a way above history.

Yet the facts of history are otherwise. The people as a whole can hardly be said to have accepted the ahistorical ontology framed by the sages and in part expressed by the system of uncleanness. They followed the path of Bar Kokhba and took the road to war once more. When three generations had passed after the destruction and the historical occasion for restoration through historical – political and military – action came to fulfillment, the great war of 132-35 broke forth. A view of being in which people were seen to be moving toward some point within time, the fulfillment and the end of history as it was known, clearly shaped the ontological consciousness of Israel after 70 just as had been the case in the decades before 70. So if to the sages of our system, history and the end of history were essentially beside the point and pivot, the construction of a world of cyclic eternities being the purpose and center, and the conduct of humble things like eating and drinking the paramount and decisive focus of the sacred, others saw things differently. To those who hoped and therefore fought, life had some other meanings entirely.

The second war proved still more calamitous than the first. In 70 the Temple was lost and in 135, even access to the city. In 70 the people, though suffering grievous losses, endured more or less intact. In 135 the land of Judah, surely the holiest part of the holy Land, evidently lost the bulk of its Jewish population. Temple, Land, people – all were gone in the forms in which they had been known. In the generation following the calamity of Bar Kokhba, what would be the affect upon the system of uncleanness?

The answer is predictable: there would be no affect whatsoever. The system would go on pretty much as before, generating its second- and third-level questions as if nothing had happened. For a brief, unreal twilight, the old pretense of a life beyond history and a system untouched by dynamics of time and change would be attempted. The result, in the history of the Mishnaic system of uncleanness, would be the hour of systemic fulfillment, the moment of the richest conceptual, dialectical achievement, a bright and brilliant time in which 200 (or more) years of thought would come to ultimate incandescence. And, at the end, Our Holy Rabbi (Judah the Patriarch) would capture the light in permanent utensils of unbreakable language. But pretense that nothing had happened, or could happen, does not make history. Things *had* happened. The system of uncleanness, unfolding beyond time and change, now complete and whole in flawless intellectual and literary structures, is set aside at the time of its perfection. The system which had denied an end time and constructed a world without end itself would fall into desuetude. History would give it its place on the crowded shelf of unused utensils, each containing its true, but implausible truths.[10]

---

[10] See my "History and Structure," *Journal of the American Academy of Religion* 45, no. 2 (1977): 161-92.

South Florida Studies in the History of Judaism

South Florida Academic Commentary Series

243039	The Talmud of Babylonia, A Complete Outline, Part I, Tractate Berakhot and the Division of Appointed Times A: From Tractate Berakhot through Tractate Pesahim	Neusner
243040	The Talmud of Babylonia, A Complete Outline, Part I, Tractate Berakhot and the Division of Appointed Times B: From Tractate Yoma through Tractate Hagigah	Neusner
243041	The Talmud of Babylonia, A Complete Outline, Part II, The Division of Women; A: From Tractate Yebamot through Tractate Ketubot	Neusner
243042	The Talmud of Babylonia, A Complete Outline, Part II, The Division of Women; B: From Tractate Nedarim through Tractate Qiddushin	Neusner
243043	The Talmud of Babylonia, An Academic Commentary, Volume XIII, Bavli Tractate Yebamot, A. Chapters One through Eight	Neusner
243044	The Talmud of Babylonia, An Academic Commentary, XIII, Bavli Tractate Yebamot, B. Chapters Nine through Seventeen	Neusner
243045	The Talmud of the Land of Israel, A Complete Outline of the Second, Third and Fourth Divisions, Part II, The Division of Women, A. Yebamot to Nedarim	Neusner
243046	The Talmud of the Land of Israel, A Complete Outline of the Second, Third and Fourth Divisions, Part II, The Division of Women, B. Nazir to Sotah	Neusner
243047	The Talmud of the Land of Israel, A Complete Outline of the Second, Third and Fourth Divisions, Part I, The Division of Appointed Times, C. Pesahim and Sukkah	Neusner
243048	The Talmud of the Land of Israel, A Complete Outline of the Second, Third and Fourth Divisions, Part I, The Division of Appointed Times, A. Berakhot, Shabbat	Neusner
243049	The Talmud of the Land of Israel, A Complete Outline of the Second, Third and Fourth Divisions, Part I, The Division of Appointed Times, B. Erubin, Yoma and Besah	Neusner
243050	The Talmud of the Land of Israel, A Complete Outline of the Second, Third and Fourth Divisions, Part I, The Division of Appointed Times, D. Taanit, Megillah, Rosh Hashannah, Hagigah and Moed Qatan	Neusner
243051	The Talmud of the Land of Israel, A Complete Outline of the Second, Third and Fourth Divisions, Part III, The Division of Damages, A. Baba Qamma, Baba Mesia, Baba Batra, Horayot and Niddah	Neusner
243052	The Talmud of the Land of Israel, A Complete Outline of the Second, Third and Fourth Divisions, Part III, The Division of Damages, B. Sanhedrin, Makkot, Shebuot and Abldah Zarah	Neusner
243053	The Two Talmuds Compared, II. The Division of Women in the Talmud of the Land of Israel and the Talmud of Babylonia, Volume A, Tractates Yebamot and Ketubot	Neusner
243054	The Two Talmuds Compared, II. The Division of Women in the Talmud of the Land of Israel and the Talmud of Babylonia, Volume B, Tractates Nedarim, Nazir and Sotah	Neusner

South Florida-Rochester-Saint Louis
Studies on Religion and the Social Order

South Florida International Studies in
Formative Christianity and Judaism